William Beatty-Kingston

Music and Manners

Personal reminiscences and sketches of character. Vol. 1

William Beatty-Kingston

Music and Manners
Personal reminiscences and sketches of character. Vol. 1

ISBN/EAN: 9783337012922

Printed in Europe, USA, Canada, Australia, Japan

Cover: Foto ©Thomas Meinert / pixelio.de

More available books at **www.hansebooks.com**

MUSIC AND MANNERS

Personal Reminiscences and Sketches of Character

BY

W. BEATTY-KINGSTON

COMMANDER OF THE IMPERIAL ORDER OF THE MEDJIDIEH AND OF THE ROYAL ORDERS
OF THE REDEEMER, STAR OF ROUMANIA, CROWN OF ROUMANIA AND TAKOVA
OF SERVIA; KNIGHT OF THE IMPERIAL ORDER OF FRANCIS JOSEPH
AND OF THE I.R. AUSTRIAN ORDER OF MERIT OF THE
FIRST CLASS WITH THE CROWN, ETC., ETC.

AUTHOR OF "WILLIAM I., GERMAN EMPEROR," "THE BATTLE OF BERLIN,"
ETC.

IN TWO VOLUMES

VOL. I.

MUSIC

LONDON: CHAPMAN AND HALL,
LIMITED
1887

TO

HENRY IRVING,

A LOVER OF MUSIC AND MODEL OF MANNERS,

𝔗𝔥𝔦𝔰 𝔅𝔬𝔬𝔨 𝔦𝔰 𝔇𝔢𝔡𝔦𝔠𝔞𝔱𝔢𝔡

WITH SINCERE AFFECTION

BY HIS OLD FRIEND

THE AUTHOR.

PREFACE.

In this book are reproduced some of the records of my experiences " in foreign parts," gathered during a period of absence from England extending over little less than a quarter of a century. A considerable portion of the term of my voluntary exile was spent in the service of a great English journal—*The Daily Telegraph*—the proprietors of which entrusted me with many a mission to Courts and Camps. In the chronicles of my journalistic career—a few of which have contributed material to these pages—Politics and War have played more conspicuous parts than Music and Manners. But those somewhat formidable topics have been rigorously excluded from a collection of personal reminiscences and word-sketches written with a desire to amuse, rather than to instruct, those who may honour me by reading them.

The child of musical parents, who taught me to sing before I could speak, and to play before I could spell, I have continually been brought into contact with musicians and music-lovers ever since the days of my early boyhood, and count amongst my dearest friends of the past and present several of the most distinguished votaries of the Divine Art. These facts must serve as my excuse for such cursory mention of myself, in connection with eminent musical composers and executants, as occurs here and there in the course of these volumes, for the manifold shortcomings and demerits of which I humbly crave my readers' indulgence.

W. BEATTY-KINGSTON.

January, 1887.

CONTENTS.

VOL. I.

CHAPTER I.

VIENNESE REMINISCENCES.—HECTOR BERLIOZ.—THE OLD OPERA HOUSE AND CONSERVATOIRE. — PEPI HELLMESBERGER. — PUPILS OF THE HOCHSCHULE. — SIGHT-READING. — JOHANN HERBECK.—THE BEETHOVEN CULT.—OPERATIC DISABILITIES.—WAGNERIAN PRODUCTIONS.—VIENNESE CRITICS.—COMPOSERS: BRAHMS, LISZT, RUBINSTEIN, GOLDMARK 1

CHAPTER II.

MUSICAL REMINISCENCES OF BERLIN.—GERMAN INTONATION.—THE LUCCA-MALLINGER CONTROVERSY.—ALBERT NIEMANN.—THE ROYAL OPERA HOUSE.—PRUSSIAN VENTILATION OF THEATRES.—THE GENERAL-INTENDANT 47

CHAPTER III.

REMINISCENCES OF PESTH.—ROBERT VOLKMANN.—A FESTIVAL OF FOOLS 90

CHAPTER IV.

REMINISCENCES OF ROME.—THE GESÙ ORGANS.—MIDNIGHT MASSES.—OPERA AND BALLET IN ROME.—RAMACIOTTI . . . 101

CHAPTER V.

ROUMANIAN LAYS AND DANCES. — THE DACIAN MINSTRELS. — PLUM-PUDDING SET TO MUSIC.—SERVIAN REMINISCENCES . 112

CHAPTER VI.

INDIAN MUSIC.—ORIENTAL VERSIONS OF THE BRITISH NATIONAL ANTHEM 147

CONTENTS.

CHAPTER VII.

JAPANESE MUSIC 163

CHAPTER VIII.

PIANOFORTE PLAYING 190

CHAPTER IX.

ADELINA PATTI AT HOME 243

CHAPTER X.

MUSIC IN THEATRES AND AL FRESCO . . . 272

CHAPTER XI.

WAGNERIANA.—STRAUSSIANA 288

CHAPTER XII.

MUSICAL AUDIENCES IN AUSTRIA, GERMANY, ITALY, AND OTHER CONTINENTAL COUNTRIES.—ENGLISH FREQUENTERS OF CONCERT ROOMS, OPERA-HOUSES, AND OTHER PLACES OF MUSICAL ENTERTAINMENT 324

MUSIC AND MANNERS.

CHAPTER I.

VIENNESE REMINISCENCES.—HECTOR BERLIOZ.—THE OLD OPERA HOUSE AND CONSERVATOIRE. — PEPI HELLMESBERGER.—PUPILS OF THE HOCHSCHULE.—SIGHT-READING.—JOHANN HERBECK.—THE BEETHOVEN CULT.—OPERATIC DISABILITIES.—WAGNERIAN PRODUCTIONS.—VIENNESE CRITICS.—COMPOSERS: BRAHMS, LISZT, RUBINSTEIN, GOLDMARK.

WHEN, some twenty-two years ago, I first made the acquaintance of Vienna—an acquaintance that rapidly ripened, on my part at least, into warm and lasting friendship—the Kaiserstadt was, as it still is, unquestionably the most musical of Continental capitals. It possessed the best operatic and symphonic orchestras, Conservatoire, choral union and established stringed quartet in Europe. One of its regimental bands—that of the Koenig von Wuertemberg Regiment—had attained such extraordinary proficiency with strings, as well as with brass and wood, that its performances alternated with those of the inimitable Johann Strauss at the Volksgarten on terms of all but absolute equality, as far as popular favour was concerned. Then it was that the

Vienna Musical Union (Musik-Verein), with its mighty orchestra of two hundred and fifty first-class instrumentalists, had just attained its maximum of effectiveness under Hans Richter's gifted predecessor, Johann von Herbeck. Until it became my privilege to attend the Concerts of the Musik-Verein, I had never even dreamed of such an executant corporation or conceived such performances to be possible. All the leading artists—all the recognised "soloists" of Vienna served in its ranks. Joseph Hellmesberger led the first, Hofmann the second violins; Dobyhal, the tenors; Roever, the violoncelli. Men of this calibre did not disdain to drudge through unknown numbers of rehearsals, even at the sacrifice of lucrative private teaching, in order to enable their less celebrated fellow-artists to achieve a perfect comprehension of the composer's meaning as interpreted by the conductor.

I well remember the enthusiasm to which HECTOR BERLIOZ gave expression *àpropos* of what he termed the "splendid self-abnegation" displayed with respect to the rehearsals of his *Damnation de Faust* by the executant members of the Musik-Verein, who, day after day and evening after evening, at the coldest time of the year, in Vienna—the week before Christmastide—sate "repeating" his numbers for four and five hours at a stretch. Berlioz, upon whom the impossibility of getting his works adequately rehearsed had weighed heavily in London and Paris, was deeply impressed by the untiring assiduity of the Viennese artists; and the final result of all this sedulous, reverent and loving preparation, which came off on a never-to-be-forgotten Sunday morning in the Imperial Redouten-Saal (18th December, 1866), fairly took him by surprise. In his excitement after the performance he was unusually profuse of quaint definitions. "It is not an orchestra, my friend," he exclaimed to me; "it is an instrument—an instrument polyphonic, automatic, and yet inspired." Later on, at the banquet given in his honour by the leading authors, artists, and dilettanti of the Austrian capital, he broke out more than once in fervid praise of the Musik-Verein's unrivalled orchestra. To Herbeck, who—"having no French"—could not understand a word that the deeply-moved maestro said to him, he ejaculated, "What players! What a leader! What musical and poetical intelligence! What noble self-effacement! How do you manage it, then, to animate two hundred bodies with one soul, and that soul, *illustre maître-de-chapelle*, not yours, but mine!"

Vienna, when the greatest of French composers visited it, was physically in a state of transition, and the accommodation provided for its musical public left much to be desired in the way of space, comfort, and even cleanliness. The magnificent new Opera House was not built—indeed, its foundations were just about being laid—and the pestiferous old Kaernthner-Thor Theatre was still the only home of the lyric drama within the precincts of the Kaiserstadt. It was an ugly, dirty, ill-ventilated den, stiflingly hot, and provided by an ingenious Court architect with the most distractingly intricate system of entrances and exits at that time in existence. To get into the house at your leisure was difficult; to issue from it in a hurry impossible. As in the case of its neighbour, the Burg, the space between the outer shell and auditorium of the Kaernthner-Thor was honeycombed by winding passages, crooked corridors, and tortuous staircases. None of these ever seemed to lead to any part of the building whither one wished to go; least of all to the street. The atmosphere inside the house was permanently sickly. It mattered not at what time of the day or night one visited the theatre—during a morning rehearsal, with its dim religious light, or a gala performance, making a heavy call upon the gas resources of the establishment—the old, musty, mephitic smell was there, conveying to at least one of the senses the impression that the quantum of interior air originally allotted to the Kaernthner-Thor Theatre by its architect had been carefully poisoned early in the century and never changed since. As a matter of fact, the orchestra was situated exactly above a peculiarly baneful drain, one consequence of which thoughtful arrangement was that, after a heavy rainfall—or, indeed, any sudden freak of the weather—the two front rows of the stalls were simply untenable by any person provided with a nose of average receptivity and susceptibility. On such occasions the mind's eye, informed by a lively imagination, could see billions of typhoid germs hovering round the members of the "Imperial Royal Court Opera Orchestra," as they sate playing in the long boarded well through every crack and fissure of which sewer-gas was assiduously working its upward way.

Little less objectionable from a sanitary point of view, and still more ignominious, ugly and inconvenient than the Kaernthner-Thor, was the old Viennese Conservatoire in the Tuchlauben. Considered in connection with musical education and training—not to mention classical Concerts and chamber performances of the highest character—that remarkable building could only be justly described as a paragon of unfitness. Two flights of a corkscrew staircase, barely five feet in width, led from a dirty stone vestibule on the ground-floor to a squalid, frowsy concert-room of a dull, nondescript colour, badly lighted, malodorous and forlorn of ventilation—the sort of room that fourth-rate provincial mechanics' institutes are wont to place at the disposal of lecturers who combine amusement with instruction, as in the case of the orrery. There was a hideous dark gallery running round three sides of this grisly apartment, close up against the ceiling, which chiefly affected the Conservatoire pupils, who would stew there, slowly and uncomplainingly, on "public nights," with an heroic endurance that I have admired and wondered at scores of times. Not that the lot of the audience in the body of the room, or on the platform itself, was strikingly preferable to that of the perspiring *alumni* aloft, for the heat was nearly as intense below as above, and the seats—small cane-bottomed chairs, mechanically fixed in rows like beads upon a string—were adjusted so close to one another as to be far more suitable for the accommodation of cherubim than of human beings. In a word, all the arrangements of that very abominable old Conservatoire were triumphs of stupidity and discomfort.

And yet, some of the finest performances to which it has been my good fortune to listen in the course of musical experiences extending over well nigh forty years, took place in the sordid and unsavoury den from which so many admirable artists have emerged, at different times during the present century, to reinforce the leading orchestras of Europe. It was in that subfusk chamber, with the thermometer steadfastly registering the Réaumur equivalent of 115° Fahrenheit, that I first heard Anton Rubinstein play the Posthumous Sonata, and lent an enraptured ear to the strains of such Liedersaenger as Hélène Magnus and Gustav Walter. There I became acquainted, musically and personally, with Epstein and Brassin, Caroline Bettelheim and Augusta Kolar, Adolphe Brodsky and Dragomir Krancevich; with Josef Hellmesberger the elder, then as now the tutelary genius of the Conservatoire, and his gifted son Pepi, who fiddled articulately before he could speak plainly, and filled the post of orchestral conductor in an opera house ere he had completed his twenty-third year. He was a lad, rising eleven, when he electrified the musical public of Vienna by playing, at one of his father's inimitable Concerts given at the Conservatoire before the most critical audience in Europe, the first violin part of Spohr's octett, and in such sort as to elicit a triple recall. Reading and execution were alike faultless. On another scarcely less interesting occasion, a few weeks later, at a Carnavalesque *Liedertafel* of the Viennese Choral Society, I heard him lead Mozart's comic sextett (stringed quartett and two horns) with admirable humour, archness, and petulance. The composition is a charming musical jest from beginning to end, and like many another subtle and fanciful joke, is easily spoilt by dull interpreters. I do not hope to hear it ever rendered again as it was given on the 15th February, 1867, in the Diana Saal, by five of the most eminent soloists then living (including Kapellmeister Hellmesberger himself, who literally played "second fiddle" to his talented child), under the leading of handsome little Pepi, arrayed for the nonce in silken smalls and stockings, knee buckles, bag-wig and powder, sword, *chapeau-bras*, and lace frills at breast and wrist. He was, indeed, a pretty sight; and the ladies who witnessed his performance at the Fasching Liedertafel were unanimous in declaring him "zum Fressen" —"à croquer"; in plain English, nice enough to be quite fit to eat.

It was this same Pepi Hellmesberger who occupied the position of *chef d'orchestre* at the Ring Theatre for some months before its destruction by fire. He was actually in the house, and on the point of taking his place at the conductor's desk, when the curtain, bellying out into the house like a half-furled wind-blown sail, discovered the stage to be ablaze, and let loose a torrent of roaring flame over the orchestra. Had the overture commenced when that awful incident took place, in all probability the instrumentalists and their youthful leader would have perished, or at the very least suffered severe injuries. Fortunately, they were still in the "musicians' foyer" under the stage, and thus enabled to effect their escape into the street through the principal stage-door without difficulty.

The last time I saw Pepi the younger was in the winter of 1876-77, shortly after the suppression of the Servian Rebellion. A few months previously, having entered upon his twentieth year, he became liable for military service, and received an official notification requiring him to present himself at the proper quarter for medical examination, as a preliminary to being drafted into an infantry regiment. To a violin-soloist, no announcement could well have been more terrible than this. Were such an one compelled to fulfil three years' service in the ranks, his fingers and wrists could not fail to lose, in delicacy of touch and flexibility, more than, in all probability, they would ever thereafter be able to regain by the most sedulous practice. The mere thought of such a calamity all but drove poor Pepi distracted, and inspired his father with courage to seek audience of the Emperor (to whose Court he had for many years been attached in a musical capacity), for the purpose of begging off Hellmesberger junior from a career so peculiarly unsuitable to him. The Emperor heard all that his faithful old servant had to say upon the subject, and then replied, "I regret, dear Hellmesberger, my inability to grant your request. My only son has to do his duty to his country as a soldier; so must yours. It seems a pity to interfere with the physical training of a great artist; but I cannot consent to draw invidious distinctions between one career and another. All I can do for your boy is to get him drafted into a regimental band instead of into the ranks. There he will have to learn to play some instrument other than that of which he is already master; but this will not give him much trouble, and he will doubtless find time to keep up his practice of the violin. But he must wear the coat, submit to discipline, and pay his proper tribute of man-service to the national defences."

As may well be imagined, Francis-Joseph's kindly and considerate concession was gratefully accepted by the Hellmesbergers, father and son; and thus it came to pass that "handsome Pepi" was buttoned up to the throat in a blue and grey uniform, with one white star on his collar, when he came to call upon me at the Hôtel Imperial soon after my arrival from Belgrade in the Kaiserstadt, just ten years ago. He had found his duties with his regiment, even under the modified conditions granted to him at the Emperor's instance, extremely irksome for a time, but seemed tolerably reconciled to them, and not a little proud of having earned a good-conduct badge. There was, of course, a humorous side to the ordeal through which he had to pass; viz., that he, indisputably the first Austrian violinist of his generation, should have had the fife assigned to him as his instrument in the band. On joining, he had been "sent up" to the bandmaster for interrogation as to his executant capacities. "What can you do, young man?" inquired that potent personage. "I can play the violin, bratsch, and 'cello, Herr Kapellmeister." "That is well—very well for a civilian, but quite useless to us, here in the regiment. Let me see. We are short of fifers. You will learn to play the fife!" And learn to play the fife Pepi did, with a rapidity that somewhat astonished his instructors.

Moreover, during his term of service he picked up a sufficient acquaintance with reeds, brasses, &c., to prove of infinite utility to him in his subsequent career. No sooner had he obtained his discharge—somewhat prematurely, through the intercession of an exalted personage

—than he was appointed *chef d'orchestre* in a popular Viennese operetta theatre, brought out a comic opera of his own composition, married a wife and took up a brilliant position in the most select musical circle of the Kaiserstadt.

The latter days of the dirty old Conservatoire were also those of my residence in Vienna, where I contracted a close friendship with Hellmesberger the elder, at that time orchestral instructor at the Hochschule, leader of the Court band and *chef d'attaque* at the Opera House, besides filling a score or so of honorary offices in connection with the teaching and practice of the divine art. Quite the keenest and most enthusiastic musician I have ever known, Joseph Hellmesberger was almost extravagantly proud of his native city's achievements in the way of advancing and refining musical culture, and correspondingly eager that every intelligent foreigner visiting Vienna with a letter of introduction to himself should be enabled to appreciate, by personal observation, the actual working of the educational and training systems which had been fraught with such splendid results to the two great institutions—the Conservatorium and Musik-Verein—of which he and every other Austrian musician, whether virtuoso or dilettante, was so justly proud. It was at his particular request that I took to "dropping in" upon the afternoon orchestral "practices" of the Conservatoire pupils, which took place twice or thrice a week under his personal direction. No musician could fail to be deeply interested by these exercises, in which the foremost rank was assigned to sight-reading. As the Conservatoire library is a very mine of old concerted works, piles of "parts" were never lacking wherewith to test the students' capacities for playing "vom Blatte;" nor did the Council of Management fail to provide the orchestral department with good store of novelties. At every "practice" a fresh score was rendered, somehow or other—for the most part, with astounding *verve* and intelligence—and the pupils always appeared eager to tackle anything and everything, no matter how cranky or complicated, that their well-loved master might please to chasten them with. On one or two occasions, when I happened to be present at the "Uebungen," Hellmesberger's greedy *alumni* even "asked for more," like Oliver Twist, after undergoing what I considered a surfeit of sight-reading.

One afternoon, during the early summer of 1868—a few days after the first production at Munich of the "Meistersinger von Nuernberg"—I chanced to call in at the gloomy old practice-room in the Tuchlauben, just as the students were settling down at their desks, with faces, as it struck me upon glancing round the semicircle, a thought graver than usual. Hellmesberger was already enthroned; but as soon as he caught sight of me he jumped up, evidently in a great state of excitement, grasped both my hands, and exclaimed—"How fortunate that thou shouldst have visited us to-day! Now I will show thee what these children can do. The full score of the 'Meistersinger' has just reached us, and I am now going to take them *a prima vista* through the overture." So saying, he gave the accustomed three quick, smart raps, and a breathless silence succeeded the clamour of tuning and chatter that had hitherto prevailed. To a music-lover, the *coup d'œil* offered by the students was a deeply interesting one. About seventy of both sexes were present, ranging between the ages of twelve and twenty, and exhibiting every facial type and variety of complexion known in the many-peopled, polyglot empire. Almost all the girl-pupils wore their hair in long, thick plaits, by the hues of which their respective nationalities could be pretty accurately determined, from the Teutonic pale flaxen and Slav hay-colour to the Magyar glossy brown and Roumanian blue-black. Oriental physiognomies abounded, a natural consequence of Vienna's geographical position upon the threshold of the East. Brighter faces than those of the dark-eyed, sallow-skinned Huns and Dacians—boys and girls alike—I have seldom seen, even in Sicily or Andalusia. The majority of the petticoated pupils was to be found in the ranks of the players upon strings; but the most promising of the French-hornists was a buxom Polish damsel of about fourteen, whose name I regret to have forgotten, whilst another handsome girl dispensed "linked sweetness, long drawn out" from the trombone, and two or three more, pink and white, golden-locked Austrians proper, had devoted themselves with conspicuous success to vanquish the difficulties of the serpent, still a favourite instrument in country churches and small provincial bands throughout the Hapsburg realm.

To say that I was surprised at the general correctness, vigour, and fire with which this heterogeneous gathering of lads and lasses interpreted one of the most laborious and intricate orchestral compositions in existence, is to describe very inadequately the sensations I experienced upon listening to the "Meistersinger" Overture, played at sight by the students of the Vienna Conservatorium. That the rendering was somewhat coarse and rough, shaky as to time here and there, and lacking in light and shade throughout, I do not contest. But not a single breakdown occurred, nor was the orchestra pulled up once by its conductor; whose face was radiant with pride and pleasure when he laid down his bâton at the conclusion of the *Vorspiel*. All he said was "Kinder, es war gar nicht so schlecht!" (Children, it was really not so bad); upon which the "children" set up a cheering and clapping of hands that obviously afforded their gifted instructor the liveliest gratification.

JOHANN HERBECK, at the time of my first fore-gathering with him, during the autumn of 1866, was the director of the concerts annually given by the "Society of the Friends of Music"—entertainments usually spoken of amongst musicians as the "Gesellschafts-Conzerte," and enjoying a well-deserved European renown. He also filled the office—one of great dignity as well as responsibility—of Master of the Court Band, or *Kapelle*, as the German idiom hath it, and was in great public favour as a composer. His income, from a Viennese professional point of view, was a comfortable one—his wife and children all he could desire—his position in the "craft" second to none. He was a man of many friends, the critics were kind to his works, and his own passionate love of music was a continual feast to him. All these agreeable conditions of his being, added together, should have made up a sum-total of human happiness, and very probably would have done so but for one draw-back. In common with ninety-nine hundredths of the Emperor-King's subjects, Herbeck was absolutely, though not irretrievably, unborn; and the consciousness of this untoward irregularity in his genetic arrangements preyed upon him incessantly, souring his pleasure in the joys of his art, the admiration of his fellow-musicians, and the ovations frequently offered to him by the great Viennese public.

My lamented friend was the son of small tradesfolk in one of the pretty hamlets with which the suburbs of the Kaiserstadt are fringed. He received a rudimentary education at the village-school, and, revealing a taste for music at an early age, was put into the church-choir. The organist happened to be a skilled musician, and under his guidance little Hans, whose aptitude for study in the one direction that interested him was a source of endless astonishment and gratification to his instructor, learnt notation in all its branches, thorough-bass, singing, the violin and one or two wind-instruments, including the serpent, at that time an indispensable item in the harmonious sum-total of provincial *Kapellen* throughout the Austrian Duchies. Young Herbeck also became an excellent organist; in short, his musical acquirements were so various and remarkable that their repute reached the ears of one or two professors and critics of the *Residenz*, and eventually led to his reception in the fostering bosom of the Conservatorium. A scholarship, agreeably supplemented by a modest stipend—wealth to the frugally-reared village chorister—was presented to him, and thenceforth his career, one of extraordinary utility as well as brilliancy, was identified with that epoch of

Viennese musical history which commenced, shortly before Emperor Ferdinand's abdication, with a strong reaction from the romantic to the classical school, and as vigorously reverted, about eight years ago, to sound-painting in tone-colour, fancy *versus* form, imaginativeness as against rule—in a word, to the hyper-romanticism of Richard Wagner and his acolytes. Herbeck, as soon as he had secured a firm grasp of the conductor's bâton, did much to revive the cultus of Beethoven, which had somewhat languished in Vienna during the second quarter of the century, and assiduously kept the works of Bach before public notice. His interest in and appreciation of Schubert and Schumann were eager and keen; but he loved the older gods better than the newer, and failed to recognise true divinity in the newest of all. Had Johann Herbeck lived to the age of Cleopatra's Needle, he would never have become a Wagnerian.

Shortly after I became intimate with him—he was then in the zenith of his musical might and professional prestige—I discovered that he was a victim to chronic dissatisfaction with the chief condition of his being. He bitterly repined at not having been born, and incessantly yearned for some Imperial conferment that might remedy Dame Nature's cruel omission in this particular respect. The Emperor, who liked his simple-hearted Kapellmeister and sincerely admired his talents, had already bestowed upon him the Knight's Cross of an Order founded by himself upon acceding to the throne, and bearing his own name, Franz Josef. But this decoration, not being one of those which impart nobility to its recipient and his descendants, was a source of distress rather than of pleasure to Herbeck, who had morbidly persuaded himself that, in endowing him with so barren a distinction, its august donor had slighted rather than honoured him. His state of mind upon this fanciful grievance was a perfect illustration of the adage "Man never is, but always to be, blest;" it almost amounted to monomania. I must say that the ireful spasms soon subsided—for Herbeck was naturally one of the sweetest-tempered, most placable of men; but when the despondent fit was on him, nothing but music had power to dispel it. If, upon any pretext—an appeal to his amazing memory about some quaint morsel of church music by an obscure eighteenth-century composer was a bait he never failed to take—he could be lured to the piano, as his fingers toyed with its keys, searching for "lost chords," or all-but-forgotten *motivi*, the clouds of melancholy would lift from his pale expressive countenance, his brows would unbend, and gradually his eyes would brighten until they positively glittered. It was at such moments that a trick he had of tossing back his hair—which, like nine German Kapellmeister of ten, he wore preposterously long and full—became prominently noticeable. With apparently no greater effort than that involved in the involuntary movement alluded to, he would recall Masses, Graduali, every variety of concerted chamber music, old operas by nobodies long since consigned to the limbo of oblivion, but in which, during his indefatigable musical burrowings, he had at one time or another detected some precious gem of melody or harmonious contrivance; mouldy P.F. sonatas in exploded styles, the names of whose writers were as utterly unknown to me as the titles of the Egyptian monarchs, let us say of the forty-ninth dynasty. With the three exceptions of Hans Richter, Dr. Hans von Buelow, and Joseph Hellmesberger the elder, I have never known any " professional" gifted with so exhaustive a musical memory as that of Johann Herbeck. Dr. Schelle and Count Laurencin —two eminent Viennese critics, of whom I shall have more to say anon—used to " cram " titles of obsolete compositions out of musical lexicons and cyclopædias, and stroll up to the Kapellmeister's rooms in the Graben—it was strolling " up" with a vengeance, for the apartment was on the fifth floor of an exasperatingly lofty house—on certain afternoons he invariably spent at home. In ten cases of twelve, his friends found him sitting at the piano, composing or arranging for the orchestra, a cigar smouldering on the instrument within his reach. Somehow or other conversation at Herbeck's was always interspersed with musical illustrations. One or other of the conspirators would adroitly lead up to the name and musical period of the particular fossil they had disinterred for the occasion; let us call him Gurgelreisser, temp. early eighteenth century. " He was perhaps a little formal and crabbed," Schelle would remark, who had only committed his name and list of works to memory that very morning, and certainly had never heard a note of his music;—" but there was good solid stuff in one or two of his concerted things. How about that *divertissement*, for instance, written for two shawms, two rebecks, sackbut and psaltery? I forget how it goes. Of course you know it, Herbeck." "You mean Opus 56, the one in E minor," would be the reply;

"now I must say I find that uncommonly laboured and stiff, even for dear old Gurgelreisser, who has written matters far more genial, as you shall hear for yourselves. The *divertissement* opens thus—*largo*, forty-eight bars, introductory—and then *allegro vivace*, the melody of which seems to me not very sympathetic." Whilst talking like this, in breaks, he would play through one *motivo* after another, exemplifying the methods of treatment, until he had more or less succinctly eviscerated the entire work. Then, jerking his hair backwards and taking a pull at his cigar, he would continue, "What I consider to be a favourable specimen of Gurgelreisser's best manner is that Sonata of his, Opus 87, you know, for Tuba Mirabilis with harp accompaniments. Listen!" And off he would go into copious extracts from another long work, with which he probably possessed an unique acquaintance. So single-minded was he, that he never suspected the traps that were laid for him on these occasions. Had he done so, nothing would have been easier for him than to turn the tables on his guileful friends by improvising *ad libitum* in the style of the school to which the composer belonged whose work they had asked him to play; for his marvellous familiarity with all the successive phases of tonality enabled him to perform the most remarkable imitative feats. I remember, on one occasion, when an old musical crony carried the joke so far as to invent the name of a composer and beg Herbeck to play a few bars of a specified work by this creature of imagination, the Kapellmeister turned upon him quite indignantly, exclaiming, "Du möchtest mich zum Besten haben; es gibt keinen Componisten dieses Namens!" (You are trying to take a rise out of me; there is no composer of that name!) It was the only time I ever saw him exhibit anything like annoyance at the extravagant tax his friends delighted in levying upon his memory; nor was I ever present when he was nonplussed by demands of this nature. To me, the universality of his acquaintance with musical compositions was an inexhaustible source of wonder and envy. No matter to what period or school they belonged—no matter what might be the nationality of their author, he knew them all. In the course of an afternoon's musical chit-chat, with P.F. *obbligato*, I have heard him play through madrigals by Battishill and Wilbye, songs by Purcell and Arne, *gigues* and *passepieds* by Rameau and Couperin, *fugues* by Albrechtsberger, Scarlatti and the younger Bachs, selections from Verdi's least-known operas, *Credos* and *Glorias* by provincial Austrian, German, and Italian organists who might have been nameless for all the musical world knows of their productions— all these, besides bits and scraps of many others, as it were *en passant*, merely to illustrate some topic or suggestion of the *causerie* going on round his huge sonorous Boesendorfer. There was but one man in Vienna—oddly enough, his dearest friend and heartiest admirer, Pepi Hellmesberger—who could cap him, play what he would; and nothing could be more interesting or amusing than to get these two great musical chiefs together in a mood to compare their classical and operatic reminiscences and test one another's memories anent such pleasing trivialities as Volkslieder, Laendler and Waelzer by the innumerable melodists, unknown to fame, with whom the

Duchies of Austria proper have abounded for the last sixty or seventy years.

Poor Herbeck! most accomplished of musicians; greatest of modern orchestral conductors—not even excepting leonine Hans Richter—and most amiable, sweet-tempered, tender-hearted of men! The predominant yearning of his perturbed soul was realised a year or two after I transferred my household gods from Vienna to Berlin; but he did not live long to enjoy the proud consciousness of having been born. Either on his fiftieth birthday, or on the occasion of his jubilee as a Court musician, I forget which, Herbeck was sent for by the Emperor, from whose presence, after a brief but thrilling audience, he came out "von Herbeck"—not only he, but the heirs of his body, lawfully begotten, for evermore. Francis Joseph I. had bestowed upon him the Third Class of the Order of the Iron Crown, which decoration carries with it the hereditary title of "Ritter," or Knight, and the predicate "von," significant of inborn nobility. I only saw the Ritter von Herbeck once after his elevation to heritable knightly rank, and found him looking thinner and sadder than ever; but his falling-off in flesh and spirits was, then, alas! due to the malady that shortly afterwards carried him off. But for his physical sufferings, as he mournfully told me, he would have been a genuinely happy man; for he had obtained his heart's desire, an Imperial homage to the musical art such as Papa Haydn himself, Mozart, and Schubert, all three Austrian-born geniuses, had never elicited from the House of Hapsburg. I spent one long, never-to-be-forgotten evening with him in his mansion near the sky, talking over old times and friends, playing with him four-handed arrangements of his later concerted works, which I had not heard rendered by the orchestra, and listening to all-but-impossible feats on the pianoforte by Epstein and Joséffy, whom he had invited to meet me. It was a late séance; supper—the chief *plat* of which, I remember, was roe-venison and cranberry-jam—lasted unusually long, and the post-cœnal palaver (as usual, with P.F. illustrations) still longer. About two we took our leave, and little Joséffy, an inveterate converter of night into day, dragged me off to an extra ante-meridianal café, where he insisted upon playing me a match at billiards (Kegelspiel) for two bumpers of hot egg-punch! I never again saw Von Herbeck. Not long after that memorable evening—at once a joyous and mournful souvenir—he died somewhat unexpectedly, and was followed to the grave by the élite of Viennese musical and artistic society. I need scarcely say that an Austrian Kapellmeister, although *primus inter pares*—not being a composer of comic operas like Johann Strauss, Franz von Suppé and Rudolf Genée, or an impresario in the concert-line, gifted with sufficient enterprise and pluck to seek fortune abroad like Hans Richter—was predestined to leave little but an honoured name and revered memory behind him. Herbeck's earnings, even when he was securely lodged upon the topmost branch of the professional tree in the most musical of European capitals, never exceeded eight thousand florins—about as many hundred pounds—a year; and upon far less than that, from a Viennese point of view, magnificent income—nearly double a major-general's pay—he brought up his sons to liberal professions, received his "friends of tried adoption" with generous and tasteful hospitality, and was ever ready to empty his slenderly furnished purse when a brother-musician in trouble appealed to him for aid. He was, I rejoice to remember, happy in his wife—a clever woman, excellent manager, and most sympathetic companion—and in his children, every one of whom turned out well, so unlike the offspring of his leading musical contemporaries in the Kaiserstadt. Two years before his death he enjoyed the supreme satisfaction of seeing them firmly and comfortably established in honourable positions, affording good prospect of life-long competence, if not wealth. Oddly enough, not one of them adopted the musical profession as a means of bread-earning; nor did their gifted father urge them to follow in his footsteps, although, in his secret soul, he deemed his own the noblest of all earthly callings, and could never be brought to understand how a man with a good ear, correct feeling for time, and a genuine fondness for "concord of sweet sounds," could possibly become an engineer, barrister, surgeon, or journalist whilst there was such a thing as a cheap fiddle to be bought or a second-hand piano to be hired, wherewith to study, practise, and serve the "Divine Art." His convictions in this respect may have been eccentric; but he lived up to them to the very last moment of his life. *Es muss auch solche Käuze geben!* a fact upon which all true musicians have reason to congratulate themselves.

During my three years' residence in the Kaiserstadt (1866-9), a strong and steadfast spirit of conservatism imparted quite a classical flavour to Viennese musical criticism, which it then pervaded, and, to no inconsiderable extent, still pervades. Without accusing the musical public of Vienna—still less the able critics who at that time formed and guided that public's opinions and judgments —of reactionary tendencies, I may be permitted to recall the fact that the amateurs and dilettanti of the Residenz, seventeen or eighteen years ago, had not long enjoyed an intimate acquaintance with Beethoven's later stringed quartets and P.F. sonatas, to the former of which *chef-d'œuvres* they had been introduced by Josef Hellmesberger, the elder, at a "Quatuor Cyklus," towards the end of the fifties, since which time he and his accomplished fellow-executants had played the mighty and monumental 130, 132, 135, over and over again, season after season, until his subscribers began to know something about them, and suspicious doubt had been transformed into rapturous conviction. With respect to the last four or five gigantic sonatas, Epstein and Von Buelow had, by persistently performing them in private houses, as well as in concert-rooms, familiarised the best Vienna audiences with them, and secured to them that precious but limited popularity among experts, which they have scarcely even yet attained in this country. It was, indeed, but a little while before the Seven Days' War, which so effectually roused Austria from her intellectual and artistic as well as her financial and commercial lethargy, that the Kaiserstadt critics and musical public *d'élite* had made up their minds that Beethoven's "higher developments" constituted the Ultima Thule of the divine art—the utmost attainable in the way of invention, science, and treatment.

In a word, musical Vienna was Beethovenesque. Schubert had his partisans, and there was a Schumann faction, pushing, eager, and dictatorial; but Brahms had made no mark to speak of, and the believers in Wagner formed so small a minority in musical circles that, but for the greater noisiness of their utterances and wildness of their appearance, their existence as a party would hardly have obtained any recognition by the "craft." Wagner—surprising as the fact may seem, viewed by the light of recent demonstrations indulged in by Vienna *àpropos* of the great composer's death—was decidedly at a discount in the Austrian capital even as lately as fifteen years ago. How slightly even his most intelligible works—I mean, of course, intelligible to the million—had taken hold of the most instinctively and instructedly musical public in Europe may be gathered from the fact that *Tannhaeuser*, from its first production on the 19th November, 1859, at the Kaernthner-Thor to the closing of that opera house in April, 1869—during, therefore, a period of ten years all but a few months—was only given forty-four times, recording an average of less than five performances per annum; whilst *Lohengrin*, brought out more than a year (19th August, 1858) before *Tannhaeuser*, was played sixty-nine times, or a fraction over six times per annum, during the eleven years intervening between that date and the "last night" at the Old House. In 1861 and 1866 it was only performed once a year—in 1867, not at all! During that year, the "Ferien" or summer vacation having lasted exactly five weeks, three hundred and thirty operatic performances took place at the Kaernthner-Thor; but the Imperial Intendant, as he himself told me towards the end of the autumn, could not spare one evening "for an opera which had hitherto entailed a dead loss of from five to eight hundred florins upon the management every time it had been given."

Vienna certainly did not take so readily to the music of the future as did Berlin. *Tannhaeuser*, for instance, had become a *pièce de resistance* at the Northern Athens when it was still "caviare to the general" in the Kaiserstadt. The latter, it is true, was alike forlorn in 1867 of an "heroic tenor" or an "heroic soprano." Gustav Walter could sing anything that had ever been written for a lyric tenor voice; but he lacked the volume of tone, and if I may say so, harshness of quality required to give due effect to the declamatory parts assigned by Wagner to his heroes. Labatt, again (*das schielende Vieh*, or "the squinting beast," was the agreeable sobriquet bestowed by the Viennese public upon this artist, in virtue of a forbidding glass eye he was in the habit of wearing), had all the productive force and metallic bray needed for the adequate vocal rendering of the *Tannhaeuser* and *Lohengrin* title-rôles; but, poor fellow, he had no ear—he has not got one yet, although he is still retained upon the staff of the Hofoper, as Herr Joel used to be upon that of Evans', " in consideration of his long and valuable services "—and sang Wagner's difficult music so outrageously out of tune, besides being a person of singularly unprepossessing appearance and utterly devoid of dramatic instinct or intelligence, that the management did not dare to put him up as the Fleshly Minstrel or the Fairy Knight. Frau Dustmann was in many respects an admirable artist; but she laboured under two disabilities, as far as the parts of Elizabeth and Elsa were concerned —her dimensions and her weight. Turning the scale at fifteen stone, and being physically characterised by an exuberance of curve almost disproving the axiom that "there cannot be too much of a good thing," she was disqualified from representing a Thuringian Princess in a decline, prematurely wasted to a shadow by hopeless love, or a young virgin Countess of Brabant "under a cloud" for sorcery and fratricide; though I have seen her play Agatha in tightly-fitting white muslin, and observed with secret relish that a conspicuously stalwart huntsman had been told off by the stage manager for the onerous duty of catching her when it became incumbent upon her to swoon, in the last act. Fraeulein Ehnn, again, who was sufficiently slight and fragile in appearance nineteen years ago to impersonate the most ethereal or anemic heroines with an outward seeming of realism leaving nothing to be desired, had not at that time come to the front with sufficient prominence to justify the "Direction" in casting her for such "heavy" parts as those of Wagner's "leading ladies;" and Fraeulein Materna was nightly displaying an uncommonly handsome pair of legs to admiring audiences at the Carl, where she was engaged at 160 florins a month to play *Beinrollen*, "with a song," in comic operetta.

Berlin, on the other hand, in the year of grace 1867, was able to put *Tannhaeuser* on the boards of the Hofoper with a cast that has never been beaten since that time, though it was equalled in all-round excellence at Drury Lane in 1881, and at the Stadttheater, Hamburg, during the same year. Of Albert Niemann as Tannhaeuser,

Betz as Wolfram, the Voggenhuber as Elizabeth and the younger Grossi as Venus, it might have been surmised with equal *vraisemblance*—so admirable was their vocal and dramatic impersonation of those characters—either that the parts in question had been expressly written for them by the great Saxon composer, or that they had been specially and providentially created for the exclusive purpose of filling those very rôles in an absolutely irreproachable manner. It may well have been that Berlin's good fortune in possessing these essentially Wagnerian artists accounted in no inconsiderable degree for the greater measure of public favour accorded to Wagner's earlier operas in the Prussian than in the Austrian capital, where they cannot with truth be said to have struck root until long after they had taken to flourish exceedingly on the left bank of the Spree. *Par parenthèse* I may observe that, with respect to his later works, Vienna more than atoned for her former *lâches*, and went far ahead of Berlin—I am referring, of course, to the respective Court opera houses of those mighty musical cities, subventioned to the tune of thirty thousand pounds a year each by their Imperial proprietors—by producing *Walkuere* just six years ago, and the rest of the Nibelungen Quadrilateral within the ensuing twenty-three months; whereas the first of German theatres has not yet, unless I am much mistaken, offered its subscribers a complete performance of the *Vorspiel und Trilogie*. Tastes change as well as times. The *Meistersinger von Nuernberg*, denounced at the time of its production in Munich (21st June, 1868) by the first of Viennese, if not of European critics, with such profuse opprobrium and scathing irony, that the musical public of the Kaiserstadt made up its mind to live and die without becoming cognisant of so abominable a work, has been performed nearly a hundred times to crowded houses in the new Hofoper, and *Walkuere* nearly as many.

If, beyond its own intrinsic merits, any collateral proof were required to establish the true greatness of Richard Wagner's music, such proof might be found in the circumstances that his most "advanced" operas, within the past decade, have stormed a theatrical citadel —that of Vienna—defended by all the champion manufacturers of public opinion on matters musical, and have established themselves solidly on the répertoire of the Hofoper; not, let me add, as sops to a powerful faction, but as *Zugstuecke*—that is, pieces that infallibly "draw" the general public. And they do draw to some purpose. The last time I foregathered with my lamented friend, Franz Dingelstedt, he informed me that the receipts of the institution over which he so ably presided, had been over twelve thousand pounds, during one season of ten months and a half, from "Wagner-nights." But throughout my sojourn in the Kaiserstadt, a "Wagner-night" at the Kaernthner-Thor was not only a rarity, but a "function" to be avoided by the habitués of the opera house, inasmuch as everybody who was anybody knew that the management only put it on the bills *pour acquit de conscience.*

Leaving professional and amateur musicians out of the question for the moment, the principal and most formidable foes in Vienna to Wagner and his compositions were the three leading Austrian musical critics of that day, Dr. Hanslick, Dr. Schelle, and Count Laurencin. No man was ever endowed by nature with a brighter musical intelligence, or a more punctilious conscience than Edward Hanslick. His taste and judgment are, in the opinion of many excellent musicians, little short of infallible; no inducement upon earth, I feel sure, would move him to write a line at variance with his convictions. And yet, when I first made this eminent writer's acquaintance (for I should mention that, as a stylist, he holds a rank second to none amongst German contemporary authors), Wagner's music was as intolerable to him as a red rag to a bull or a puddle to a domestic cat. He could find no virtue in the man or his works. Possibly there was little enough discoverable in the former, from a social or conventional point of view. But Dr. Hanslick, no little to my surprise, was to all appearances irremediably insensible to the surpassing beauties, and even technical excellences, of the latter. Nothing, from a literary point of view, could be more enjoyable than the eloquent invectives elicited from him by Wagner's innovations; nor has there probably ever been written, before or since, so brilliant or truly "slashing" a musical criticism as that contributed by him to the *Neue Freie Presse* immediately after the *première* of the *Meistersinger*. It was, indeed, such a splendid piece of work that I sent it in translation to the *Daily Telegraph*, four columns of which journal were devoted to its reproduction in "minion" type, with the result, I have no doubt, that innumerable untravelled music-loving Britons contracted a life-long prejudice against the noblest, most genial, and most melodious of Wagner's lyric dramas. Some of the definitions with which this remarkable critical analysis sparkled were exquisitely felicitous—that, for instance, of "infinite melody;" "the recognised resolving of every convenient form into a shapeless, sensually intoxicating tinkle—the substitution of vague, incongruous melodising for independent, shapely-limbed melodies." Wagner's method of utilising "infinite melody" is also powerfully, if inimically, described. "A small *motivo* is struck up. Before it has had time to grow into a proper melody, or theme, it is bent, broken, set higher or lower by means of continual modulation and inharmonious shoving about; then carried on a little bit, then chopped up into pieces and cut short again, then repeated or imitated, now by this, now by that instrument. Anxiously shunning every resolving cadence, this toneless and muscleless figure flows forth into the Immeasurable, ever renewing itself out of itself . . . . The melody is not entrusted to the voices, but to the orchestra; where, being 'infinite,' it is wound out as though it were passing through a spinning-jenny. This melody-weaving orchestral accompaniment constitutes, in reality, Wagner's coherent and substantial sound-picture, the voice being compelled to accommodate itself to the accompaniment by also weaving phrases into it, half declaimed, half sung. This method of composition is diametrically opposed to that hitherto employed by every master. Heretofore, the melody for the voice was the first thing conceived by the sound-poet—the *positive* thing, to which the accompaniment (however free or complex in treatment), was made subordinate. As a rule, one could divine the accompaniment, or *an* accompaniment, to the given melody for the voice; and the accompaniment thus, in some sort, became one's own unsubstantial property. Under the Wagner 'method' the voice-part is not only something incomplete, but is, in fact, *nothing at all;* the accompaniment is everything—is an independent symphonial creation—is an orchestral *fantasia* with *ad libitum* vocal accompaniments."

Dr. Schelle, Hanslick's successor on the old *Presse*, when Michel Etienne persuaded the leading Viennese critic to enlist under the banner of the *Neue Freie*, was a less impulsive and passionate writer than Hanslick. A profoundly erudite musician and confirmed "classicist," his enmity to Wagner as a composer was of a colder, but no less deadly character than that of his illustrious contemporary. He was a man of delicate health, weak digestion, infirm of body and of temper; the calm, order, and symmetry of the "old school" of music soothed his nerves and refreshed his spirit, whilst the fervid agitations and restless tentativeness of Wagner's compositions vexed his soul, clashed with his convictions, and sometimes worried him to the verge of frenzy. To the end of his days—he died quite suddenly three years ago—he strove against tone-painting and its prophet with a stern, implacable doggedness peculiarly his own. Regarding Wagner as the Mammon of unrighteousness, musically considered, he fought him "wherever found," after the manner recommended by Artemus Ward for invariable adoption towards the Red Man. Almost his last important critical effort was a series of masterly *feuilletons* upon the Stage-Tone-Play *Parsifal*, and its rendering at Bayreuth. These articles were written with undiminished power, but betrayed a consciousness in their accomplished author that he was no longer combating on the winning side, as of yore, but vainly striving to sweep back a resistless wave of hero-worship. During my residence in Vienna I saw a great deal of Dr. Schelle, who was a difficult man to know intimately, by reason of his retiring habits and constitutional shyness, and learnt to esteem him very highly, not only as an able musical critic, but as a man of absolute truthfulness and sensitive honour. To those for whom he entertained a liking he was, moreover, a delightful companion, teeming with information and anecdote, rendered piquant by the flavour of his own dry, caustic humour.

Count Laurencin, a quaint and memorable figure in Viennese musical circles for more than a quarter of a century, whose verbal comments upon compositions and performances were the terror of "the profession," and who wrote his criticisms with a pen dipped, figuratively speaking, in gall and sulphuric acid, was another inveterate, irreconcilable anti-Wagnerian. This bitter but eminently knowledgable little gentleman may still be alive, although he was pretty old when I last sat beside him during a quartet rehearsal at Joseph Hellmesberger's seventeen years ago. If he be, I doubt not that the recent bereavement sustained by musical mankind left him unmoved, save, perhaps, by a sour spasm of rejoicing that he had nothing more to fear from Richard Wagner's productiveness. The critical Count, a natural son of the Emperor Ferdinand, but so indifferently provided for by his august father that he was fain to eke out his slender means with the modest salary paid to him for his contributions to a second-class Viennese newspaper, was so diminutive of stature as almost to belong to the dwarfish category, dark of complexion, with glittering eyes, gleaming teeth, and an angry expression of countenance that by no means belied his disposition. When listening to, or discussing Wagner's music, he was apt to foam slightly at the mouth, and to grind his teeth in a highly alarming manner. Under the influence of Mozart, or even of Papa Haydn, the ferocity of his look would something abate; but, under the most soothing circumstances, he was only, as it were, "lying by for a chance to bite." Musicians are proverbially irritable folk, but Count Laurencin was the most choleric of his tribe I ever met—and Richard Wagner was his "favourite foe."

Amongst the composers well known to fame, whose personal acquaintance I made during my residence in the Kaiserstadt, were Johannes Brahms, Franz Liszt, Anton Rubinstein, Karl Goldmark, and Robert Fuchs. My first meeting with the author of the *German Requiem* took place in the bosom of a singularly unmusical family, endowed by nature, however, with an infinite capacity for hero-worship. Every member of this household, from its head, the erudite, grizzled "Herr Doctor" —a veritable mine of scholarship and science, but barely able to distinguish "Gott erhalte unsern Kaiser" from "Ach, meine liebe Augustine"—down to its youngest *cadette*, a merry, flaxen-haired girl of sixteen, to whom melody and rhythm were inexhaustible sources of perplexity, except in so far as they served to facilitate and even promote the recreation of dancing, regarded Herr Brahms with undisguised admiration, and paid him that sort of reverent homage which lay-folk of a devotional turn, however ignorant of the religious mysteries embodied, so to speak, in an exalted ecclesiastical functionary, are apt to offer up to a high priest or archbishop. One and all, however, my friends the W——s were most excellent, worthy, and hospitable people, counting amongst the *habitués* of their dinner-table many of Vienna's artistic and literary celebrities, and possessing the inestimable social talent of keeping their guests in good humour and well entertained. Their circle, at the time the privilege of frequenting it was accorded to me, included Etienne and Friedlaender, the co-proprietors of the *Neue Freie Presse*, Vienna's leading journal for the past twenty years—Uhl, Wachenhusen, Spitzer and Speidel, feuilletonists of the first water— Gustav Walter and Caroline Bettelheim, stars of the Imperial Opera House, Professor Joachim and his gifted wife, then the first Liedersaengerin of the day, and other shining lights of music, the drama, and the plastic arts, too numerous to recapitulate in this place. Of this intellectually and artistically luminous circle, Johannes Brahms, whenever he joined it, became at once the central point and chief personage—partly in virtue of the prestige earned for him by his indisputable genius, and partly by reason of his own innate masterfulness of disposition, which enabled him, in eleven cases out of twelve, to take and keep the lead in society, no matter of what class. An imperious man, restrained from self-assertion by no reluctance to wound his neighbours' sensibilities, if he be endowed with real talent, and have done things universally acknowledged to be great, finds little difficulty in establishing himself as a social despot amongst people of average brains and courage. Having a rough side to his tongue, and being quite unscrupulous with respect to his use of it, his domineering is frequently submitted to by those who are his equals in intelligence and his superiors in breeding, but either too timid or too indolent to resist his assumption of superiority. Such an one, when I first met him some eighteen years ago, was Johannes Brahms—loud, dictatorial, a little too obviously penetrated with a sense of his surpassing greatness, violently intolerant of opinions differing from his own, curiously blunt of speech and "burschikos"—a German adjective comprehensively descriptive of the roughness characterising University manners throughout the Fatherland—but none the less a jovial spirit, strongly addicted to the pleasures of the table, and taking keen delight in highly-salted "after-dinner" stories, of which he was an ever-ready narrator, at once boisterous and unctuous. As long as he was allowed to have his own way, without let or hindrance, whether in an oracular or anecdotical mood, he was an exceedingly amusing companion, being extremely well read, clear-headed, and humorous. But he could not stand competition; a shared social throne had no charms for him, and other people's brilliancy "put him out." When by any extraordinary accident he found himself relegated to the position of "the other lion" who "thought the first a bore," his irritation too often betrayed him into actual rudeness towards people for whom he had the highest regard. At one of the W——s' select musical parties I remember an instance of how badly he could behave, even to such a man as Joseph Joachim—a prince of executant art and his intimate personal friend. Joachim had very amiably volunteered to play, and there happened to be no violin music handy except one set of the Beethoven P.F. and Violin Sonatas (that dedicated to Salieri), which was brought by our hostess to the great *virtuoso* with the request that he would ask Brahms—she had not the courage to do so—to take the pianoforte part. Turning towards Brahms, Joachim smilingly asked, "Dear master, will you vouchsafe to play this with me for the amusement of our friends here?" "I am not an accompanist," growled Brahms, and abruptly turning his back upon Joachim, strode angrily off into another room. The Hungarian violinist merely shrugged his shoulders, and looked around for a volunteer pianist. I may perhaps be pardoned for mentioning *en passant* that I had the good fortune to be accepted as Brahms' substitute, much to my gratification. Nobody except myself seemed the least surprised at the latter's pettish outburst and *sortie*. To a look of inquiry I was unable to suppress, Joachim replied, "It is his way when he is vexed; he means nothing by it;" and this view of the incident was evidently the one adopted by all present.

To FRANZ LISZT, the greatest pianist the world has ever known, I was presented by Herbeck, when the potent Abbé visited Vienna upon the occasion of the production by the Gesellschaft der Musikfreunde of his *Legend of St. Elisabeth*, a truly gruesome work. In introducing me, the Viennese Kapellmeister said—"This, strange to say, is an Englishman who loves and understands music," and I shall never forget the kindly, compassionate smile that relaxed the somewhat severe expression of Liszt's strongly-marked features as he listened to—from his settled point of view—so improbable a statement. It was a smile that seemed to say, "Very likely you believe so, you poor good Herbeck, because you are the kindest fellow alive, and the most easily taken in; but I know better!" To me personally he was, then and afterwards, uniformly gracious, never, however, conversing with me about music, of which I have no doubt he held that my nationality debarred me from knowing anything whatsoever. But I was more than once admitted to the priceless privilege of hearing him play in private during his sojourn in Vienna and subsequently in Rome, where his countryman and most intimate friend, Archbishop (afterwards Cardinal) Haynald—himself an excellent pianist—afforded me several opportunities of "sitting reverently at the Great Man's feet" when His Reverence—I mean the Canonico, not the Prelate—was seated at the piano.

One evening during the Œcumenical winter, at a musical *soirée* given by the Princess O———, Liszt's Symphonic Poem "Tasso," arranged for two pianos, happened to be lying on one of the magnificent instruments that stood side by side—head and tail—in the Princess's music-room, where some sixty or seventy personages of Roman society were assembled, amongst them the Canon of Albano. Whilst chatting with his hostess, Liszt picked up the "Tasso" arrangement by chance, asked her whether she had heard it, and on receiving a reply in the negative, said that he would gladly make it known to her, if she could find any one amongst her guests to play it with him. There were several Italian pianists, virtuosi and amateurs, present, but none of them would venture to attempt so difficult a work at sight, especially in conjunction with its composer, of whom one and all evidently stood in awe. Archbishop Haynald (he had not then received the red hat), whose rooms were next to mine at the Albergo di Roma, and who had placed his excellent grand piano at my disposal immediately upon his arrival in the Eternal City, came up to me and said, "*Hoeren Sie mal, mein Lieber!* you have played a good many hard pieces (*schwere Stuecke*) at sight with me during the past six weeks. Are you afraid of Liszt? He wants somebody to take the second piano with him, and try his 'Tasso.' I should like to do it myself, but am afraid of the fatigue. What do you say? Will you make the attempt? The thing is difficult enough—more than enough." I thought of Liszt's dubitative smile, when Herbeck had introduced me to him as an Englishman who "knew music," and at once replied, "Will your Grandeur vouch for me? I am not afraid of the great man, for the truly strong are generally merciful; and if I break down, not being a professional pianist, I shall manage to survive the disgrace of failure." Haynald took me by the arm and led me up to the illustrious compatriot, saying, "Franz, thou knowest this young man. He can read music well; he has done so with me again and again. He is ambitious to play with thee, and has the audacity to essay thy 'Tasso'! Wilt thou try him on my recommendation?" "Certainly I will," replied Liszt; and, after addressing a few kindly, reassuring words to me, forthwith took his seat at one piano, motioning me to the other. I felt as I suppose men feel when they have been told off for a forlorn hope and are awaiting the signal to advance. However, I contrived somehow to follow the Canon's superb leading, and not to put him out; the "fearsome foursome" went off without a hitch, and when it was over Liszt held out his hand to me, smiled benignly, and said only three words, "Herbeck avait raison." On the 11th of April, 1886, when my London home was honoured by his presence, he reminded me of our "quatre-mains" in Rome, more than sixteen years ago, and told me that he had written to Cardinal Haynald the same day, telling his Eminence that he (Liszt) was going to lunch with the English amateur who used to play pianoforte duets with the Archbishop of Kalocza during Rome's last winter under the Papal *régime*. I mention this fact as an instance of the clearness and tenacity of his memory at the age of seventy-five, only three months before his death. On the same occasion he alluded to several musical *ana* of that memorable winter, incidents which I had completely forgotten, and especially recalled to my remembrance the excellent playing of a Polish pupil of his, then a stripling of twenty, now a prosperous P.F. teacher, and the father of half-a-dozen children; also of his (Liszt's) having played one evening at poor Harry Arnim's to Prince Frederick of Hohenzollern, the King of Roumania's younger brother, upon whom Liszt's inimitable extemporising produced no visible impression whatever. "And no wonder," added the great *virtuoso*, "for all the Hohenzollerns I have ever known cared nothing for music, which old Prince Albrecht once told me he regarded as 'an expensive noise.' That was the man who once said about his own son, Albrecht the younger, now Regent of Brunswick, 'He cannot be a true Prussian Prince, for he does not admire women, never gets drunk, and even plays the organ!' (*spielt sogar die Orgel*)."

I cannot bring these notes to a conclusion without reminding readers that the dead composer to whom they refer was one of the most disinterested, generous and charitable men who ever lived. At least one-half of his enormous earnings, which may be reckoned by hundreds of thousands of pounds, has been given away to the poor, the suffering and the unfortunate; to encourage struggling talent and commemorate surpassing genius; to further the culture of art, spread its doctrines far and wide, and promote its intelligent worship in every civilised European country. To Franz Liszt, in common with the late Ludwig von Wittelsbach, belongs the honour of having extricated Richard Wagner from a slough of despond and dilated his heart with joyful hope when it was all but broken by despair. When Liszt did Wagner the greatest service one composer could do another he knew full well that the disappointed, soured Saxon musician disliked and distrusted him; but that knowledge did not deter him from carrying out his magnanimous purpose. For this alone mankind was his debtor—and for how many more noble deeds? For scores which have reached public cognisance, and hundreds of which he never breathed a word, even to his most intimate friends. What life had to give was his —love, friendship, popularity, dignities, distinctions and ample means, which last he held in trust for the deserving poor. Franz Liszt's was a beautiful career, teeming with light, sweetness, and beneficence.

To those who have not been so fortunate as to hear Liszt perform I may observe that his playing always was in every way extraordinary, and in several respects uniquely so. Not only had he vanquished every technical difficulty contrived by composers for the pianoforte up to his time, but had invented hundreds of new ones, some of which nobody but himself has as yet succeeded in overcoming. To him, even the most intricate and laborious of these latter were obviously mere child's play, costing him absolutely no perceptible effort. It was—that is, to any conscientious pianist thitherto inclined to "fancy himself" as a performer—at once inimitable joy and bottomless despair to hear Liszt extemporise when strongly moved by some more than unusually sympathetic theme or happy fancy. After listening, awe-stricken and breathless, to one of those unequalled musical utterances, marvels alike of invention and execution, the revulsion of feeling experienced by a pianist of the class above alluded to was little short of crushing, suggesting grim vows of never again laying finger on key, of advertising one's favourite "grand" for sale at an unprecedented sacrifice, and of foregoing throughout life all musical enjoyments save that derivable from a Liszt improvisation. Perhaps the most wonderful feature of his playing was his touch, or rather, plurality of touches—pianists will understand what I mean—one as light as a falling snow-flake or the flutter of a butterfly's wing, another as rich as Genoa velvet of triple pile, a third as clinging as a young lover's first kiss, a fourth as hard and bright as the blow of a diamond-headed hammer. He could make the instrument, to others a machine of readily exhaustible tone-resources, do anything—sing, talk, laugh, weep, and mimic orchestral effects without number. There never was and probably never will be another such genius, of the executant order, as the slender, romantic-looking Magyar—Siegfried Wagner's grandfather—who was once the most general and successful admirer of the fair sex in Europe, the object of an adoration that frequently led him into strange and even tragical adventures, and expressed itself, on the part of his fair votaries, over and over again, in extravagances of action no less comical than repulsive. The infatuated maid of honour at the court of Saxe-Weimar, whose peculiar personal flavour of stale tobacco mystified all her friends and fellow-courtiers until an accident one day revealed the astounding fact that she permanently wore in her bosom, as a sacred relic of her musical idol, an old cigar-stump that Liszt had thrown away in the street under her very eyes—she had reverently picked up the unsavoury morsel, enshrined it in a costly locket enriched with the monogram "F. L." in brilliants, and suspended it round her virgin neck, whence it steadfastly gave forth the sickly reek that so long perplexed the Grand Ducal Household—that fascinated Fraeulein, I repeat, was not the only damsel of high degree, by many a score, whose head had been completely turned by the inimitable *improvisatore*. I have seen the proudest beauties of the Austrian aristocracy crouching round him on the bare boards of a concert-room platform, in attitudes with which the love-sick maidens of *Patience* have made the British public familiar, and positively gloating upon his expressive and animated countenance. I have seen stately Roman princesses seize his hand and rapturously kiss it *à plusieurs reprises*, despite his manifest efforts to disengage it from their clutches. Never was an artist so petted by "the sex;" but successive generations of fair enthusiasts strove in vain to spoil him. He always held his own with them—and the only mistress to whom he was immovably constant is the Divine Art of Music, with which he kept up the tenderest of *liaisons* for more than half-a-century.

Anton Rubinstein I first met at Hellmesberger's "mansion near the sky" in the Tuchlauben, where the quartet rehearsals of Vienna's "primo violino assoluto" used to come off on Wednesday and Friday afternoons. Having been jocularly recommended to him by our host as "ein geschickter Umblaetterer," I was permitted to "turn over" for him whilst he played the P.F. part of his B flat trio—perhaps the most strikingly Mendelssohnian of all his instrumental works—and more than once nearly got into trouble because I could not keep my eyes from wandering to his wonder-working hands from the pages upon which my attention should have been riveted. The hands themselves, I must admit, were by no means "things of beauty," though eminently capable of imparting "joy for ever" to those who can appreciate really magnificent P.F. playing. It appeared to me, I remember well, little short of a miracle that Rubinstein should be able to achieve such intricate and delicate feats of execution and touch with fingers so short—compared to those of other great cotemporary pianists—and so bluntly tipped; but I soon got used to the marvels of his *presto pianissimo*, though how he contrives to combine a maximum of velocity with a minimum of pressure is still a puzzle to me whenever I hear him play. After Liszt, he is unquestionably the finest pianist and most ardent musical enthusiast I have ever known. Like the great Hungarian, he is heard to the greatest advantage in private, surrounded by a small number of unquestionable musicians and unfettered by any social restrictions. He abhors evening dress, and the enforced abstinence from smoking of a fashionable *salon* is utterly intolerable to him. If his quick eye detect a "profane" in the room, or if his portly cigarette be not smouldering in a corner of his mouth or on the piano convenient to his hand, he does not, cannot play his best. How many highly-polished instruments he has irretrievably ruined by allowing his cigarettes to burn long corrugated grooves in their surface whilst he has been wrestling with extemporised difficulties of his own imagining, I will not venture even to surmise. At such times, however —when the rosewood is slowly calcining and emitting a pungent scent that, as I have more than once noticed, exercises a painfully depressing influence upon the spirits of the suffering pianoforte's owner—Rubinstein plays with a passionate vigour, intensity of feeling, and subtlety of interpretation that are peculiarly his own. He is, indeed, altogether a creature of impulse — short-tempered, distractingly crotchety, and totally reckless, when annoyed, with respect to anything he may say or do. But to his friends, whose name is legion, he is the kindest, most genial, and generous fellow living, and the money he earns so deftly with his fingers has always hitherto run through them like water. He has made four or five fortunes and spent them; urgent need of ready cash has too often prompted him to turn out crude and slovenly "pot-boilers" instead of the ripe and ornate work that no composer of the present day can produce in a condition of more perfect finish than he can.

Karl Goldmark, whose acquaintance I also made through Joseph Hellmesberger during the winter of 1866-7— when the Kapellmeister was preparing the first "Goldmark'sches Streich-Quatuor" for production in the course of that season's *Cyklus*—was at that time a meek little man of thirty-four, but already slightly bent and grizzled, timid and retiring in manner, of apologetic address, shabby appearance and humble bearing. Before Hellmesberger took him up and made his works known to the musical public of the Austrian capital, Goldmark had undergone many trials and disappointments, as well as no little actual privation. Although his chamber-music and songs made a decided hit shortly after I came to know him, it was not until nine years later—and then only through his steadfast friend's influence with the Intendant of the Imperial theatres—that his grand opera, *Die Koenigin von Saba*, a work teeming with gorgeous Oriental colour, was brought out at the Hofoper. Goldmark's was one of those gentle natures that are intensely grateful for the least encouragement. A word or two of judicious praise anent any work of his composition would at any moment dispel the settled sadness of his expression, and cause his dark features to brighten with lively pleasure. I have often watched him during rehearsals of his quartets and quintets, sitting quite quiet in a corner and not venturing to make a suggestion when anything went wrong, though his eyes would flash joyously enough when the performers happened to hit off the exact manner in which he wished his meaning interpreted. A less talkative person, for a musical composer, it would be difficult to discover. Even when he was amongst his professional brethren, who were for the most part extremely kind to him, he would nervously shrink from mixing in conversation and open his lips to no one but his cigar for hours at a stretch. If abruptly addressed, he was wont to cast a deprecatory glance at his interlocutor, as though he would mildly exclaim, "Don't strike me, pray; but you may if you will!" That being "the sort of man he was," it is not surprising that I failed to become very intimate with Karl Goldmark, although I heartily admired some of his compositions, and was, for a long time, ready at any moment to develop a strong personal liking for him. But it is easier to shake hands with a sensitive plant and elicit a warm responsive grip from that invariably retiring vegetable, than to gain the friendship of a man afflicted with unconquerable diffidence; so, after several futile attempts to break down Goldmark's barriers of reserve—by which I am afraid I made him exceedingly uncomfortable—I resolved to confine my attention to his music, which, for the most part, is well worth studying and highly satisfactory to the cultivated musician's ear.

CHAPTER II.

MUSICAL REMINISCENCES OF BERLIN.—GERMAN INTONATION.—THE LUCCA-MALLINGER CONTROVERSY.—ALBERT NIEMANN.—THE ROYAL OPERA HOUSE.—PRUSSIAN VENTILATION OF THEATRES.—THE GENERAL-INTENDANT.

WHEN I first made its acquaintance, nearly twenty years ago, Berlin was not the capital of the German Empire, but of the kingdom of Prussia. It numbered barely half as many inhabitants as it boasts at the present day; and, musically considered, only ranked as the second, if not as the third city in the Fatherland. With respect to all institutions and performances connected with the divine art, Vienna was considerably ahead of Berlin, whilst Leipzig ran it hard for precedence, and Munich followed it close at heel. The "modern Athens"—a sobriquet bestowed upon Berlin, half in jest, half in earnest, by the most literary and artistic of all the Hohenzollern kings, Frederick William IV.—was at that time forlorn of a High School of Music, whilst the noble Conservatoires of Vienna and Leipzig were flourishing exceedingly and turning out dozens of accomplished artists yearly; its "Symphonie-Conzerte," organized and conducted by antique pedants, could not bear comparison with the admirable "Gesellschafts-Conzerte," given every Sunday throughout the season by the "Friends of Music" at the Imperial Redouten-Saal in the Kaiserstadt, or with the orchestral feasts served up weekly, under the direction of Karl Reinecke, in the ancient armoury of the good old Saxon city of Leipzig. In the matter of opera houses, Berlin and Vienna were about on a par up to the year 1868; the theatre on the Opernplatz, and that situate at the Kaernthner-Thor, as far as heat, lack of ventilation and evil smells were concerned, presented but minute and unimportant differences; Vienna had the better orchestra, Berlin the better singers; and both houses, being the property of monarchs who respectively subventioned them to the tune of some £30,000 a year—and who, moreover, happened to be fervent admirers of the Terpsichorean art—devoted their energies quite as vigorously (if not more so) to the production of magnificent ballets as to the attainment of excellence in operatic performances. As far as the respective leading characteristics of musical taste in Berlin and Vienna are concerned—leaving Leipzig out of the question, as a neutral territory in which no particular school predominated, but all things beautiful, old or new, classical or romantic, were equally welcome and cherished—Berlin exhibited a predilection for the music of intellect; Vienna for that of feeling. The Wagner Cultus was solidly established in Berlin several years before it took firm root in Vienna. Perhaps I may go so far as to say that the Berlinese inclined to seek instruction in music, whilst the Viennese only sought for pleasure; and that the public of the Prussian capital, in its attitude towards art and artists, was the more critical, that of the Kaiserstadt being by far the more sympathetic. It is in such *nuances* as these that the intrinsic differences existing between Northern and Southern temperaments, even in people of identical race, find expression. Prussian severity and Austrian indulgence are as plainly perceptible to the dispassionate foreign observer in connection with musical performances and compositions as in relation to military and civil administration, social observances and popular habits. In his amusements as well as in his occupations there is always present to the typical Prussian's mind the desire to improve himself—that is, to derive some personal advantage from whatsoever pursuit he may be engaged in for the time being; whereas the average Austrian is naturally disposed to take his work as easily as may be compatible with circumstances, and his recreation for recreation's sake, unalloyed by any moral consideration or interested *arrière-pensée*. The Prussian public, in its musical and dramatic appreciations especially, lacks sympathy for works exclusively belonging to the sentimental category, and excelling in expression rather than in form; whilst that of Vienna is somewhat supersensitively *en rapport* with sound-exponences of feeling, played, sung, or spoken. With respect to the capacity for judgment that is the offspring of study and cultivation, there is little to choose between them. They are both eminently musical, in that sense of the word which has of late years come to be so thoroughly understood in London and is still utterly uncomprehended in Paris. Berlin has the sounder judgment—Vienna the finer ear. Oddly enough, both publics are tolerant in vocal performances, of faulty intonation to an extent that, times without number, has caused me infinite surprise. Wagner, whose acquaintance with his countrymen's characteristics and qualities was at once profound and exhaustive, has accounted satisfactorily for this apparent anomaly in one of his luminous letters to Arrigo Boito, *e.g.*, "from a physiological point of view, by the fact that the Germans lack the true methodical voice-gift"—that is to say, the gift of producing the voice in such a manner as to ensure correctness of intonation. To this shortcoming he ascribes "the mighty influence that, for a century past, Germany has exercised upon the perfectation (*Vervollkomnung*) of music; for the creative force of a people exerts itself in the direction in which Nature has been a niggard of her gifts to it, rather than in that indicating lavish liberality on her part." Judging by the seeming indifference of Berlin and Vienna audiences to singing out of tune, one can only infer that this national insensibility of ear is the corollary of the other national shortcoming alluded to by Wagner.

In the latter part of the year 1866, when I first became closely intimate with the musical life of Berlin, there were not three *prime donne assolute* in all North Germany whose intonation was irreproachably pure, and whose vocalisation was not more or less clumsy and laboured; nor was there a single *primo tenore* capable of adequately rendering a part profusely ornamented with *fioriture:* let us say that of Don Ottavio, Almaviva or Otello. Pauline Lucca reigned in the Berlin Opera-house with undivided sway at that time; her subsequent rival, Mathilde Mallinger, was still "leading lady" at Munich, and the feud between these two eminent songstresses—which ultimately drove Frau von Rhaden to break her life-long engagement at the Prussian Hofoper and incur a very heavy pecuniary penalty—was undreamt of by either. The sprightly Viennese was then at the zenith of her professional career. The splendid quality of her voice was unimpaired, her production of it unimpeachable, her intonation all but faultless. But how was she supported on the first operatic stage of the new-born North German Confederation? It would be difficult to do justice to the turpitude, musically considered, of her lyrical colleagues, save by indulging in far stronger language than could possibly be approved of by my readers. The object of the modern German school of singing—as attained and exemplified by the *personnel* of the Berlin opera company seventeen years ago—was manifestly to develop power at the expense of quality. It appeared to take no account whatever of flexibility, *mezza-voce* production, and tone-colour. Consequently, at the time I am referring to, all the tenors at the Hofoper roared, and all the *soprani* (except Pauline Lucca) squealed. The one class of singers was as reckless as the other with regard to the *summum bonum* of all vocalisation—namely, an unflinching fidelity to the middle of the note—and yet they were tolerated—nay, vociferously applauded—by audiences especially pluming themselves upon the possession, if not the monopoly, of high musical culture and keen critical acumen.

From 1866 to 1878 this besetting sin of German operatic artists—viz., singing out of tune—characterised the concert-room singer and drawing-room amateur, as well as the exponents of the lyric drama. I well remember, at a concert I attended shortly after the conclusion of the Nikolsburg Peace Treaty—it was given by the pianist Joséffy, then a juvenile phenomenon, who subsequently developed into one of the most accomplished executants in Europe—a select audience of Berlin *dilettanti* enthusiastically recalled a good-looking songstress for performing a lengthy and elaborate *cavatina* by Rossini exactly an eighth of a tone below the key in which it was accompanied by the concert-giver. As far as amateurs were concerned, a German Fraeulein " of society " who habitually sang in tune was as remarkable a rarity—I speak, of course, only of my own distressing experiences in the *salons* of the Fatherland—as a truly melodious bull-frog. Fortunately "At Homes" with " a little music " are not so common a form of entertainment in Germany—or anywhere else upon the Continent, for that matter—as they are in this beloved isle; and foreigners, however long they may reside in Berlin, seldom acquire sufficient intimacy with native families, to be subject to the *peine forte et dure* of young ladies' vocal performances. But when I was a dweller in the Modern Athens, it was possible for any alien with what is conventionally termed " a good ear for music," to get his teeth very punctually set on edge at the Hofoper or the Sing-Akademie any night of the week throughout the winter season; nay, at the former institution all the year round, barring an interval of a few weeks' "Grosse Ruhe" during the maximum vehemence of a Boreal summer's furious heat.

It took me some time, and more suffering than I

should care to endure again, to realise the stern fact that an Art Institute of the first class, liberally subventioned by the Prussian Royal Exchequer, and so cordially supported by the Berlin public that, from a financial point of view, it really had nothing to wish for, was unable to secure the services of vocal artists capable of singing in tune. As a musical Englishman, I had for many years shared one of the most extensively circulated and rarely challenged delusions formerly obtaining in my native country, viz., that Northern Germany in general, and Berlin in particular, were the head-quarters, so to speak, of modern musical culture. In the days of my youth, that assumption was one of the articles of faith of a creed honestly and resolutely believed in by innumerable British musicians and lovers of music who had never lived in Germany. These worthy persons—it is always worthy persons who are indissolubly wedded to error—not unreasonably imagined that, because the Fatherland had produced the greatest composers of the eighteenth and nineteenth centuries, the present German school of singing must be the best, the German ear the most finely attuned, the German taste the most pure, and the German vocal executants the most accomplished. Admitting the correctness of these deductions, it would be fairly logical to derive from them the further belief that all these excellences should have attained fuller development in the Prussian capital than anywhere else. But after a few months' sojourn in Berlin, during which I spent at least four evenings a week in listening to operatic or concert-room performances, I was compelled to recognise the fallacy of the theories I had taken for granted during the unsophisticated period of my existence above alluded to; and I eventually arrived at the conclusion—which I have not seen any reason to change up to the present day—that State theatres in Germany, as far as the provision of efficient vocalists is concerned, did not keep pace with the musical requirements of the age. Their managers, cultivated and conscientious gentlemen, who labour under the disadvantage of being salaried Court officials, are not at liberty to obey their inspirations in the matter of engagements. Their position as functionaries of the State, highly paid, titled, decorated, and enjoying all the social consideration accorded in Germany to members of any Imperial or Royal Household, necessarily renders them somewhat more indifferent than is consistent with the interest of the theatre-frequenting public to the purely artistic merit of the performances given at the institutions under their control. It also leaves them forlorn of any personal, pecuniary object in securing the mere commercial success of those institutions; whilst the absence of competition with these latter deprives Royal Intendants or Directors-General of an important stimulus to exertion. Moreover, they may not pay the prices that English and American impresarii eagerly offer for first-class talent. Finally, they are confined to Germany for their choice of artists, the German language—although probably of all European tongues the least suitable to the lyric drama—being insisted upon as a *sine quâ non* by the august personages who "run" opera houses in the Fatherland. Under these circumstances, it is obviously next to impossible that they should retain in the service of their *imprese* any stars of the greater magnitudes, even of German birth, supposing the said stars to be gifted with the small modicum of intelligence required to suggest to them the expediency of learning Italian—or even English, nowadays—inasmuch as from £1,200 to £1,500 a year is the outside remuneration they are authorised to offer to a *prima donna assolutissima* or leading tenor-singer. They are, consequently, compelled to fall back upon the front rank of mediocrities—highly-instructed and hard-working mediocrities, excellent musicians for the most part, and frequently admirable actors, but to whom, as a rule, is lacking the inestimable inborn gift of singing in tune.

Of artists such as these—with the shining exceptions of Pauline Lucca and Marianne Brandt—the vocal executant staff of the Hofoper at Berlin was exclusively composed when I first became an *habitué* of its suffocating precincts. For some weeks I hardly ever attended a performance without falling into an ecstacy of astonishment at the moderation of the Berlin public's artistic requirements and the unboundedness of its endurance. To offences, as well of omission as of commission, which would have elicited showers of petty vegetables from the auditorium of a second-class Italian provincial theatre, Berlin audiences constantly accorded their approval (on the principle that "silence gives consent") and not infrequently their plaudits. I repeatedly heard Herr Fricke—the leading *basso profondissimo* of the Hofoper in 1867, who, by the way, still occupies that distinguished position—sing his whole part through a fraction of a tone below pitch. Every musical ear in the house must have suffered a long agony under that torture; but I could detect no sign of disapprobation or murmur of remonstrance. Herr Fricke was an accomplished musician and clever actor, endowed by nature with a splendid voice; a gifted painter in water-colours, and a most amiable man of excellent private character to boot. Friends of his have assured me that he has always been totally unconscious of the defect in his physical organization which incapacitated him from singing in tune, or rendered his doing so at rare intervals the strangest and most unforeseen of accidents. He was—and doubtless still is—such a worthy fellow and "quick study," had so wonderful a memory, and exceptional a knowledge of stage "business," was so indefatigable, conscientious, ready to oblige, popular among his colleagues; in fact, so thorough a gentleman and efficient an artist, except in the matter of his constitutional inability to sing exactly in the keys prescribed to him by operatic composers—that, when I knew him, he was regarded by the management of the Hofoper as a main pillar and support of that establishment. But all his positive and negative qualities, admirable as some of them were, could not have availed to maintain him in his position as the typical Sarastro, Falstaff, Commendatore, Marcel, Pogner, &c., &c., of the Berlin Opera-house, but for the fact that the Berlin public was content to put up with him. It did more; it liked him, and virtually endorsed his chronic discordances. The professional critics treated him with undisguised tenderness; society *dilettanti* shrugged their shoulders whenever I ventured to utter a mild protest against his faulty intonation, and replied, " But he looks so well on the stage; he is such an intelligent, trustworthy actor; besides, where can we find a better than he in Germany now-a-days?" It was upon such grounds as these that Berlin tolerated a singer who invariably put every concerted machinery with which he had to do out of gear, and whose *soli* cried aloud to Apollo for vengeance. Its admiration for Mathilde Mallinger, two or three years later, was similarly founded. She was an excellent actress, endowed with a voice of singularly unpleasant quality, and with an ear well nigh as defective as that of Herr Fricke. And yet an important section of the Berlin musical public pitted her against Pauline Lucca, and carried their partisanship to such lengths that they eventually succeeded in giving the latter artist mortal offence—with the result that she turned her back upon the German capital in utter disgust!

I have above pointed out one or two of the shortcomings characterising the organization and performances of the Berliner Hofoper at the time I first made its acquaintance, some three months after the conclusion of the so-called Seven Days' War. Those shortcomings, I have good reason to believe, are as conspicuous now as they were then; for the Hofoper is conducted upon strictly Conservative principles by an aristocratic ex-Guardsman, to whom innovations are an abomination, and who is at once as autocratic and thrifty as was the great Frederick himself, when that many-sided monarch played—and played successfully—the part of an operatic impresario. Eight years ago, I was still a resident in the German capital, where my abode had been fixed in the autumn of 1871, as I then believed for the remainder of my mundane existence; and the drawbacks above alluded to were at that time as apparent as they had been at any period of the preceding decade. More so, indeed; for the Hofoper had been bereaved of its one pearl of great price in the *prima donna* line, and was on the point of losing a gem of minor lustre but unquestionable value, by which the said pearl had been more or less efficiently replaced ever since the Lucca-Mallinger controversy had resulted in Frau von Rhaden's indignant repudiation of her Berlin engagements. Pauline was gone, having vowed by all her gods she never would return; Mathilde was going, her voice having completely collapsed under the strain of leading Wagnerian soprano-parts, and had solemnly announced her intention of exchanging "endless melody" for spoken dialogue. The *prime donne* still on the permanent staff—not one of them was indisputably *assoluta*—were Frau von Voggenhuber-Krolop, the wife of the comic baritone, a good declamatory singer and clever dramatic actress, but by no means exceptionally favoured by nature as to voice or person; Fraeulein Grossi, a singularly handsome woman, whose singing never failed to remind me of an excited peacock's screeching, and whose extraordinary good looks probably justified her, in her own opinion, for the commission of sins uncounted, dramatic as well as vocal; and Fraeulein Lilli Lehmann, a striking-looking young lady with a harsh soprano, a faulty ear, and considerable command of execution alike lacking in spontaneity and finish; but, in spite of all these disadvantages, the only "Coloratur-Saengerin" of any moment at the disposal of the Hofoper management. To have heard these three ladies simultaneously, sustaining important parts in one and the same opera—let us say, *Don Juan*—may be described as a quite unparalleled musical experience, not to be forgotten, nor ever recalled to mind without a shudder. Upon them, however, the Berlin Opera-house has been for several years past dependent for the execution of all the leading soprano parts in its extensive répertoire, lyrical as well as dramatic. In fact, as far as *prime donne* are concerned, it has never rallied from the loss of Pauline Lucca, for which it had to thank the injudicious partisanship of Mathilde Mallinger's irrepressible admirers.

For many months before that crowning calamity befell the management, a war of opera-going factions had raged in the German capital. Musical Berlin was split into two camps, the denizens of which burned with mutual animosity. Those upon whose banner the name of Lucca was inscribed were the more numerous and socially influential. On the other hand, the Mallingerites were the more energetic, persevering, unscrupulous. Long and bitter was the contention between the followings of these rival sirens, whose tempers caught fire at the angry passions of their respective votaries, and more than once brought them into vehement collision on the stage in the presence of the public, when they both happened to be singing in the same opera. They could hardly be decently civil to one another, even when the "business" of their parts required them to be tenderly affectionate. In vain did the distracted Intendant, Herr von Huelsen, strive to conciliate either of them, and to keep on tolerably good terms with both. They were not to be talked over by *him*, nor even by the kind old monarch, his master, who over and over again tried to persuade them to conclude an armistice, personal and factional, in their own interests as well as those of art. If glances could have slain, they would both have died a hundred deaths whenever they had to act together. I used to watch the two irate little ladies with a mixture of amusement and alarm, when they were "on" at the same time. The disdainful looks they flashed at one another were, from a spectator's point of view, irresistibly funny, and yet suggested the apprehension of something terribly imminent, in the way of *voies de fait*, to any one acquainted with the reckless impulsiveness that was the only characteristic, perhaps, they possessed in common. One could never know, at such moments, what might happen; nor would the *habitués* of the stalls and side-boxes have been greatly surprised if Cherubino and Susanna had exchanged bites instead of kisses, or if Dames Ford and Page had broken off their plot against the Fat Knight's peace to indulge in an animated scratching and slapping bout. This uncertainty imparted an anxious interest to all the performances in which Mesdames Lucca and Mallinger were simultaneously engaged, as far as the audiences were concerned; but it made the manager's life a burden to him, and brought about an altogether intolerable state of affairs behind the scenes.

Meanwhile, "in front" and outside the theatre, the "Pauline" and "Mathilde" factions chronically vilified and not infrequently belaboured one another with infinite spirit and persistency. The worshippers of Elsa (one of Frau Mallinger's happiest impersonations) made it their business to wait, hundreds strong, by the stage-door in the Opernplatz until Zerlina—in which character Pauline Lucca was simply inimitable—issued therefrom, in order to hoot and pelt her. On one occasion some cowardly cad threw a stone at her carriage just as she had entered it, breaking one of the windows and inflicting a slight cut upon her right cheek. Again, when the Mallinger made her appearance on the stage, she would be saluted with a storm of hisses and whistlings by a packed house of Lucca enthusiasts, every man Jack of whom was so fired by the conviction that his idol was the most fascinating, soul-subduing songstress and actress in creation that he found himself unable to tolerate the presence of any other *prima donna* upon the Hofoper boards. Once or twice—notably, one dreadful evening when the Mallinger was playing Susanna to her detested rival's " farfallone amoroso "—the performance came to a dead stop, and the curtain had to be lowered in the middle of the action of the piece, owing to the absolutely riotous behaviour of the antagonistic factions. Some minutes later on, when—the disturbance having been partially quelled by the energetic interference of the police—the curtain again rose, discovering Cherubino and Susanna "as before," Frau von Rhaden considerably astonished the audience by advancing rapidly to the footlights, withering her persecutors by such a look of indignant contempt as no one present had ever theretofore seen gleaming from her bright blue eyes, and scornfully exclaiming, "You are very badly bred people! I am not accustomed to be insulted; pray understand this, once for all!"—with which she turned her back on the house and quitted the stage; nor could she be induced to return to it that evening. Indeed, but for the entreaties of an exalted personage, from whom she had received countless proofs of esteem and affection, that hot rebuke would have been her final farewell to the Berlin public. She had formed the resolve to abandon, at once and for ever, the scene of her greatest triumphs; but that resolve was modified, in deference to the highest influence in the land, personally brought to bear upon her that very night before she left the theatre. However, the insolent ingratitude displayed towards her by the Berlinese, whom she had served so long and so faithfully, rankled in her wounded spirit, and eventually instigated her to break her contract with the Hofoper management—thereby forfeiting her pension-rights and incurring a heavy pecuniary penalty—and to shake the dust of Berlin from the soles of her feet. As soon as it became known that she was really gone, both factions were stricken with consternation, and the organs of the Mallingerites were profuse in penitential utterances, whilst the Luccaites ceased from troubling, and the calm of discomfiture reigned throughout the auditorium of the Opera-house. Frau von Schimmelpfennig (Mathilde Mallinger, about that time, espoused an impecunious Prussian Junker rejoicing in that somewhat remarkable patronymic) remained mistress of the field—sole and absolute "leading lady" of the Hofoper company—but speedily wrecked her voice by too assiduous devotion to Wagner's declamatory parts, and was compelled, in her turn, to leave the stage from which her admirers had driven a far greater *cantatrice* and dramatic artist than she.

Looking back with my mind's eye to the scanty array of tenors affected to the service of the State and the delectation of the public in the Berlin Hofoper within the past twenty years, I see one massive and comely form towering above a feeble herd of pigmies. Ever since I have known that establishment, Albert Niemann has reigned supreme upon its boards—over vocalists of his own category, of course. Once, I have been assured by hundreds of more or less trustworthy persons, he possessed a magnificent voice; an organ of inimitable beauty and power; but not in my time. Ere I first heard him sing, he had sacrificed that priceless gift of Nature to Wagner and conviviality. I only know him, in his public capacity, as the finest tragic and romantic actor living of those connected with the lyric drama, as a man of extraordinary, splendid *physique* and noble bearing, and as an exceptionally accomplished musician. In private life I have found him an eager and skilful sportsman (like another famous *tenore robusto*, Ernest Nicolini, he is enthusiastically addicted to all kinds of fishing), a well read and highly entertaining *causeur*, and the most jovial of boon companions at table. But of his voice's glory, as it must have been when it raised him, an unknown young strolling actor, with surprising suddenness to the uncontested leadership of Germany's "heroic" tenors, I know nothing. My first experience of his vocalisation was acquired during his performance of the title-rôle in *Tannhaeuser*, towards the close of the 1866 autumn. It was a painfully disappointing one. His voice, even then, was nothing more than a splendid ruin. He had torn it to tatters by persistent shoutings at the top of its upper register, and undermined it by excessive worship at the shrines of Bacchus and the Paphian goddess. Although his intonation was generally correct, its rare departures from central truthfulness being exclusively ascribable to fatigue—never to any shortcoming in his sense of tunefulness, which has always been exquisitely keen—his "production" was characterised by a huskiness and scratchiness infinitely distressing to listen to. In these respects it has suffered but little change, either for the better or the worse, since the occasion referred to. When he made his London début three years ago at Her Majesty's Theatre in the declamatory part of Siegmund (*Walkuere*) his delivery was not appreciably hoarser or harsher than it had been sixteen years previously. Untravelled metropolitan *dilettanti*, who had heard and read of Albert Niemann as the first tenor singer of the Fatherland, could hardly believe their ears whilst listening to his husky declamation, with all the cracks, flaws, and roughness to which his Berlin admirers have for so many years past been accustomed that they have long ceased to regard them as defects, and not infrequently speak of them in respectful rather than critical terms as "Niemann's individual peculiarities of production." But the musical and dramatic judges of this city were unanimous in their recognition of his surpassing abilities as an interpreter of the Wagnerian ideal, in which speciality, despite his vocal shortcomings, he still knows but one rival throughout the length and breadth of Germany—to wit, Hermann Winkelmann. Although he is well advanced in his fifty-sixth year the splendour of his *physique* and the youthfulness of some of his attributes— for instance, the rich bright golden hue of his flowing hair and luxuriant beard, the luminous limpidity of his light blue eyes, the elasticity of his gait, and the uprightness of his lithe yet stalwart figure—are altogether unimpaired. He and the German Crown Prince, to my mind, are absolute types of comely and vigorous German manhood. Both these magnificent men have the true heroic look and bearing. By a quaint coincidence, they are identical in age, stature, and complexion.

Albert Niemann was born at Magdeburg in January, 1831. Like his brother-tenor and fellow-fisherman, Nicolini, he is the son of an innkeeper, and was an unmanageable boy, gifted with great physical strength and exuberant natural spirits, recalcitrant at his studies, and devoted to athletic sports. When he was seventeen his father bound him to an engine-maker, although by that time he had already made up his mind that his vocation was that of the sock and buskin. A few months later he suddenly vanished from his workshop, and presently turned up under a pseudonym at Dessau, as a "super," soon to be promoted to small speaking parts, and subsequently to a leading post in the chorus of the Hoftheater in that artistic little provincial capital. His first serious instruction in the science of music and in the art of vocalisation was imparted to him by the Ducal Hofkapellmeister, Fritz Schneider, who, having "spotted" his remarkable musical aptitude, taught him "the rudiments," free, gratis, and for nothing, as the saying goes. For a few years he led a jovial, wandering life, readily obtaining short engagements (he would not accept long ones) at the minor opera houses of North Germany, at one of which it happened, when he was about four or five and twenty, that Von Huelsen, the General-Intendant of the Royal Theatres in Prussia, heard him sing, and shortly afterwards summoned him to Berlin, where the means of further instruction and improvement were generously placed at his disposal. The late King of Hanover subsequently sent him to Paris to study under the great Duprez, and on his return to Germany engaged him at the Hanover Court Theatre. When the Guelphic realm was annexed to Prussia in 1866, Niemann became a permanent member of the Royal Operatic Company at Berlin, of which he has ever since remained the one "fixed star" of the first magnitude that, in the opinion of his worshippers, age cannot dim, nor custom stale. He has had two beautiful and talented wives, the actresses Seebach and Raab, from one of whom he was divorced after (it is whispered) having projected her into space through a first-floor window in a moment of temper brought on by the breaking of a favourite Japanese vase. Musicians, like poets, are a *genus irritabile;* and Berlin regarded this feat as an amiable eccentricity on the part of its handsome favourite.

Having devoted a considerable portion of this chapter to an exposition of the executive shortcomings and blemishes that have characterised that important musical institution, the Royal Opera-house at Berlin, ever since it became intimately known to me—some twenty years ago—I think it but fair to point out some of its more salient merits and excellences before essaying to record other souvenirs connected with music in the Prussian capital. In many respects the Berliner Hofoper renders invaluable services to art and its votaries on the one hand, and to the German public on the other. Its management is inspired and guided by two fine, wholesome principles, which govern its routine work and animate its enterprises—absolute catholicity in art and generous encouragement to native talent, or, to put the case in more familiar imagery, Free Trade to composers and Protection to executants. Unlike certain operatic *imprese* in Paris and other great French cities, it uncompromisingly recognises the great fact that musical compositions are of no nationality, and acts upon that eternal truth with unimpeachable consistency. Its patriotism, which is vigorous, but not bigoted, asserts itself in the employment of German artists, officials, and handicraftsmen throughout all its departments, and in the use of the German language for all its vocal performances. Further than this, its spirit of nationalism never prompts it to exercise monopoly. Within my remembrance the Hofoper has produced a large number of works by French composers, for instance, with no less care and outlay than it has bestowed upon those of German origin. Bizet's *Carmen,* and Délibes' *Le Roi l'a dit* were brought out upon its boards, magnificently mounted and with its best cast, at a time when no Parisian manager would have dared, for his life, to propose the production of Wagner's *Lohengrin,* or Goetz's *Der Widerspenstigen Zaehmung.* Angrily excited as was German popular feeling against France and Frenchmen during the terrible struggle of 1870-71, the *chefs-d'œuvres* of Gounod,

Auber, Halévy and Méhul were not even temporarily withdrawn from the répertoire of the Royal house, but appeared on the bills in their due turn (according to certain prescribed customs of the establishment) and drew, so the General-Intendant subsequently informed me, audiences quite as numerous and sympathetic as those which attended performances of *Die Zauberfloete* or *Der Freischuetz*. In no European opera house—above all, not in that so long and conservatively directed by M. Halanzier—have Rubinstein's operas been so splendidly put upon the stage, so favourably received and so frequently given. I have even heard Michael Balfe's *Bohemian Girl*, under the German title of *Die Zigeunerin*, far better played and sung in the house on the Opernplatz than it had thitherto (within my personal experience) been rendered in London—in a word, as carefully and intelligently as it has in later years been performed by the Carl Rosa Opera Company.

Another admirable feature of the Berlin Opera-house is its paternal solicitude for the material welfare and mental tranquillity of the members of its staff, no matter of what artistic rank or bureaucratic position. To every person enlisting under its banner it offers a sure subsistence for life, only forfeitable in case of misconduct or voluntary retirement from the establishment on the part of the individual engaged. This system of superannuation pensions, although by no means organized upon an extravagant scale, is found to work advantageously to the institution. The prospect of securing a sufficiency, if not a superfluity of means in old age, is a great attraction to respectable people to accept engagements at moderate salaries, and fulfil them conscientiously. It proves also a stimulus to general good conduct, and the most efficient of checks to the heat of temper and whimsicality that characterise so many musical and dramatic artists. It enables the obscure carpenter or humble dresser, as well as the renowned leading tenor or *chef d'orchestre*, to consider himself as *inamovible* as a judge or a Government clerk, and to contemplate his future, up to the very day of his death, with an equanimity which is the offspring of a comfortable certitude that, come what may, he is provided for in this world. It facilitates discipline—always a main object in every Prussian institution, Royal or private—and imparts a hierarchical *cachet* to the relations between all classes of the Hofoper's *personnel*, obviating a great deal of the vehemence from above, and impertinence from below that make themselves so unpleasantly manifest behind the scenes of most German theatres. Many of the assured positions connected with the Hofoper invest their occupants with honorific titles, to which all Germans, and especially the Prussian variety of that race, attach enormous value and importance; and the effect of this ingenious arrangement, based upon a solid foundation of human vanity, and costing absolutely nothing to its constructors, is to foster a high standard of behaviour in the persons glorified by it. The be-titled vocalist, instrumentalist, box-keeper or check-taker, considers it imperatively incumbent upon him to live up to his predicate; and the super, scene-shifter, or machinist, looking far forward down the long vista of years, perceives it to be faintly possible that he, too, may attain a post ready fitted with a prefix, and regulates his conduct accordingly. As a matter of fact, all these privileges, real or imaginary, extended to members of the Opera-house staff in virtue of the Sovereign's proprietorship of that theatre, contribute in no inconsiderable degree to the aggregate of efficiency with which the enterprise is carried on. Everybody on the establishment has a more than weekly, monthly, or even yearly inducement to do his or her duty to the very best of his or her ability, and to bear him or herself irreproachably in private, as well as public life. The concrete result of this state of things, is that order and discipline, punctuality and decorum prevail throughout every department of the Hofoper. Considered as a piece of executive and administrative mechanism, it functions with the unswerving exactitude of a first-rate chronometer.

Perhaps the permanency of appointments to the Opera-house staff *does* exercise a somewhat too fossilising influence; for instance, upon the Terpsichorean department, and that of the singing supers. Sylphs of sixty and grandmotherly fairies are by no means uncommon apparitions in the course of the Hofoper ballets; the pension system also has a tendency to keep aged demons and infirm sprites before the public until the time of life at which they become qualified for the advantages of retirement. If I remember aright, forty years' continuously active service entitles the *ballerina* to cease from capering, and the *figurante* to be at rest. Long before these artists have, however, completed the term in question, they have ceased to contribute, to an appreciable extent, to keeping up any audience's illusions with respect to the uniform juvenility of the *corps de ballet*. Paint and padding work wonders, as every one knows; but when, as I have more than once observed at German Court Theatres—three generations of a dancing family figure simultaneously upon the stage, no spectator unendowed with extraordinary force and elasticity of imagination can be reasonably expected to accept the managerial implication that all the fays or *almées* displayed behind the footlights have at least one characteristic in common—that of youth. On the other hand it cannot be denied that veteran *figurantes* are invaluable for the example of precision they set to their daughters and grand-daughters in executing the more complicated manœuvres of a ballet *ensemble*. They are the ballet-master's most trustworthy *aides-de-camp*, and take by far the greater part of his troubles off his hands, not only by their ready understanding and exact fulfilment of his directions, but by keeping their young colleagues in order. Still, from the general public's point of view, their venerable aspect is decidedly out of keeping with the characters assigned to them, and a lavish display of sexagenarian charms is the reverse of exhilarating to the spirits. For obvious reasons the ravages of extreme old age are less noticeable in the *personnel* of the chorus than in that of the ballet; but any *habitué* of the Berlin Opera-house can hardly have failed to notice that its peasants, noblemen and bandits, when verging upon senility, as is their wont by reason of the pension-system, experience no inconsiderable difficulty in keeping their voices up to concert-pitch. Patriarchs cannot be justly reproached with singing out of tune; but the management of a musical institution has no right to persistently harass the ears of its supporters with defective intonation. In weighing the advantages to be derived by the audience from a very old chorus-singer's ripe experience against the disadvantages resulting from the decay of his physical powers, the former will be found to kick the beam as far as public opinion is concerned—even in Berlin, where regular opera-goers are surprisingly tolerant of shortcomings that would be vehemently resented by London audiences.

With respect to its administration, stage-management, and orchestral performances, the Hofoper of Berlin is on a par with that of Vienna. I can offer it no more comprehensive tribute of praise and admiration. Its "plant," in the way of costumes, appointments, and stage accessories, is the most complete and valuable in existence, and constitutes one of the most interesting sights to be seen in the German capital, comprising, as it does, the wherewithal to equip an entire company for over a hundred operas and between thirty and forty ballets at, so to speak, a moment's notice. The arrangement of these accumulated treasures is simply admirable—a triumph of intelligent and painstaking organization. That of the armoury, in particular, may fearlessly challenge competition by one and all of the celebrated national collections of weapons and military trappings to which Murray and Baedeker devote pages upon pages of elaborate description. From the Grecian hero's spear down to the Prussian Guardsman's Mauser rifle, every variety of arm is displayed in this magnificent museum, the special pride and glory of His Excellency the Intendant-General. Need I say that its contents are kept spotless and burnished to a maximum of brilliancy, or that the post of chief-armourer to the Royal Opera-house is one of the most important, responsible, and dignified in that establishment? The armoury, as well as the *garderobe* and scene-repository, is located in the enormous building occupying the greater portion of the vast Opern-platz and containing a theatre as large as Drury Lane, a concert-room but little smaller than St. James's Hall, and all the departmental offices except that of the chief manager, Herr Botho von Huelsen, whose *bureaux* are situated in the Behren Strasse, hard by the seat of his immediate dominion, and facing the back of the Emperor's unpretending palace, Unter den Linden. The Opera-house, in fact, is self-sufficing, a miniature *imperium in imperio*, submitted to the rule of a knowledgable and benevolent despotism, and comfortably accommodating its administration, bureaucracy, army, Court, &c.— as well as a magnificent library and collection of manuscripts—under its own roof. The institution domiciled within its walls very nearly realises the Prussian ideal, *i.e.*, a minimum of expenditure and maximum of efficiency. I say very nearly, because the concrete result of all the intelligence, conscientiousness, and economy brought to bear upon the Hofoper by its management, is too frequently a mediocre—now and then even an absolutely bad—rendering of a good opera. That this should be so appears at first sight scarcely less surprising than regrettable. The manager, and everybody administratively connected with him, do their best, but are hampered in their efforts by circumstances over which they have no control. The orchestra, too, does its best, which is practically unsurpassed by the achievements of any other Continental orchestra. Finally, the vocal artists do *their* best—which, unfortunately, is not *the* best. "And why not?" will not unnaturally be asked.

The answer is that the German public will have its amusements cheap. However full the *salle* of the Hofoper may be—and it is crowded at least five times a week—the prices paid for its places do not, and cannot defray the expenses of an establishment carried on upon so large a scale and offering so great a variety of entertainments to its frequenters. Above all, they do not permit the management, even with the assistance of the Royal subsidy, to make it worth the while of first-class vocalists to accept engagements of any but a "starring" or transitory nature at the Berlin Opera-house. It is the six shilling stalls, three shilling pit, and shilling gallery, in a house holding barely two thousand people when crammed to the ceiling, that compel the authorities to fall back upon inexpensive songsters, who are for the most part accomplished musicians, but who also, as a rule, sing out of tune.

Looking back to a course of assiduous opera-going and concert-attending in Berlin, extending over eight consecutive years, were I called upon to record, with meat-lozenge condensity, the characteristics of Berlinese musical entertainments which have left the strongest impressions upon my memory, I should do so thus:— 1. Instrumental excellence; 2. Vocal mediocrity;

3. Overpowering heat; 4. Triumphs of anti-ventilation, architectural and administrative; 5. The conceivable maximum of public susceptibility to draughts. Terseness, I know, is lacking to my definitions of the last two impressions; I confess my inability to propound them in fewer words. The temperature prevailing within the Hofoper and chief concert-rooms of the German capital during performances was little short of maddeningly high in my time—the sort of heat in which a person of lively imagination might be justified in expecting thermometers to explode like well-warmed soda-water bottles, scattering quicksilver spray around them in every direction. As for the respiratory arrangements at that time obtaining in buildings dedicated to the service of musical art, they may be not unfairly described as constituting the practical negation of every ventilation theory that has ever yet sprung from the human brain. Whether the sensitiveness of the Berlin musical public to draughts generated this state of things or was its offspring I shall probably never know. This problem, like that of the Greek sophist concerning the precedence of hen or egg, is "one of those things no fellow can understand;" and as its solution would probably not augment the aggregate felicity of my readers to any considerable extent, I will crave their permission to forbear its further consideration in this place. For the fact that, during my sojourn in Berlin, any irruption of fresh air into the *auditorium* of the Hofoper or Sing-Akademie during a performance was invariably regarded by the audience for the time being with feelings of undisguised consternation and resentment, I am ready to pledge my solemn

assurance. Many and frequently ludicrous have been my personal experiences of this peculiarity in the Berlin musical public. The following true story may serve to illustrate that public's attitude towards ventilation, as it has been steadfastly maintained (so, at least, say the Hofoper traditions) from the days of Frederick the Great down to the period of which I am writing. Moreover, I am assured that it is unchanged at the present moment.

Some eight or nine years ago, a series of unusually bitter onslaughts, succeeding one another at brief intervals throughout a whole winter season, was made upon the " Intendantur "—an impersonality comprising in itself the management and administration of a theatre —of the Hofoper by the political, artistic, and comic press of Berlin. Herr von Huelsen was arraigned upon all sorts of charges—innumerable sins, of omission as well as of commission, were ascribed to him—he was solemnly caricatured and grimly ridiculed, in verse and prose, with that cold and cutting ill-nature which is the typical Prussian humourist's notion of fun. The Royal Court Theatre Director was reproached for engaging inferior artists, for reviving obscure works that nobody wanted to hear, for failing to produce novelties of indisputable merit, for perpetrating anachronisms in the setting and mounting of pieces; and, finally, for stewing the public quite insufferably in the theatre submitted to his rule, " all for want," as the *National Zeitung* was wont to reiterate about once a week, " of a little, simple, elementary ventilation, such as the merest tyro in architecture or ordinary mechanics could apply to the Hofoper within a few hours, and at a nominal expense." Upon this lack of ventilation—which, by the way, was not at all peculiar to the Hofoper—Berlin journalism, heavy and light alike, was down with remarkable force and pertinacity. The auditorium of the Opera-house was portrayed as a Roman calidarium; its stalls occupied by nude perspirers, and its stage by emaciated ballet-dancers, worn to mere shadows by a tropical temperature. Counterfeit presentments of Herr von Huelsen in the characters of a stoker, of a gardener in the act of "forcing" rows of flowers arranged to represent a theatrical audience, of a "hermetical sealer" (this was a very subtle specimen of pictorial satire, calling for elaborate explanation in the way of foot-notes), and of several other more or less ludicrous personages, abounded in the weekly "Witzblaetter," causing that gentleman to writhe and his friends to beam with smiles.

The much-exercised Intendant-General, having fumed and fretted under journalistic castigation for several successive weeks, made up his mind quite suddenly one morning that, with the venerable Emperor's permission, of obtaining which to any innovation involving real increment of public comfort in a Royal establishment he felt tolerably certain, he would at least quash for ever one of the special Press indictments brought against him, to wit, that he was an inveterate stewer and suffocator of his fellow-subjects within the precincts of the huge theatre on the Opern-platz. "Stifling no longer makes them happy, it seems; they would rather have their pores shut than open; they have developed a sudden objection to carburetted hydrogen, and exhibit strange yearnings for oxygen and ozone." Thoughts like these, I have reason to believe, fluttered through the great man's brain as he sate brooding in his "three-pair front" Behren Strasse 2, on the forenoon in question, and prompted him to sally forth, cross the street to the private entrance of the Palace, and ask for a special audience of the Hofoper's exalted proprietor. What passed during his interview with that truly great and good man I am precluded from disclosing, partly by the dictates of discretion, and partly by the fact that I know nothing whatever about it. The concrete result, however, of the Kaiser's privy confabulation with his Intendant-General was that the latter incontinently sent for one of the Court Architects, and that a few days later mysterious scaffoldings began to crop up here and there on the exterior surface of the Opera-house, much to the perplexity of the Berlin "knowing ones," who—well assured that the Royal Theatre was in perfect repair, within and without—cudgelled their brains in vain to divine what could possibly be the object of the operations in course of execution upon the outer shell of that building. As far as the local press and the general public were concerned, the secret was well kept; but a friendly chamberlain divulged it to me one evening at an august tea-party, in a burst of confidence which, I am happy to believe, was not altogether undeserved, inasmuch as I have kept his counsel upon the matter rigorously from that day to this.

Herr von Huelsen had obtained the royal permission to ventilate the *auditorium* of the Hofoper, and to expend the important sum of six thousand thalers (£900) in so doing, the money to be supplied from the *Kœnigliche Schatulle*, or Privy Purse. Neither His Majesty nor the Intendant-General, as I was informed, looked forward over-hopefully to the effect of scientific ventilation upon the *habitués* of the Opera-house; but the latter, for personal reasons, was eager, and the former benevolently willing, to try the experiment, which accordingly was carried out in the *ad libitum* but thorough-going manner for which skilled German artisans are so justly renowned. Weeks elapsed, and by degrees the mysterious scaffoldings disappeared one after another, until at last the Hofoper's roof and sides reassumed their normal aspect. Happening to call at the Intendantur one afternoon about that time, I took occasion to inquire how the new ventilating apparatus was getting on. "Attend the performance of *Lohengrin* (*Hohe-Preise*) next Tuesday evening, *geschaetzter Herr Redakteur*," was the reply, "and you will witness the *début* of our never-sufficiently-to-be-admired hygienic innovation. The public as yet knows nothing of what we have done in the interest of its health and comfort. We shall take the audience quite by surprise; pleasantly, we hope. Of one thing at least we are sure by anticipation— namely, that we shall leave no doubt upon the mind of any one present as to the practical efficacy of the arrangements now completed for the sufficient airing of His Majesty's Opera-house. Enough for to-day, worthiest sir! I have no more to communicate." This hint— more, perhaps, in the manner of its delivery than in its mere matter—seemed to me fraught with promise of entertainment. On the following Tuesday, accordingly,

I was in my accustomed stall at seven precisely, just in time to see my friend Carl Eckert take his place at the conductor's desk and look over his acolytes with a circular and severely-inquiring glance before executing the smart double rap that never failed to concentrate their attention upon the tip of his ebony bâton.

It was, I well remember, an exceptionally cold, raw evening of that early so-called "spring" which, in Berlin as well as in London, is almost invariably so much more killing a time of year than the deepest depth of winter proper. As was, and I believe still is, always the case on a Wagner night, the house was crowded throughout; fashion in the side-boxes and dress-circle; science and dilettantism in the stalls, abundantly provided with spectacles and full scores; various grades of the musical *bourgeoisie* in the three tiers of upper boxes, and a host of appreciative proletarians in the cheap and capacious gallery. By the time the overture had come to an end every place available to the general public was occupied, and the temperature had risen to its customary tropical degree of elevation. "If this," I found myself thinking, " be the result of the new ventilation system, the Emperor, save for the honour of the thing, might just as well have saved his money." Had the audience been exclusively composed of orchids they could not have been more congenially accommodated in the way of atmosphere. Henry the Fowler, however, had scarcely taken his seat under the shade of the Justice Tree, the public having meanwhile settled down to enjoy and perspire in compliance with hallowed Hofoper traditions, when suddenly piercing jets of iced air invaded the house from every direction simultaneously. The effect in the stalls was that of a lively breeze; persons located higher up in the house described their experiences to me subsequently as varying between a moderate gale and a circular wind-storm of no inconsiderable violence. Looking round me at my immediate neighbours, I observed that amazement sate upon their brows. Obviously they failed to realise by what uncanny enchantment their favourite musical sudarium had thus malignantly been transformed into a Cavern of the Winds. Presently surprise was succeeded by indignation. Scores of men rose in their places, shouting "Es zieht! es zieht!" —which may be freely rendered in our vernacular by "What a draught!"—turning up their coat-collars and putting on their hats. Still the ventilating apparatus continued to function with undiminished efficiency, the audience waxing angrier and angrier every second, and utterly heedless of the performance steadily going on upon the stage, until symptoms of a theatrical riot began to make themselves unmistakably manifest, and the more nervously-disposed of the spectators quitted the house in considerable numbers. From his snug stage-box on the ground tier the Intendant-General had calmly watched the rising of the tempest from the time at which, in obedience to his command, ventilation had been let loose upon the Emperor's lieges in all its horrors. When he deemed that the "psychological moment" had arrived, he leaned back in his velvet *fauteuil* and spoke some word of power to a subordinate. In less than a minute the breezes subsided as suddenly as they had arisen. The fiat of Æolus had gone forth; Notus,

Eurus, Auster, and Zephyr ceased to inflate their cheeks, and a dead calm settled down upon the interior of the Opera-house, so lately resembling the "vexed Bermoothes" in more than one essential respect. "It is all over!" ejaculated somebody in authority; "it will not occur again; the highly-honoured public is exhorted to resume its seats!" This the highly-honoured public did with laudable promptitude; and a quarter of an hour later things were again as though ventilation were but a vague theory—a scientific dream—instead of a terrible reality, teeming, like Pandora's box, with all the ills that flesh is heir to.

Thus swiftly and conclusively (as far as I know) terminated the enterprising Intendant-General's experiments in the direction of keeping the Berlin Opera-house cool during performances, and supplying its frequenters with atmospheric refreshment. The costly apparatus with which he had endeavoured to effect that purpose may still exist, just as it was set up at the period above referred to, and even be available for use at a moment's notice; but I do not believe that the experience of which I was an amused witness during the first act of *Lohengrin*, "when this old hat was new," has ever been renewed; nor is it likely—unless the Hygienic Exhibition should have suggested an entirely "new departure" in this particular respect to the sons of the Fatherland—that theatrical ventilation will very readily become a German national institution.

As my friend the General-Intendant of the Prussian Royal Court Theatres is really a remarkable personage, a few words about him may not come amiss in this place.

Botho von Huelsen, the scion of a warlike race and *arrière-petit-fils* of one of Frederick the Great's favourite generals, entered the military profession at the age of seventeen as a Royal Cadet, obtaining a commission in the Guards a year later, and thus starting fairly on the high road to Prussian honours, distinctions, and " good things" in general. There is no Court post or State office of a non-political character to which a Prussian Guardsman may not aspire; nor is there anything surprising in the fact that a lieutenant in that *corps d'élite* should be selected by his Sovereign to occupy a position giving him equal rank with the Grand Officers of the Household, such as the Lord High Chamberlain, Master of the Horse, Grand Seneschal, Master of the Ceremonies, Grand Huntsman, Sewer and Carver, although these officials, with one or two exceptions, are noblemen of princely rank, occupying the posts in question by hereditary right. In a word, the Prussian path to social greatness runs straight through any one of the messrooms of the Guard Army Corps, and has led Botho von Huelsen, a penniless younker, to the highest summits of prestige, influence, and glory attainable by a patrician-courtier in the Hohenzollern realm.

Young officers in the Prussian army are, as a rule, apt to be smartly snubbed, and even sternly reprimanded, if they display a chronic tendency to hang about the *coulisses* of theatres and cultivate the "demoralising" society of actors and actresses. Herr von Huelsen's theatrical proclivities, however, although manifested when he was still a member of the Cadet Corps—and consequently subjected to rigorous supervision as far as his private recreations and associates were concerned—not only failed to get him into scrapes, but proved the foundation of his fortunes; thus aptly exemplifying the saying that "One man may steal a horse, whilst another may not look over a gate." Soon after he joined the Alexander regiment he earned a more than garrison reputation as an amateur actor by playing "leading lovers" in drawing-room comedy, and as a manager by directing musical-dramatic entertainments given by the officers of that renowned corps every winter in their barracks. Before he came of age he had written several farces and burlesques, three of which were performed, by Royal permission, in the concert-room of the Berlin Schauspielhaus before audiences consisting of the Court and *fine fleur* of Prussian Society. These performances brought Von Huelsen directly under the notice of Frederick William IV., an enthusiastic patron of the drama, who was so strongly impressed by the dramatic and managerial abilities of the youthful Guardsman that, during the representation of *Mohr, Rekrut, und Jesuit*—one of Von Huelsen's best efforts—he remarked to his chief aide-de-camp: "There is the making of an excellent theatrical manager in that young fellow." These words, spoken in 1841, bore fruit ten years later. Meanwhile, Von Huelsen stuck to the army, although he obtained no promotion whatsoever; indeed, when he eventually retired after seventeen years' actual service he only held the rank of lieutenant. But his social talents were the means of exempting him to a great extent from the dull routine of regimental duty, inasmuch as they led to his selection by officers in high command to fill the comparative sinecure of "personal aide-de-camp." In this capacity he served the 1848 campaign in Denmark on the staff of Count Waldersee, and assisted in suppressing the Revolution in Saxony a year later, conducting himself with conspicuous gallantry.

In 1851, three years after his marriage to Countess Helene von Haeseler, a beautiful and accomplished young heiress, Von Huelsen achieved the topmost height of his ambition. The then General-Intendant of the Royal Theatres, Von Kuestner, having fallen out with a member of the Royal Family respecting one of the leading *figurantes* at the Opera-house, offered his resignation to the King, who accepted it without a moment's hesitation, much to the surprise of Kuestner, who deemed himself indispensable. Frederick William IV., however, had not forgotten Huelsen, and jumped, so to speak, at the opportunity thus afforded him of planting "the right man in the right place." Berlin could not at first believe its ears when it learnt that Kuestner had been pensioned; its surprise knew no bounds when that startling piece of intelligence was supplemented by the announcement that a lieutenant of His Majesty's Guards had been "commanded" to take up the succession of so mighty a magnate as the "Koeniglicher Hof-Theater-General-Intendant." Von Huelsen at once resigned his commission in the army and entered upon his new functions on June 1, 1851, having received a few days previously his appointment as Royal Court Chamberlain, giving him access to the King's private apartments at any hour, and many other valuable social privileges.

His inauguratory address to the *personnel* of the Court Theatres was as Prussian in spirit as the veriest military martinet could have desired it to be. He harangued the singers, actors, dancers, and supers in the right regimental tone, as though they had been soldiers instead of stage-players, exhorting them to observe a strict and uniform discipline, and promising them absolute justice at his hands. Under his *régime* the "Court Artists" soon found that there was an end to the comfortable, easy-going ways to which they had grown accustomed during his predecessor's tenure of office. All sorts of abuses that had hitherto been tolerated were swept away with an iron hand; the shortcomings and anachronisms obtaining in the costume and property departments were abolished; ruthless reforms were enforced in every branch of the "Royal Endowment," and military order, regularity, cleanliness and punctuality reigned supreme over an institution which, for two or three years before Huelsen's appointment, had exhibited alarming symptoms of deterioration and incipient decay.

In all respects, except the engagement of really first-class artists—in which matter a Prussian Court Manager is fettered by all manner of restraints unknown to *impresarii* of the purely commercial variety — Herr von Huelsen has made the Berlin Opera-house and Schauspielhaus absolute models of what such institutions should be. Their *répertoire* is enormous, and every one of its items is capable of being set, mounted, and played at twelve hours' notice. The Hofoper ballets can confidently challenge European competition, even that of Vienna and Milan. The orchestra of the opera is of great power and fine quality; as to choruses, singing and acting supers, stage effects, &c., everything goes as smoothly and accurately as though the whole machine were moved by clockwork. As a stage-manager, Herr von Huelsen has proved a thousand times that he can hold his own with Chronegk of Meiningen, or even with Henry Irving; which is saying a good deal. He has been an indefatigable worker, and, according to his lights, an apostle of Progress and Development—a steadfast encourager of native talent, in authors as well as in artists, and a good friend to "the profession," only exacting from singers and actors, no matter how distinguished their position therein, entire obedience to the rules and regulations prevailing in the Royal theatres under his direction. His services have been on more than one occasion munificently acknowledged by the German Emperor, who bestowed upon him the predicate of "Excellency" in 1874, accompanying that high honour by the *grand-cordon* of the Crown-Order, created him a Grand Chamberlain in 1882, and the following year (on the occasion of Von Huelsen's Jubilee) nominated him Knight Grand Cross of the Red Eagle, than which there is only one more exalted decoration in Prussia. The autographic letter in which this conferment was notified to its recipient, concluded as follows: "It is my hearty wish that by God's grace you may long be enabled to fill your honourable office with undiminished vigour and activity. Your grateful King; William."

It is probable that the London manager of a "Royal" theatre, however distinguished his services to the musical and dramatic arts, might live to an extremely advanced age without being summoned to Windsor for investiture with the Grand Cross of the Bath. That is a honour to which even a veteran warrior like Colonel Mapleson, or a fervent patriot like Mr. Augustus Harris, can hardly venture to aspire with hopefulness, however highly they may appraise their intrinsic claims to distinction at the hands of their Sovereign. The decoration in question, however, is the exact equivalent, *cæteris paribus*, of that bestowed on the leading Berlin manager by the mightiest of Continental monarchs; and a striking illustration of the social estimation in which music and the drama are held abroad may be derived from a glance at the list of Imperial and Royal Orders of Chivalry, of which Herr von Huelsen has been made a member, in recognition of his managerial merits, by fifteen European Crowned Heads. He is a Knight Grand Cross of the Russian Order of St. Stanislas, of the Saxon Family Order of Ernestine, of the Hessian Order of Philip the Magnanimous, of the Wuertemberg Order of Frederick, of the Italian Order "Crown of Italy," of the Baden Order of the Zaehring Lion, of the Swedish Order of the Northern Star, of the Oldenburg Family Order, of the Luxembourg Order of the Oaken Crown, and of the Danish Danebrog Order. He is also Knight Commander of the Hohenzollern Family Order, of the Russian "St. Anne" in brilliants, of the Austrian "Leopold" and "Iron Crown" (both carrying with them the title of Baron), of the Saxon "Falcon," the Hessian "Lion," the Belgian "Leopold" and the Anhalt "Albert the Bear." Such are the dignities attainable in the Fatherland by a theatrical manager, than whom—when arrayed in gala uniform, his manly breast adorned with multi-coloured ribands and cuirassed with sparkling crosses, *plaques*, and *crachats*—Solomon in all his glory was not a more gorgeous being. Truly, his salary is only six hundred a year; but he could not be more heavily laden with honours were he a three-fold millionaire. Besides, there are pretty pickings, no doubt, connected with the supreme direction of half-a-dozen subventioned theatres, *en tout bien et tout honneur*. On the whole it may fairly be assumed that any comparison instituted between the position and circumstances of Herr von Huelsen and that of the manager of any London Royal Opera-house can hardly fail to result advantageously to the Berlin Intendant.

[Since the above lines were written, Botho von Huelsen, " ein treuer Diener seines Herrn," has joined the majority. He died peacefully and painlessly at his Berlin residence on September 29th, 1886.]

CHAPTER III.

REMINISCENCES OF PESTH.—ROBERT VOLKMANN.—A FESTIVAL OF FOOLS.

It was during my third visit to the stately and hospitable capital of Hungary, that I became personally acquainted with Robert Volkmann, whose fame as a composer had at that time (1867) but just reached public cognizance in Vienna, where, during the foregoing winter season, Hellmesberger had produced for the first time the gifted Hungarian's *Erstes Streich-Quatuor* in G minor (opus 14) —a work that caused no small sensation amongst the musical virtuosi and amateurs of the Kaiserstadt. At the time I refer to he was no longer a young man, and the story of his life had thitherto been one of bitter disappointments and harassing privations. During early manhood and middle age his countrymen had refused to recognise his genius, which gave birth to compositions they were incapable of understanding—for the art of music, until very lately, was but little cultivated in Hungary, and the Magyars, as a rule, were stolidly indifferent to any strains save those of their national dance, the czardàs—and his extreme poverty precluded him from either publishing any of his works on his own account, or paying executants to play them at concerts or private musical entertainments. A few years before the date of my introduction to him, he had, however, succeeded in persuading a publisher established in Pesth to print some of his songs and concerted pieces (amongst them the stringed quartet above referred to and two noble trios, op. 3 and 5, the shining merits of which have of late years obtained universal acknowledgment), upon terms of remuneration that barely enabled Volkmann to keep body and soul together by furnishing him with the minimum amount of nourishment upon which an adult human being can contrive to exist. Throughout a considerable portion of that period of Hungarian national stagnation during which the Constitution was suspended, Robert Volkmann was practically the bondsman of this close-fisted publisher, whose payments for his successive works took the form of a wretched pittance, scarcely sufficient to defray the rent of a dismal garret in Buda and the cost of exiguous daily rations, consisting chiefly of bread, cheese, and vegetables. During the severe Hungarian winters, Volkmann frequently lacked the wherewithal to purchase fuel—an expensive article in the Kingdom of the Five Rivers—and, his clothes being too shabby to wear in the streets by daylight, he was compelled, in order to keep up the circulation in his extremities, to pace up and down his miserable garret for hours at a stretch, or to remain in bed. That his productiveness was comparatively speaking small under such conditions of hardship cannot be wondered at; what works he did compose, however, during those years of tribulation, became the property of his leasor, whom they were destined to enrich. Volkmann, himself, never got anything by them but scanty food, sordid raiment, and a lodging at which a London footman would turn up his nose with scornful indignation, were he required to occupy it whilst "in service."

The early spring of 1867 was a season of patriotic rejoicing and feverish emotion for the Hungarian nation. For eighteen years Hungary had been dealt with as a conquered country; all the political and administrative institutions had been in abeyance, and the heel of oppression had not been lifted from her neck for a single hour. Austrian military reverses in 1866, however, compelled Kaiser Franz Josef to make large concessions to his Magyar subjects, the concrete outcome of which was a transaction between the moieties of the Dual Realm which has endured to the present day, and may possibly last for many years to come. One of the most strikingly manifest results of this transaction was the "King's" visit to Pesth in the character of a Constitutional monarch —his first appearance in the Magyar capital since the days of his boyhood. It was my special mission to witness his reception and the fêtes given publicly and privately in honour of the reconciliation achieved between victors and vanquished. Pepi Hellmesberger, with his customary intelligence, had made arrangements to give two concerts during the week of national elation, knowing full well that the capital would be thronged with representative Magyars, free-handed and pleasure-loving, their pockets full of paper currency destined to be squandered in recreation and revelry. I accompanied the "quadrilateral of harmony" under his command to Pesth, and punctually attended its first performance at the Redoute, where I lighted upon my old friend Camillo Sivori, attracted to the twin-cities by the prospect of a golden harvest, and found myself included, through Hellmesberger's influence, in an invitation addressed to the "musical and literary celebrities honouring Pesth with a visit" by Heckenast, the leading publisher of the Hungarian capital, to a supper-party at his mansion in a street with a polysyllabic, and, to any tongue save that of a born Magyar, unpronounceable name. Heckenast, an enlightened and liberal patron of the arts, had at that time but recently "discovered" Robert Volkmann, and taken the luckless composer under his protection. He happened to mention, in the "artists' room" at the Redoute, that we should meet Volkmann at supper, and Hellmesberger at once suggested an agreeable surprise for the latter—with whose gloomy past he was acquainted—in the shape of a post-cœnal performance of the G minor quatuor by the Viennese quartet party, the members of which, having rehearsed the work a day or two before in view of a private concert for which they had been engaged by Count George Karolyi, had it, so to speak, at their fingers' ends. The genial suggestion was adopted by acclamation, and as soon as the concert had terminated, Heckenast's guests, some twenty in number, were conducted by their host to his residence, where they found Volkmann and one or two other local notabilities awaiting them.

A glance at the great Hungarian composer sufficed to convince any observant person that he had before him a man of sorrow, acquainted with grief. His bowed shoulders and sad, lustreless eyes told a tale of excessive application, toil at the desk and immoderate consumption of "midnight oil." A heavy, drooping, grizzled moustache enhanced the melancholy expression of his countenance, furrowed by the pencil of care rather than of time, and "sicklied o'er" with a sallow pallor by long years of confinement to small rooms, insufficient nutriment and lack of exercise. His chief characteristic appeared to be an invincible shyness, almost amounting to painful timidity. To me he conveyed the impression of a nature, originally gentle and diffident, that had been subdued by ill-luck and unkind usage to a chronic condition of self-depreciation and hopelessness. To my endeavours to draw him into conversation he replied with discouraging brevity, in low and hesitating tones. His black clothes—too manifestly a *ci-devant* gala suit, indued only upon occasions of exceptional pomp and moment—were threadbare and of strangely antiquated cut. Even Hellmesberger's kindly jesting and inexhaustible flow of apposite anecdote failed to brighten Volkmann's mournful visage with even a fleeting smile, until our host's good cheer and generous wine had somewhat thawed the ice of his inborn reserve and habitual low spirits. Towards the end of supper, when cigars had been lighted and champagne was flowing freely, he began to take part in the conversation, which was of an extraordinarily animated and brilliant character, dealing mainly with the two topics in which every one present was more or less keenly interested—music and the political resurrection of Hungary. It was in commenting upon the latter, rather than upon the former, that Volkmann displayed knowledge and eloquence of no ordinary calibre. In speaking of the public men by whom the transaction with Austria had been brought about, he let fall a few masterly sketches of character revealing a depth of psychological insight that took most of his hearers by surprise. Upon the potentialities of music, as a descriptive art, he made some very striking remarks, never at any considerable length, but, like a meat-lozenge, containing much essential force compactly propounded. Commenting, for instance, on the Wagnerian theories, he observed: "Music, like painting, is imitative, not reproductive. Her imitations are necessarily addressed to persons gifted with musical apprehension, just as those of painting appeal only to the eye that is appreciative of colour or form. Her graphic power is not indicative of concrete facts, but of their characteristics, and makes itself readily manifest to the ear that is at once receptive and cultivated. Even that ear requires, in nine cases out of ten, to be prepared for the recognition of a tone-description by a certain amount of information, conveyed to the intelligence in the ordinary manner. . . . . A mere melody is seldom able to tell its own story intelligibly. I mean, of course, the story its composer intends it to tell. *Tempi*, phrasing, and harmonic treatment are more available, as musical narrators —or, rather, describers—than tunes. The inevitable formality of a tune fetters its faculty of depicting ideas, circumstances, or actions, all of which may be recognisably sketched in sound by imitative figures and instrumental combinations. . . . . That information other than oral is indispensable, in descriptive music, to the hearer's perception of the meaning sought to be conveyed to him, is beyond a doubt. For instance, the special significance of certain rhythmical mannerisms and accents in our national music cannot but be lost upon those who possess no acquaintance with Hungarian history, traditions and manners. In my own attempt to describe musically the ordinary incidents of a day's life in a Hungarian frontier-stronghold of the olden time, I feel confident that I have made my tone-sketches comprehensible to such of my countrymen as may be endowed with musical understanding. To the average foreign musician my special meanings can only appear in the light of eccentricities in tonality."

It was long past midnight when Hellmesberger suddenly rose in his place and exclaimed, "Enough talk for the present. Let us have some music. Sivori is dying to play us something classical of his own composition; and I—I have brought with me a new quartet by a young composer whose name I forget—he is a mere boy and none of you have ever heard of him—which I and my comrades here would like to play to Volkmann. Heckenast, I know you have a four-sided desk somewhere in this hovel of yours; produce it, and let us get to work. We will play in the next room, opening the folding doors, and my Englishman shall turn over. Our audience—including the *maestro*, who looks so comfortable that I would not have him disturbed for the world—shall remain in here and listen, if they please to do so." Sivori laughingly begged to be allowed to hear the "new work" before contributing his mite to the entertainment, and without further delay the prearranged "surprise" was put into execution. Volkmann sat ensconced in a huge arm-chair, smoking a powerful Partagas, his eyes half-closed, and his whole attitude expressive of that blissful state of body and mind, hight *kief*. As the executants commenced the spirited Allegro with which his G minor quartet opens, every eye was turned towards him. He started up, as though stricken by an electric shock, hastily put down his cigar and clutched both arms of the *fauteuil*, looking about him confusedly, like one suddenly awakened from a deep sleep. Presently, he sank back into his seat, covering his face with his hands; and when we next caught a glimpse of his sad grey eyes, they were wet with happy tears. Never before or since that memorable night have I heard the quartet—perhaps his most passionate and romantic composition for strings—so magnificently played, or so enthusiastically applauded. At its close, a shout of "Eljen â Volkmann!" was raised by all present, and Heckenast called upon his guests to drink "the Master's" health in brimming bumpers of Roederer. Rendered speechless by glad emotion, Volkmann could only express his gratification by repeatedly pressing the artistic hands that had wrought him such paramount pleasure, his cheeks glistening the while with "unfamiliar brine." A little later, when he had recovered his self-possession, he sat down to the piano of his own accord and held us spell-bound for some twenty minutes with an improvisation "on a heroic subject" (which I recognised years after in his *recueil* of "Musical Poems," intituled "Visegrád"), ever to be remembered by the survivors of that joyous company as an extempore production of unique beauty and indescribable fascination.

During my brief sojourn in Pesth on the above-mentioned occasion and in connection with the so-called "Reconciliation Week," I underwent a very curious and exceptional musical experience, chiefly worth recalling because so pre-eminently illustrative of the wild excitement then prevailing throughout all classes of Hungarian society, and finding vent in extravagances of action that struck me at the time as all but incompatible with sanity of mind in their perpetrators. One of the fêtes organised by the patricians and artists of Pesth in honour of the great national rejoicing was announced under the amazing title of "A Fools' Evening, given by the Committee of Folly," and came off one Sunday evening in the Grand Redoute, with the co-operation of over five thousand persons of both sexes, one and all earnestly bent upon proving themselves, in appearance and behaviour, bereft of their senses. The entertainment lasted ten hours; and I am bound to say that, from beginning to end, it was an uninterrupted and kaleidoscopic display of more or less humorous insanity. I could fill half a dozen pages with a *catalogue déraisonné* of its anomalies and absurdities; the space at my command, however, only permits a brief reference to those eccentricities which partook of a specially musical character. After the possessor of a voucher (himself necessarily travestied into some maniacal seeming) had passed the ordeal of examination by the Committee, stationed on the grand staircase, he was received with triumphal blasts, at the main entrance to the hall, by a "Mad Orchestra" consisting of ten bugles, eight side-drums, and *one violin*. Deafened and dizzy with the incomparable din of this braying and thumping cohort, he passed through a flame-coloured wicket into the Redoute, converted for the nonce into the semblance of a gigantic menagerie, its walls lined with dens of the most approved pattern, their grated doors flung wide open. Returning for convenience from the third to the first person, I may state that the first question which occurred to me as I glanced round that astonishing apartment was, "Where are the wild beasts?" A second later they "jumped to the eye," as the French idiom hath it, on a raised platform at the further end of the hall, pent up in an enormous built cage some twenty feet high, and constituting an orchestra, eighty in number, assiduously engaged in performing *The Beautiful Blue Danube*. The disguises were admirable, and had been allotted to the wearers in such sort as to intensify the general incongruity suggested by furred and feathered music-makers. For instance, the leading flautist was an elephant, whose aspect whilst diligently blowing his *Querpfeife* under his trunk was irresistibly comical. The triangle was being gravely tingled by a Royal Bengal tiger of alarmingly truculent mien; a portly old lion, his tail comfortably adjusted across his knee, led the violoncelli; a solemn pelican was tooting the French horn, its mouthpiece inserted in the side of his bill; the drums were being administered to by a mild-eyed grey bullock of the true Banat breed; side by side, amongst the first violins, were a bear, a colossal perch, and a frog of prediluvian dimensions; the two bassoons were deftly handled by a mammoth spider and a shiny sturgeon, whilst a giant prairie tortoise clashed the cymbals as though that were the exclusive function to fulfil which was his inborn mission in life. The leader, a famous German *chef d'orchestre*—appeared as a gorilla of unexampled hideousness, quite the most appalling creature my eyes had ever thitherto beheld; and he conducted with a mimic knotted club formidably suggestive of "homicide with intention." The whole tableau was irresistibly provocative of convulsive and inextinguishable laughter. Moreover, facing this zoological band, at the opposite end of the hall was installed another "full" orchestra, consisting of life-size puppets set in motion by machinery, and occupying the lid of a Brobdingnagian musical box, the inside of which was tenanted by a real live military band in full play, so that its strains, produced by an unseen agency, seemed to proceed from the dolls, whose conductor, a singularly limber automaton, rivalled his *dos-à-dos*, the gorilla, in wildly energetic action. Taken in connection with the practice of the divine art, the orchestral menagerie was the funniest sight a musician could hope to look upon in the flesh. Of the puppet band one wearied readily; not so of the harmonious wild beasts, whose "infinite variety" custom " could not stale."

CHAPTER IV.

REMINISCENCES OF ROME.—THE GESÙ ORGANS.—MIDNIGHT MASSES.—OPERA AND BALLET IN ROME.—RAMACIOTTI.

My acquaintance with the Eternal City—a close and loving one, at least on my part—began and ended under the Papal dispensation. Royal Rome is unknown to me. When I last sojourned within her venerable precincts, she was the capital of the Catholic world; since which time she has possibly gained in vitality, but certainly lost in dignity, by becoming the *chef-lieu* of a single nation—a mere centre of fussy, futile politics and fashionable mundane vanities. If there was anything that the ecclesiastical *régime* prevailing throughout the Papal States only sixteen years ago more especially abominated than another, it was innovation. To remain at a stand-still, gravely, serenely, decorously, was the height of authority's ambition—I mean, in all secular matters, such as administration, science, literature, and the arts. Progress and emancipation were highly objectionable words to the clerical dignitaries who comfortably ruled the Roman roast in anti-Œcumenical days; for those worthies held them to be convertible terms with Iconoclasm and Anarchy. It is not exaggerative to say that a passive dislike to new things and ideas pervaded Roman society, civil as well as religious, at the time I refer to. Prosaic architecture, "impressionist" painting, narrative music, the revelations of chemists and geologists, the bold conjectures of modern philosophers and eager enterprise of Latter-Day journalists were all regarded with distrust and apprehension by the upper and middle classes, who sided almost unanimously with stone against stucco, Raphael against Maret, Bellini and Donizetti against Berlioz and Wagner, the Fathers against Faraday and Darwin, Machiavelli against Schopenhauer, and the "Osservatore Romano" against the "Perseveranza." Owing to this prevalent indisposition to accept or even tolerate novelty on the part of its native inhabitants, rich and poor, Rome—whilst the Cross-Keys banner still floated above St. Angelo—was the most old-world capital in civilised Europe. Its conservatism may have been at some time or other, before I became familiar with its characteristics, more artificial than real, or less voluntary than compulsory. But it had become a second nature to all sorts and conditions of Romans when I lived among them and got, by their own admission, to know them well.

The attitude of the Papal Government towards music in particular, whether sacred or secular, was a curious combination of the inflexible conservatism above alluded to, of celibate prudery and cynical indulgence. In all musical performances of a public character, at church as well as in theatres and concert-rooms, the influence of this quaint blending was plainly apparent. I have heard hundreds of masses with orchestral and organ accompaniments in Roman churches, and can confidently assert that nine-tenths of them were by old and comparatively obscure composers, such as Morales, Carpentrasso, Ruffo, Festa, Pierre de la Rue, Vittoria and Anerio, the remaining tenth being chiefly by ancient and distinguished writers; for example, Palestrina, Carissimi and Allegri. I do not remember hearing anything, belonging to this class of work, more modern than Jomelli and Paisiello. But, in the matter of voluntaries, almost unbounded license was allowed to the organist, who might and did, as his fancy happened to prompt him in that direction, introduce airs from nineteenth-century operas, and even popular melodies, into his reminiscences or arrangements of sacred strains. I was particularly struck with some startling contrasts of this kind afforded by a splendid performance given in honour of the Bambino—an effigy of the Infant Saviour usually kept in the church of Ara Cœli—at which I was fortunate enough to be present on New Year's Eve, 1869, during a brief interval between two important sessions of the Œcumenical Council. To this function, celebrated in the Gesù, one of the most gorgeous fanes in Christendom, all the Royal personages then in Rome had been specially invited. Pius IX. himself sang mass, and pronounced the benediction. It was an occasion of extraordinary solemnity and splendour; but to me, I confess, its most interesting feature was the music. Then—strange as it may appear, for the first time, though I had already spent several months in Rome — did I hear really good singing and admirable, soul-enthralling organ playing.

The Gesù is possessed of three organs, not very powerful or rich in combinations, but exquisitely sweet-toned and in perfect tune—at least, they were so sixteen years ago; one in either wing, or arm of the cross in the shape of which the church is built; the third just above the main entrance opposite the high altar. On these charming instruments, for more than an hour before the Pontiff's arrival at the church door, did three accomplished organists successively play voluntaries, movements from masses, and selections from familiar Italian operas. As soon as the final resolution of some glorious old fugue—the subject of which seemed to be struggling in the toils of counterpoint, like Laocoön with the serpents—had died out amid the solemn thunder of the pedal pipes, a sweet melody from *Lucia*, *L'Italiano in Algeri*, or *Ernani* would steal upon the ear from another quarter in all the plaintive tenderness of a mellow wooden flute-stop. And then, almost before this insinuating song had melted away into silence, its last lingering note would be drowned in the joyous chords of some sturdy old "Jubilate," square, simple, and just sufficiently aping the fugal form to interest the scientific musician, while delighting the not-scholastically trained ear. It was, indeed, a plenteous regale of sound, thoughtfully arranged and tastefully served. Meanwhile, flitting forms arrayed in white and violet vestments were lighting up the countless candles round the Holy of holies till the sheeny marbles of the great altar flashed again with prismatic reflections. Suddenly, while an inspiration of supreme tunefulness was enthralling my senses in the purest of raptures, heavy curtains were let fall over the gallery windows, shutting out the golden sunbeams and enveloping the body of the church in mysterious shadow, whilst the altar illumination of tapers shone out with tenfold brilliancy. As a *coup de théâtre*, it was the most splendid effect I had ever hitherto seen introduced into an ecclesiastical spectacle. Soon afterwards the venerable Pope arrived, attended by a gorgeous *cortège* of Cardinals, Bishops, torchbearers, Swiss Guards, Roman Senators and Knights of Malta. His advent was greeted by a fine choral rendering of a sprightly antique *motivo*, accompanied by silvern bells, triangles innumerable, all three organs and twelve trumpets. The church itself was magnificently decorated with Gobelin tapestries, velvet hangings and a profusion of fresh flowers; and in front of the altar was displayed the Bambino himself under a blaze of concentrated light. As Pio Nono crossed the threshold of the Gesù five hundred muskets clashed, brought sharply to the " Present ! " by the battalion on duty within the sacred edifice. The whole effect, to eye and ear, was simply inimitable and never-to-be-forgotten.

A painful contrast, in the way of musical entertainments of an ecclesiastical order, to the above performance in the Gesù, was afforded by a Midnight Mass I was induced by treacherous persuasion to attend on Christmas Eve at San Luigi dei Francesi. My betrayer, I need scarcely say, was an Englishman who had " done the thing himself." Roman friends never advise you to indulge in recreations of that class. If you ask them what they think of such diversions they are apt to shrug their shoulders, slightly shake a significant fore-finger and smile a caustic Italian smile. It is your Briton or American who "knows Rome" that will insist upon your seeing and hearing everything most inconvenient and costly to be seen and heard, and will even go with you—should you require the inducement of company to persuade you, against your better judgment, to sacrifice time and comfort upon the altar of morbid curiosity—cynically resolved that, suffer what he may, you at least shall not be spared one drop of that bitter cup he has already drained to the dregs. On the 24th December, 1869, a peculiarly malignant compatriot had fervently assured me that, at San Luigi dei Francesi, I should hear strains of celestial harmony and contemplate a dazzling illumination in celebration of the Nativity Morn. It was a wet night. On such occasions conveyances vanish from the streets of Rome with mysterious unanimity. Before I got to the church I was moister than is compatible with unalloyed physical comfort, and a ten minutes' episode of exposure to rain on the broad steps, whilst striving to wriggle my way through a motley throng of damp Zouaves, peasants, pickpockets, and professional beggars, brought me to a condition of humidity that could scarcely have been surpassed had I been dipped bodily into the Tiber. After much labour and tribulation I at length succeeded in entering the sacred edifice. The first vileness that assailed one of my senses was a mosaic of stenches, amongst which were chiefly distinguishable the malodours of garlic, incense, candle-snuff, boiling grease, damp cloth, and shoe-leather. The next, outraging another sense, was a nondescript noise, respecting which I soon had to ask myself, What may this be, that offends my ears and, in less than a minute, has worn out my patience? Is it, haply, the heavenly harmony promised to me? are these the sublime strains that could not by any possibility fail to transport my ravished soul to realms of bliss? It was; they were! Any score or so of blind-beggars, British-born and musically proclivious, picked up at random in London streets and set to intone a Catnach ballad in, say, sixty verses, could have matched, in every respect, the performance of the San Luigi choristers on that dread Christmas Eve. Moreover, there was an altogether intolerable organ, quivering with senility, and divided against itself—one of its registers being an eighth of a tone sharper than the other, and both wofully out of tune. Upon this instrument of torture some organist in his novitiate had been instructed to do his worst; and most conscientiously did he fulfil his mission. For instance, whenever the choir had dismally drifted into the tonic chord, he would burst out joyously into that of the two dominants, or wail a plaintive relative minor. None of his dissonant vagaries, however, for a moment disturbed the choristers, or hindered them from plodding doggedly on with gruesome sonority, more nasal than laryngean. The effect was indescribably bewildering— something like a tale of Hoffmann illustrated by Retzsch and set to music by the fiddler-fiend who once appeared to Tartini in a dream. Thus, methought, must they sing in Dante's Fifth Circle, where circumstances over which its inmates have no control render their manner of passing the time exceptionally repugnant to their feelings and tastes. Only to those endowed by

Providence with nerves of oak and triple brass is it given to endure much of such Tartarean grunting, aggravated by the discordant spasms of a bad organ writhing under unskilfully administered persecution. After suffering a brief and unmerited agony, I struggled forth into the rain with all the haste and eagerness of one pursued by the Avenger. Ever since that fearsome experience I have been accustomed to think of the Christmas Eve choral service performed at San Luigi dei Francesi as the Stomach-ache of Sound.

Extremes meet—a proverb happily exemplified by the circumstances that the very same Papal authorities who were so genially tolerant of operatic airs in church, declined to permit the performance of certain operas in any Roman theatre until they had undergone a searching revision at the hands of the Pontifical Censor (a singularly straitlaced Monsignore, whose acquaintance I made during my sojourn in the Eternal City), frequently resulting in sweeping alterations of their plots, dialogue, and even names, for reasons only apparent to the ecclesiastical mind. Titles of works which are household words in every country of Europe suffered a police change when at Rome in the days of Pio Nono. A meaningless alias was bestowed upon our old friend *Rigoletto*; the *Traviata* was modestly transformed into *Violetta*; *La Forza del Destino* became *Dorina*, and so forth, in at least a dozen instances. The quality of the performances by no means atoned for the liberties taken with text and title. It was uniformly execrable, for the management, considering anything good enough for the merely musical public of Rome, concentrated all its energies, intelligence and outlay upon the production of attractive ballets, to which the reverend Quæstor and his tonsured subordinates entertained no kind of objection on the ground of morality or decorum. In Rome a ballet of this description used to run—and probably still does so—through a whole season, filling the Tordinone every night, and hummed, more or less loudly, by the entire audience. Italians will not be deterred from giving tongue to their likes and dislikes with a freedom unknown to us frigid islanders; and, sitting in the Apollo stalls amongst the *principini*, I used to hear the airs of *Brahma* (the ballet of that Œcumenical winter) chanted all around me by dandies of the first water, very seldom under their breath. As a rule Roman society did not attend the opera to listen to the music, but to chat, flirt, and exchange scandals. Having philosophically made up their minds that they were doomed, as far as the singing was concerned, to be *strappazzati*, or put upon and tormented, the nobles and wealthy *bourgeois* resigned themselves cheerfully to their fate, and treated the theatre as though it were a drawing-room in which a private musical-party was being held; *i.e.*, they never paid the least attention to the performance provided for their amusement, but indulged in *chiacchere* to their hearts' content.

To the native circles of Rome, in Papal times, classical music was all but unknown. Not even by combining the professional and amateur executant resources was it feasible to get up a stringed-quartet party. Very few of the Roman matrons or virgins were pianists; and those few, with a brilliant exception or two, played insignificantly or viciously. There was but one good fiddler to be met in Roman salons—Ramaciotti, a fine artist and polished gentleman—and *he* was only "in society" as *le mari de sa femme*, having espoused a marchioness whose family and friends, whilst deeply resenting his musical talent, tolerated his presence at their receptions upon her account. Arthur Strutt—most genial, learned, and hospitable of Anglo-Romans—made him known to me soon after my arrival, and during the ensuing six months we "made much music" together, greatly to our mutual satisfaction and comfort. The German Club was the centre of culture and exercise in matters musical. Its weekly gatherings were not unfrequently honoured by a visit from the inimitable Canonico, Feréncz Liszt, whose favourite pupils, from time to time, made their social *début* at that jolly rendezvous of art-students, diplomatists, travelling celebrities, and good fellows of all nationalities. It was there—not at the Sala Dantesca, Rome's only concert-room—that I first heard Sgambati and Ketler, two of Liszt's *alumni* who have since then earned European reputations as exponents of his works. The one really musical salon of Rome was that of the Princess Pallavicini, to which my kind old friend, Cardinal Haynald, himself an excellent pianist and ripe musician, procured me the *entrée*. But, with the exception of Ramaciotti, Sgambati, and Pinelli, a nephew and pupil of the Roman violinist, all the performers at the "Pallavicini Wednesdays" were of foreign birth and training. Of course, in so cosmopolitan a city as Rome, first-class amateur pianists and vocalists abounded throughout the winter season. Pre-eminent amongst the former was Mrs. Astor, the mother of Willie Astor, then studying sculpture in Tadolini's studio, and now U.S. Minister at the Court of King Humbert; amongst the latter Mr. Odo Russell, then Second Secretary of the British Legation at Florence, but residing at Rome *en mission spéciale*, and afterwards Lord Ampthill, G.C.B., a Privy Councillor and H.B.M. Ambassador to the German Emperor. " Tempora mutantur, et nos mutamur in illis!"

CHAPTER V.

ROUMANIAN LAYS AND DANCES.—THE DACIAN MINSTRELS.—PLUM-PUDDING SET TO MUSIC.—SERVIAN REMINISCENCES.

I HAVE been more than once impelled by certain troublesome and recurrent doubts to ask myself the question, Is there, or has there ever been, such a thing as Roumanian Music? It was a difficult question to answer, for more than one reason. In the first place there is unquestionably something about the songs sung and the dances played throughout the length and breadth of the Dacian lands (which comprise Bessarabia, the Bukovina, and a considerable portion of Transylvania, as well as the Kingdom of Roumania proper, whilom the United Principalities of Moldavia and Wallachia) that reminds the discriminating ear of Turkish, Hungarian, and Slavonic strains. This circumstance is readily to be accounted for by the fact that Dacia, for a thousand years past, if not more, has been an oppressed and downtrodden land, the favourite battle-ground of Eastern Europe, surrounded on all sides by warlike and rapacious neighbours, whose favourite recreation it was to overrun the "sweet and lovely country" (scûmpa tseâra si frumoâsa), carry off its sons and daughters into slavery, and every now and anon, annex it altogether. The Roumanians of the Middle Ages, as well as of a more modern epoch, although they frequently fought their invaders with great gallantry and resolution, were nearly always in a state of vassaldom, writhing under the armed heel of some neighbour mightier than themselves. It is not to be wondered at that their successive conquerors made deep impressions upon their manners and customs, and even imparted various foreign flavours to their national music. That they retained their language—originally the "army Latin," or *lingua franca*, commonly spoken in the foreign legions of the Roman Empire—(two of which colonised Dacia in the time of Trajan)—is an extraordinary illustration of the instinctive race-conservatism exemplified in Western Europe by the Welsh, Scotch Highlanders, Bretons, Basques, and Swiss Roumanians. Of course, Hungarian, Polish, and Turkish occupations of Roumania forcibly introduced a large number of foreign words into the Dacian vernacular; indeed, when I first began to study Roumanian, exactly twenty years ago, *sub consule Cusa*, twenty-four per cent. of its total vocabulary consisted of Magyar, Slav, Turkish, and even Greek importations, the remaining seventy-six per cent. being of pure Latin origin. I may observe—for the fact is an interesting one, though it certainly has nothing to do with Roumanian music—that since Roumania practically shook off the Turkish yoke in 1866, her leading philologists—amongst them Prince Jón Ghîca, her present representative at the Court of St. James, Basil Alecsandri, her Poet Laureate and Minister in Paris, and Majorescu, formerly her Minister of Education—have been assiduously engaged in purifying the Roumanian tongue and ridding it of the "barbarous" idioms that had crept into it in the manner above indicated. Their efforts have been so far crowned with success that the *limbâ românâ* of to-day only contains about five words of alien origin in every hundred, retained in deference to popular convenience; and, freed from the cramping trammels of the Cyrillic alphabet, is as well-ordered and learnable a literary language as either of its first cousins, Italian or Spanish.

To return, however, to the subject of this chapter. Ultimately I made up my mind that there *was* such a thing as Roumanian music—music, that is to say, which, despite its borrowed "tricks and manners," and frequent suggestions of Hungarian and Turkish influence, steadfastly displays certain melodic characteristics peculiar to itself, as distinctly recognisable, let us say, as the Magyar rhythm *alla zoppa* (or scale with two superfluous seconds, a harmonic minor with a sharp fourth), or the fundamental droning fifth of the Celtic music. It is difficult to describe these characteristics intelligibly; that they exist I shall endeavour to demonstrate. Such as it is, the music of Dacia is essentially, almost exclusively, melodic. Harmony does not enter into its being; it has never created a vocal duet, trio, or part-song; its horas (*derivatur* chorus) are sung in unison, the time being marked by the stamping of feet and swaying of bodies as the singers hold hands in a circle and revolve, like English village children to the strains of "Here we go round the mulberry-bush." Roumanian music, in common with that of all peoples who have suffered long and cruel subjugation, is for the most written in the minor mood. There are some exceptions; but they are of modern production, and owe their genesis, as I have ascertained, to gipsies, not to pure-blooded Dacians. These latter, by the way, in their patriotic anxiety to prove that emancipated Roumania is " up to time " in the gentler arts of civilisation, have taken to composing a vast amount of the weakest rubbish that ever put forward a claim to rank as vocal or instrumental music. Nothing more rickety or wishy-washy than the *doine* and *hore* of Scheletti, Ventura, and Michael Poliso has ever been fabricated by the British drawing-room ballad manufacturer, whose capacity for uttering musical platitudes I had deemed unrivalled until I became acquainted with the works of the above-mentioned gentlemen.

The genuine Roumanian music, with its elementary accompaniment of a pedal-point that is not necessarily in tonic relation to the key of the melody it underlies and supports—with its rugged intervals, quaint flourishes or *agrèmens*, and plaintive semitonic wailings—is extremely ancient; so much so that if you ask a vocal peasant what might be the age of the ditty with which he cheers his bullocks on their ploughing way, it is ten to one that he will answer you, " *Acel cantic, Domnul?* That song, my lord? It is as old as the Devil "—a reply suggestive of a somewhat exceptional antiquity in a popular melody. Until very lately, none of the national airs had been notated; for their conservation from the fourteenth century, in some cases, down to the present day, Roumania has to thank her wandering minstrels (*laotari*), who have transmitted them with perfect accuracy—so, at least, it is believed—through generations innumerable of the "sons of Trajan" (fii Trajanului). These airs belong to three categories; *cantice batrineste,* that is, historical or legendary ballads; *doine,* love-songs and elegies; *hore,* lively lyrics, much of the class that used to be popular in after-dinner circles when English society was convivial and chirpy, *i.e.,* stanzas with a chorus; the difference between the British and Roumanian lyric of this kind being that the burden of the former is sung, whilst that of the latter is danced. There is, moreover, a fourth sort of air, having some analogy to our Christmas Carol; it is called *colinda,* and is sung in unison by bands of children, on Christmas and New Year Eves, under the windows of the Boyars' houses. Two of these *colinde* — "Florile Dalbe" (Strange Flowers) and "Plugul" (The Plough)—are of unknown antiquity, and very dear to the heart of every true Roumanian. A gentle melancholy runs through words and music alike; indeed, this is the case with all the genuine Roumanian songs and dances, whether their *tempi* be slow or rapid. During my long sojourns in Moldavia every now and anon I happened upon a *hora* of an unmistakably rollicking character—"Am un leû" is a shining example of these exceptions to the rule—but on inquiring carefully into the origin of these cheerful airs I invariably found that they hailed from Transylvania, where the influence of Magyar musical joviality had been effectively brought to bear upon the languorous plaintiveness of the Roumanian melodic method.

Of the *cantice batrineste* several that enjoy especial popularity deal with the predatory exploits of certain celebrated bandits (Heiduki) who flourished in the sixteenth and seventeenth centuries, and are still looked up to by the Roumanian peasantry as heroes of only a thought less historical interest than Stephen the Great, Michael the Brave, and Vlad the Cruel. Village youths and maidens are never weary of listening to the wild adventures of Gianul, Stepan Boujor (Stephen the Poppy), Tunsul (the Shaven), Andrii Popa (Andrew the Priest), and Groza (the Terror), of whom they are accustomed to speak as *omeni buni* (worthy men), or *puii de zmei* (sons of giants). Gianul is to the Roumanian Legends what Robin Hood is to our own ballad lore. He robbed the rich to give to the poor, exhibiting extraordinary daring and ingenuity in the execution of his predatory feats. I have no idea how many verses there are in the celebrated song that bears his name and professes to chronicle his principal achievements. All I can say about it is that I have never succeeded in hearing the end of it, though I have listened to it, more than once, for an hour at a stretch. Probably the leading *laotari*, who are ready enough at improvisation, extemporise additional verses to this favourite ballad whenever they find their audience deeply attentive to their lays. Were any drawing-room vocalist to attempt the singing of the adventures of Robin Hood in a hundred and thirty-five verses or so at a London evening party he would of a certainty be voted the most intolerable bore that ever disgraced humanity; but I have never known "Gianul" to pall upon Roumanians of any social class, no matter at what dismal and unseemly length it was droned out by Nick the Moldavian or Gregory the Nightingale, Roumania's most accomplished minstrels in my salad-days—alas! long past.

Of the *Doine*, or love-songs, it may with truth be said that their name is legion. Few of them, however—that is, of the ancient, characteristic ones—are procurable in print, although every *laotar*—I had almost written, every Roumanian—knows them by heart, and Alecsandri, Eminescu, Bolintineanu, and other modern poets of Dacia have written beautiful words to them. Alecsandri's "Dorul" is a lyric descriptive of the passion which Roumanians are wont to say they alone of all the Latin peoples can feel—a blending of regret, hope, pain, and love, alleged to be fatal (sooner or later) to those who experience it in all its fulness. To this class of tune there is always a second part, but no burden, as in the case of the *cantic batrinest*, or the *hora*.

Let me say a few words about the instruments upon which these tunes are generally played. The violin and Pandean pipes take the melody in turns; the accompaniments are played upon a sort of guitar, upon the ciombalan, a thing of wood and wires, like an upright zither without a back, and upon an instrument shaped like a clarionet, but keyless, and pierced by half-a-dozen holes at most. Amongst the peasants this is used as a solo instrument, in both senses of the word *solo*, for it is the only one they have any skill in. In tone it somewhat resembles a bass flute, and I am not guilty of exaggeration, I believe, in saying that thousands of Roumanian shepherds and tillers of the soil play it—as well as it can be played. It "lends itself" very congenially to the execution of a popular *hora*—hight "The Tribute" for some mysterious reason which I have never been able to discover.

There is, probably, no country upon the Continent of Europe in which music, considered as a social recreation interchangeable between persons belonging to the higher classes, is less assiduously cultivated—more steadfastly neglected would, perhaps, be the more accurate way of putting it—than Roumania. At the very height of the "fast and furious" fashionable season in Bucharest, one admitted to the penetralia of Boyar society may attend half-a-hundred evening parties without being called upon to make pretence, amid a ceaseless buzz of small-talk, of listening to "a little music." As a rule, nobody belonging to them by right of birth or position sings or plays in Roumanian *salons*. Politics and *petits soins* monopolise the drawing-room energies of the Dacian stronger sex—coquetry and *caquetage* those of the weaker. Upon the rare occasions when the musical element is, for some special reason, introduced into the unwritten programme of a *soirée*, at which "one dances not," the *laotari*, or native minstrels, are hired for the night and stationed in a roomy, divanned ante-chamber, through which the guests must pass on their way into or out of the reception-rooms. There, at brief intervals, they sing the wild melodies of the country, or play quaint arrangements of popular airs, familiar and dear to every born Roumanian, from about nine P.M. (the Dacian dinner-hour is six, and dinners seldom last more than a couple of hours) till one, or at the latest two A.M. You are by no means expected by your hostess or host to pay any attention to the musical entertainment thus provided for your delectation; still, it is "the thing" to encourage the *laotari* from time to time by strolling into the apartment occupied by them, and listening for a few minutes to their inspiring strains whilst half reclining, cigarette in mouth—in some of the more old-fashioned Boyar palaces a chibouk will be offered to you in the "minstrels' room"—upon a divan luxuriously bespread with velvety Moldavian rugs. The minstrels themselves, Roumanian gipsies to a man, are an extremely sensitive and excitable folk of highly-wrought temperament, subject, as a matter of course, to reactions of dismal flaccidity. When their efforts to please are unheeded for any length of time, their spirits are apt to flag and their playing to become slack and nerveless. To a few attentive listeners however—especially to such as are not too indolent or stuck-up to express appreciation by a little judicious applause—they rise as readily as a hungry trout to a fly, and brighten into deft and stirring execution with that inexhaustible enthusiasm which only fires the souls of genuine inborn musicians.

The *laotari*, as I have already observed, are gipsies to a man, in the literal as well as conventional sense of that definition—for, with few and unimportant exceptions, female singers and players are rigorously excluded from the so-called "minstrel brotherhoods" at present enjoying private favour and public celebrity in the "fair and lovely land" of Basil Alecsandri. These "brotherhoods" pride themselves somewhat inordinately upon a strict observance of the traditions orally communicated to them and to those who came before them, from generation to generation for five or six centuries past. One or two of the provincial *laotari* bands, unacknowledged by the chiefs of the minstrel "mystery," admit songstresses to participation in their performances; but such Master-Singers as Niko Moldoveanûl (Nick the Moldavian), or Grigor o Rucinôara (Gregory the Nightingale) would scorn to tolerate the presence of petticoats amongst the tuneful fraternities submitted to their sway.

Of yore the *laotari* were far more important personages than they are now. Their profession—chiefly owing to the confidential nature of its supplementary branches—was a highly lucrative one. Not only were they Minnesingers—whose periodical rounds throughout the country afforded the wealthy provincial Boyars the only artistic recreation then available to the Dacian squirearchy—extempore poets and musical *improvisatori*, but purveyors of news in ante-journalistic days, and, to boot, trusty go-betweens in all the secret negotiations of love. In their hands were the threads of countless family intrigues, as well as of not a few political conspiracies; and they were seldom, if ever, known to betray the confidence reposed in them. I am writing of imperative and all but lawless times, when Boyars were not to be trifled with, and the *laotari*, knowing full well that any indiscretion might cost them their heads, or subject them to the irreparable inconvenience of impalement, inflexibly kept their own council and made a good thing of so doing. In nine cases out of ten, their arrival upon an estate was a welcome interruption to the tiresome monotony of rural life, and furnished the profoundly-bored Boyar with an indefensible pretext for indulging in a congenial burst of revelry and jollification. Messengers were despatched in all directions to the neighbouring landowners, charged with invitations to a round of banquets and *hora* bouts, organised as a natural consequence of the *laotari's* advent. At these feasts, the minstrels, stationed in a semi-circle behind the amphytrion's chair, and picturesquely arrayed in dark velvet jerkins and scarlet caps, sang alternately their newest and oldest lays, or improvised upon themes propounded to them by the chief personages of the company, or chanted extempore couplets, dealing humorously with the special characteristics of their auditors. Considerable licence was accorded to them, as to the mediæval jester. It was an understood thing that no offence was to be taken at the witticisms—however personal and pungent—of the "privileged Tsigani." Thrice during the afternoon's and evening's performance—which, comprising the long-protracted *hora* that succeeded the vocal part of the entertainment, generally lasted many hours—it was the prerogative of the leading *laotar* to hand his cap, bowing profoundly to his host, who, after dropping into it his own tribute, passed it on to his male guests, and when it again reached him, after having gone the round of the table, restored it to its owner with a kindly, "Pouftich, brat!" (Take this, brother!) Good store of broad silvern *yakussars* and eke of sparkling golden ducats caused the gaudy head-gear to weigh heavily as the dark-eyed, brown-skinned gipsy took it deferentially from the hand of his benefactor, and without even glancing at its contents—for such was the behaviour prescribed by *laotari* etiquette—poured them into the leathern pouch hanging from his untanned girdle.

When I first knew Roumania, long before its Royal and railway days, when Boyars still ruled the land, and serfdom, though legally abolished, was practically a Dacian "institution" by no means devoid of vitality, the *laotari* retained some brilliant vestiges, in outward appearance at least, of their pristine smartness and prestige. Now-a-days they have come down in the world, like their patrons, the country squires, whom universal suffrage has reduced to nonentity. Not, as in the "good old times," do they perambulate the provinces in glossy velvet jackets and gay crimson *kaciule*, secure of an hospitable welcome and generous guerdon at every provincial magnate's château. They may be seen hanging about hotels in the larger Roumanian cities, or in suburban pleasure gardens (like the Herestreu at Bucharest), of which they constitute the chief attraction. Three or four of their best "brotherhoods," each under the leadership of a famous tenor-singer or supremely gifted fiddler, abide permanently in the capital, where during the fashionable season they are in considerable request at diplomatic dinner parties, and at the evening receptions already alluded to. According to the numerical strength of the band engaged, from five to ten pounds will remunerate their services for a spell of, say, six hours in duration; but a guest at such an entertainment may, without committing any breach of the social law, bestow upon them *largesse*, when leaving the house of his host. Their dress, as a rule, is that of the average Dacian counter-jumper, subfusk in hue, relieved perhaps by a bright scarlet, blue, or pea-green necktie, the solitary outward and visible sign of their congenital fondness for gaudy colours. When not actually playing, they bear themselves cringingly. The brightest things about them are their restless eyes, from which sparks of their innate wildness flash out now and anon, in strange contrast to the prosaic seediness of their attire and spiritless servility of their attitude. But, once launched into the rendering of some fantastic *doina* or rollicking *hora*, a surprising change accrues to their demeanour and facial expression; they draw themselves up cheerily—almost proudly —and take free elbow-room with the gestures of emancipate men, joyously conscious of their natural gifts and developed powers; their lugubrious physiognomies are illuminated by beaming smiles; the droop, as though by magic, vanishes alike from shoulders, eyelids and mouth-corners. It is then that the art he all unreasoningly loves transfigures the *laotar* from a limp loafer into an eager executant of the strangest strains that ever startled and fascinated a cultured musical ear. Not one of these minstrels possesses the least knowledge of the elementary rules of harmony, or is acquainted with even the rudiments of notation. They make music as the birds do, they know not why or how; but from them many a Western composer might pick up valuable hints anent novelty of thematic treatment, so quaintly subtle and exquisitely delicate are the modulations and enharmonic transitions they contrive to extract from their instruments, often poor in quality and always eccentrically heterogeneous in combination. One peculiar characteristic of the music they play and sing I may mention here. It is for the most part—vocal as well as instrumental—*doina* as well as *hora*—cast in the minor mood, and actual discords are frequently employed in the *laotari* concerted arrangements to enhance the intrinsic gloom of the melody, with a weird and singularly impressive effect.

Nine years have elapsed since my last sojourn—one extending over several months at a stretch—in the principalities, since that date promoted to the rank of kingdom; but during the previous decade, I had enjoyed many opportunities of becoming well acquainted with Roumanian music and minstrelsy. At one time I knew every eminent *laotar* in Moldavia, if not in Wallachia, by sight, and was—for a *strainû* (foreigner)—tolerably familiar with the artistic specialities of all the "stars," instrumental or vocal, working the country from Suczàva to Galatz. Of the many roaming minstrel-bands with which it was my good fortune to foregather in the course of my own successive wanderings through the "scûmpa tseâra si frumoâsa" between the years 1865 and 1875, the "brotherhood" submitted to the sway of Nick the Moldavian, was in every respect the most remarkable. It consisted of eight performers, each of whom could play more than one instrument, and with really extraordinary ability, whilst one and all were tuneful and passionate singers. I first came upon them, very late at night, in a summer-garden, the abode of vociferous frogs, myriads in number, and never weary of croaking batrachian part-songs in every vocal register, from the gruffest of basses to the shrillest of trebles. Thither some of my Boyar friends conveyed me, to sup under the dark blue canopy of a Roumanian midnight sky, and to hear the best minstrelsy in all the land. As we were sitting in a bosky nook, dimly lighted by one stearine candle, defended from the breezes by a crystal sheath, we became aware of dusky faces peering in upon us from among the rustling green leaves. It struck me, I remember, that if the owners of such ominous physiognomies earned their daily bread by honest means, Dame Nature must have done them a cruel wrong. The situation seemed precarious; suddenly the frog-choruses themselves, to my ear, acquired an intolerably menacing vehemence. Whilst I was anxiously scanning those dingy visages, in the faint hope of detecting a ray of mansuetude in at least one gleaming eye, they all broke out into merry smiles; off went a fiddle with a humorous flourish; tink-a-tank twangled the double-necked guitar under the deft fingers of Niko Moldoveanûl; a flutey tooting revealed the presence of Pandean pipes, uncommonly mellow in quality; and Nicolai Terranûl (Nicholas the Peasant), a slender young Tsigan, with crisply curled black hair, and eyes like dark brown opals, stepped forward, bowing with all the grace and ease of a practised courtier, and sang one of the gayest predatory ballads of his *répertoire* in a throstle-throated, truly admirable manner.

The "Peasant" and the "Moldavian" could both fiddle distractingly well, besides singing in such sort as to stir the heart and charm the ear, and playing the ciombolanû—a sort of upright zither, plucked at with a plectrum—quite inimitably. To either of them a page of printed notes would have been about as intelligible as a chronological brick from Mesopotamia. Of their comrades, one in particular—a withered gipsy, exactly the colour of an ancient copper kettle, with revolving wild eyes—was the original genius of the "brotherhood." His instrument was the fiddle, upon which he could imitate exactly the tones of the flute, Pandeans, and three-holed reed—the genuine Dacian peasant's solace and only musical "familiar." This incomparable sound-mimic was, moreover, a composer and improvisatore, extravagantly proud of his compositions, which seemed to me the ravings of insane tonality, though there was unquestionably "method in their madness." When he extemporised, his "brothers" accompanied him by ear and intuition, hitting off the just harmonies with a surprising prescience of the most improbable melodic transitions. In all his rhapsodies there were real tunes, cast in the oddest of rhythms, but correct in form and intelligible enough to a quick musical ear. The copper-coloured, wizened Tsigan had queer ways of his own. His ordinary attitude in the company was retiring, not to say furtive; but when he detected appreciativeness in his audience he would edge his way through his fellows to their front, jerk his chin down upon his fiddle like some extremely aged and supernaturally wily bird, roll his eyes, wink, and grin a saffron grin. Then, dropping his bow lightly on the strings, he would conjure therefrom, with the supplest of wrists and most dexterous of fingers, such weird sounds as I, for one, have never before or since heard produced from any combination of wood, catgut, and horsehair.

The remaining members of the brotherhood were, avowedly, a second guitar, second-fiddle, three-holed pipe, grunter, and Pandeans. I say avowedly, because those were, so to speak, their official attributes in the band; but it appeared to me that each man could, at a pinch, play his neighbour's instrument, and others as well. He of the Pandeans was a gipsy version of Don Quixote; very long, very brown, very dried-up, very loose-jointed, with a face chiefly consisting of converging nose and chin, set off by a pair of dark sad eyes, bovine rather than human. All of this artist's flesh that I could see, reminded me, in colour and texture, of South American dried meat. He had a curiously lugubrious way of piping, as though conscious that it was his doom to forward his own process of desiccation by blowing his inward self into the reeds fringing his under lip. Judging by his facial expression whilst dealing with the lower tones, each one of them might have been fraught with his death-warrant. As a player, you could not have looked upon a more melancholy man; and yet, when it behoved him to sing, he could smile quite genially, whilst giving out rich, velvety bass notes from the deepest depths of his lank, cavernous chest. I found him a pleasant fellow to talk to, profoundly interested in his art, and childishly curious with respect to the music of other lands. So, indeed, were they all; and I shall never forget the rapture of attention and glow of excitement with which they listened to some sketchy souvenirs of Wagner, Berlioz, and Liszt, which I played to them on a dreadful old grand piano one day, when I had bidden them to my hotel for the entertainment of a few friends. It was a treat to observe their intense appreciation of harmonic methods and treatments absolutely new to them, and to listen to their intelligent attempts to fish out the novelties on their own instruments afterwards. In conclusion, I cannot forbear mentioning what struck me at the time as a fine trait—artistic and chivalrous—of those untutored but gifted Roumanian minstrels. They refused their fee, when dismissed for the evening, saying that what I had taught them more than paid for their humble service, without counting the pleasure they had experienced in hearing "undreamt-of sound-wonders." Of such stuff were the Dacian *laotari* when I knew them!

Throughout a period of absence from "my own, my native land," extending over well-nigh a score of years, it was my lot to spend Christmas more than once in places that, even from the modern British tourist's point of view, may be classed as "out-of-the-way," and amongst people having no cognizance whatsoever of our Christmas symbols or of the fare we deem peculiarly appropriate to our family celebrations of the chief Christian anniversary. When compelled by circumstances over which I had no control to pass the festive season in some "foreign part" belonging to the category above alluded to, I invariably made an effort—prompted thereto by those old associations which exercise so irresistible an influence upon Englishmen wandering far from home—to get up a genuine, thorough-going Christmas dinner for my own delectation and that of any other Briton who, like myself, happened to be enduring temporary exile within my reach. Need I say that plum-pudding constituted the leading—nay, the one indispensable feature of these *symposia?* The mince-pie I have always regarded as an institution of secondary importance; whereas plum-pudding is an absolute essential to the due observance of the Nativity feast. As far as I am personally concerned, this axiom only holds good when Christmastide comes upon me abroad. In these isles I never eat plum-pudding at that or any other season; for I do not like it, and it disagrees with me in a quite surprising manner. But I have consumed it—or something more or less like it—on the 25th of December in Berlin, Vienna, Rome, Versailles (at a memorable Christmas banquet, eaten within hearing of the guns of Mont Valérien, and in the company of twenty Englishmen well-known to fame, *entr'autres* William Howard Russell, Alfred Austin, the late Lord Ampthill, Hilary Skinner, and poor Bob Landells), Belgrade, Pesth, and Bucharest. It is of an exceptionally quaint plum-pudding experience that accrued to me in the last-named capital—commonly known to Mudie's subscribers as "The City of Pleasure" —that I now propose to give some account.

At the time to which I refer, the State which has lately blossomed out into Royal rank under the style and title of the Kingdom of Roumania was a fief of Turkey, officially known as the United Principalities of Wallachia and Moldavia, forlorn of railways, badly-off for roads, and governed in a happy-go-lucky sort of way by an intelligent but curiously dissolute Hospodar, hight John Alexander Cusa. The Roumanians were in many important respects a long way behind the inhabitants of Central and Western Europe; several arts of modern civilisation were unknown to them; they were as ignorant of plum-pudding, for instance, as is the unborn babe. Yes; strange and even unnatural as it may appear to English apprehensions, the Dacians of '64 were as good and happy as it was in their nature to be at Christmastide (their Serbatóre Craciunului, by the way, comes off twelve days later than our Feast of the Nativity) without the stimulus to virtuous conviviality that is afforded by plum-pudding. Having ascertained that such was the case by painstaking inquiry, and being detained by the exigencies of a special mission on the banks of "sweet Dumbovizza" during the festive week, I resolved that I would have an indisputable English plum-pudding for my Christmas dinner, or know the reason why. I may as well say at once that I fulfilled the latter moiety of my resolve as completely as the fondest heart could wish—but not the former.

I had set up house—or rather, rooms in somebody else's house—in a modest kind of way, and engaged a native cook who, being a gipsy as well as a Moldavian, was musical to the core. Meticka (the Roumanian diminutive for Demetrius) could play the fiddle or *ciombolán* with excellent taste and spirit, and sing right tunefully with a soft light tenor voice that would have made the fortune of a French or German hero of operetta. He was also an adept in the somewhat primitive culinary science of Moldo-Wallachia, and could turn out a dish of *uâ impletatâ* (stuffed egg-plant) as well as the Hospodar's *chef* himself. A cheerier cook than Meticka— one freer from professional prejudices or more eager to please his master for the time being—I never encountered. Instead of scowling at suggestions after the approved manner of his kind, he received them with genial smiles; and the less he understood them the more energetically did he endeavour to carry them out. In spite of one or two startling surprises I had experienced, resulting from his failure to give practical expression to my theoretical instructions, I had faith in Meticka. I deemed him capable of compounding and cooking the plum-pudding *in prospectu* upon which I had fixed my mind's eye; the more so that a happy fancy, as I believed, had inspired me with an expedient for guarding him against any of the errors of interpretation or shortcomings of memory that had frustrated his previous efforts to realise my wishes.

It happened that I had with me, nestling in a secret drawer of my travelling-desk, a maternal grand-aunt's recipe for the composition of an inimitable plum-pudding. Throughout my wanderings *per mare per terras* I had never parted from this precious document, regarded in my family with deep reverence as the abiding record of a sublime revelation especially vouchsafed to a gifted ancestress. I translated the muniment in question into current Roumanian, and—early in the third week in December—proceeded in person to purchase each several ingredient incident to the preparation of a pudding which, for me, was invested with the hallowed character of an heirloom. This done, it became incumbent upon me to induce Meticka to learn by heart the text of my deceased great-aunt's instructions "How to make a Christmas Pudding," as well as the names of that dainty's component parts and the proportions in which they were to be utilised. After I had recited all these details to him in my most impressive manner, I added, " Now, my good Meticka, is there not some easy, popular air in your *répertoire* of national melodies to which you could adapt this recipe? I think that, were you to sing it about the house for a week or so—say as frequently as you are in the habit of favouring us with "Doi ochj" or "Cinel, cinel"—you might, so to speak, make it a part of your own being, and thus obviate the possibility of forgetting the least of its prescriptions." His dark eyes sparkled with intelligent joy as he replied, "Beloved sir, there is such an air. You must know it well, for all the *laotari* (minstrels) sing it, and it is the delight of the Boyars. 'Am un leû' will take any words; it is an elastic tune. Leave it to me, *domnû;* in an hour your pudding-words shall fit it like a glove!"

It may be as well to mention here parenthetically that the favourite lay of Roumanian peer and peasant alike—probably because its leading incident is one eminently calculated to enlist the national sympathies—is intituled "Am un leû, s'am se'l bé," and embodies a salient Dacian instinct with remarkable exactitude in its first verse, which may be roughly Anglicised as follows:—

> I've a piastre—'tisn't mine—
> Traderideridera.
> Nevertheless I'll spend it in wine—
> Traderideridera.
> That being done, my conscience may tell
> Me whether I have done ill or well—
> Traderi, derideriderideridera;
> Houp là! deridera!

These spirited words, and others to follow, dealing with petty frauds in a light-hearted temper which is highly appreciated in the *scúmpa tseára si frumoása* that gave my musical Meticka birth, are set to a no less spirited tune—almost the only Roumanian melody known to me that is composed in an exclusively major key; and, as he reminded me, I had certainly heard it a few hundred times during my sojourn in the Principalities, then drawing towards its close.

Meticka committed the recipe to memory; and, having skilfully adjusted its items and edicts to the above popular melody, went about the house for a day or two more tunefully than ever, singing it at the top of his voice in fifteen verses or so. If I remember aright the opening stanza ran thus:—

> Fâinâ, grasime, amestecat;
> Lemâe zagharisitâ si patrat,
> Stafide, migdale, mai multe ouû,
> Smochine, bere, pucin rachiû:—

or, in the vernacular—

> Flour and suet, sugar and spice,
> Candied lemon-peel, cut into dice,
> Currants and eggs and almonds a few,
> Raisins and beer, and brandy, too:—

with the "Traderiderideras" all in their proper places, and the jocund "Houp là!" to wind up with. On Christmas Day, Meticka became almost oppressively vocal with the pudding-song. As the dinner-hour approached, his confidence in the proximate realisation of all the promise so melodiously set forth by that ditty rose to joyous certainty, until the "Houp là!" of his refrain became, as it were, the triumphant outcry of irrefragable conviction. As I heard him thus proudly carolling in the fulness of his heart, I murmured complacently "My Christmas pudding is an accomplished fact."

When, however, the pudding made its appearance on my table in due succession to *carne de bouŭ fripta* (roast beef) and *curcán fertu* (boiled turkey) it proved to be a gruesome porridge, thick and slab, brownish-grey in colour, studded with dark glutinous knobs of evil aspect, and singularly malodorous. All the precautions of the careful Briton—all the minstrelsy of the trustful Dacian had only resulted in this revolting compound. With a mournful smile I unhesitatingly conferred it upon Meticka, whose spirits were effectually damped by an heroic attempt to consume it, and made up my mind, once for all, that (even when set to music) plum-pudding was not achievable in Roumania by faith or works, or both combined.

In stating my conviction that the Servians are the most unmusical people in Europe I trust that I do that nation of pig-breeders and plum-growers no very heinous wrong. No kind of art at present flourishes in Servia, nor in those adjacent countries to which, despite Berlin Treaties and other solemn international compacts, she still persists in putting forward a shadowy claim. According to the Servian Ethnographical Society—which, I may say parenthetically, is *imperium in imperio*, a power in the youngest of European kingdoms—Servia is to its Slav neighbours what the dog, from a railway-traffic point of view, is to other domestic animals, as set forth in that inimitable drawing of Keene representing an old lady on the platform of a station, surrounded by pets in cages and hutches, and a porter holding up a tortoise demonstratively to her view whilst explaining the tariff to her in the following lucid terms: "The stationmaster, mum, he says as cats is dogs, and rabbits is dogs, and parrots is dogs; but this here tortus is a hinseck, and he won't make no charge for it." Similarly, to the ardent Czillak patriot, Bulgaria is Servia, and Bosnia is Servia, and the Herzegovina is Servia, not to mention Croatia and Montenegro. Admitting the correctness of his view (only because it suits me to do so for the time being), I say again that Servia, in the most comprehensive sense of the word, is unmusical—nay more, that it is the converse of musical. What it produces in the way of vocal and instrumental noise is the negation of music, eminently calculated to split rocks rather than to soften them, and fully equal, not only to rend the knotted oak, but to saw up that monarch of the forest into planks. During my repeated and, on more than one occasion, protracted sojourns in the Principality—that was its rank until a few years ago, when it promoted itself to the rank of Kingdom—I have frequently, much too frequently, heard male Servians grunt and female Servians squeal, under the pretence of singing, in a manner that would have done distinguished credit to the most vociferous hog of all the bristly herds that constitute the staple of their national trade; and it has been my dismal fate, times without number, to listen to Servian military bands, doing such deeds of terror with brass and wood, as have blanched my cheek and chilled my blood. But no sound of strictly Servian origin that has ever reached my ears could be justly described as musical. It must have been a typical Czillak whom Shakespeare had in his mind when he wrote, " The man that hath not music in his soul, and is not moved by concord of sweet sounds, is fit for treason, stratagem and spoil." As a matter of fact, those are the pursuits for which Servians display an aptitude altogether undeveloped in them as far as the production or appreciation of melody and harmony are concerned. So inveterately indifferent are they to the charms of Polyhymnia that the itinerant concert-troupes annually making their rounds through Eastern Europe and looked for at certain seasons with joyful eagerness by the inhabitants of such out-of-the-way towns as Temesvar, Debreczin, Hermannstadt and Crajova, never dream of crossing the Danube to Servia, well aware that musical performances are permanently at a discount in that singularly inartistic realm. Even the gipsy minstrels, who swarm throughout the Lower Banat on the opposite bank of the great river, steadfastly refrain from expending any portion of their earnings in the ferry-fares between Semlin and Belgrade; sorrowful experience having taught them that the brightest fiddling, gayest piping, and most tuneful singing is incapable of extracting a single copper from the baggy pocket of any human being indigenous to the Servian capital. On calm summer evenings, whilst strolling along the riverward ramparts of Belgrade Citadel, you can faintly hear the merry strains of the Zigeuner playing and singing in the hotel-gardens of Semlin to generous and appreciative Austro-Hungarian audiences, supping *al fresco* in those leafy retreats with wild minstrelsy *obbligato* until far into the night. But the sallow songsters shun the right bank of the river, where Save and Danube meet. They might sing themselves dumb within the precincts of a Belgrade inn, at or after supper time, and yet fail to earn a plaudit or a penny. This they know; and it effectually checks even their errant impulses and enterprising spirit, for they are as greedy of appreciation as of gain.

In all Belgrade there is not a concert-room—no, not even in the Konak, or Royal Palace, the illustrious occupants of which, from Milosch down to Milan, have one and all been as radically unmusical as their subjects. I once spent three months at a stretch in that city, and was on unceremonious visiting terms with several of its leading families; but I do not remember to have seen a pianoforte in any Servian house, or to have elicited a single admission of partiality to music from any Servian dame or damsel. One morning, whilst breakfasting with the lamented Prince Michael—a man of great natural gifts but few accomplishments, to whom, strange to say, music was an offence—the conversation happened to turn upon the state of the liberal arts in Servia, and I took occasion to ask His Highness whether any of the ladies attached to the Court circle were musically inclined, and, if so, who might be the most skilled executants, vocal and instrumental. He replied, without a moment's hesitation, "Really, I do not know. I believe my cousin Catherine plays the piano; but I have never heard her do so, for she knows that I dislike every kind of music." The Prince's peculiarity in this respect being notorious throughout Belgrade society, I need scarcely say that music was strictly tabooed at the entertainments given from time to time by the members of the Corps Diplomatique, whenever—which was but rarely—their banquets or soirées were honoured by His Highness's presence.

If, in the preceding paragraphs, I have succeeded in conveying to my readers anything like an adequate notion of the hopeless unmusicality characterising the Servian nation, they will assuredly not be surprised to learn that such reminiscences as I have retained of music and musicians in Belgrade are exclusively connected with the foreign element of that capital's population. When I first paid it a brief visit, nearly twenty years ago, the mighty fortress for the possession of which Moslem and Christian have so often and fiercely fought in times long past, was still in the hands of the Turks, and the first music, or that which was intended to be so, produced for my especial delectation, as the honoured guest of the worthy old Pasha in command of the garrison, was of a nature to all but petrify me with astonishment and consternation. Having gleaned from the British Diplomatic Agent, with whom I was staying, that I was a music-lover, His Excellency Ali Riza, bent, in the fulness of his heart, upon giving me the greatest artistic treat of which he could dispose, despatched the full band of the artillery regiment constituting the bulk of his garrison, to the court-yard of the British Agency at an early hour of the morning after the banquet at which he had entertained me with profuse Oriental hospitality. This band, some forty strong and brass to a man, except the drums and a peal of silver bells intermingled with horse-tails, received orders to take up a position exactly under the bedroom window of the newly-arrived English Effendi, and there, at precisely seven A.M., to open upon him with the March of Sultan Mechmet—by many degrees the most vigorous concerted piece in the Ottoman military orchestral *répertoire*. The English Effendi was slumbering profoundly when this visitation burst upon him with all the terrors of the unknown and unexpected; but had he been a hybernating dormouse, or one of the Seven Sleepers, the preliminary blast and thump of *Mechmet* would have awakened him with more than lightning-like promptitude. The first thought that flashed across my bewildered brain, as I started up in bed, was that I had been shot out of a gun of large calibre; the next, presumably suggested by the blare and braying of the trumpets and trombones, that the end of all things was at hand, and the inconceivable clamour assailing my ears was an announcement of that consummation confided to wind instruments of an altogether supernatural class. Collecting my scattered wits at the expiration of a few hideous seconds devoted to incoherent conjecture, I got upon my feet and staggered to the window, peering nervously through which I took in the whole dread reality at a glance. There they were, forming a hollow double circle, in the centre of which stood the gorgeous bandmaster, leading with his hand in lieu of a bâton—two score swarthy, wiry, deep-chested Arnauts, blowing, beating, and jingling at high pressure, and looking as if they could go on doing all these things for unnumbered hours without turning a hair. I may say with truth that I had never entirely realised what cymbals were capable of, in the way of poisoning human happiness, until I heard that band play. Nor had I been aware that any tune could be harmonised in such sort that its accompaniment should exclusively consist of discords. As "long I stood there, wondering, fearing," I learnt all this and a good deal more, equally discomforting. Presently the bandmaster, looking upwards in a spasm of inspiration, brought on by a more than usually deadly dissonance—at that particular moment the brasses were playing simultaneously in at least six different keys—caught sight of my face at the window. Instantly a lurid smile illumined his tawny countenance; he waved his hand more frantically than before, and spoke some word of power to his bandsmen, the immediate result of which was an explosion of noise to which their previous achievements in that line had borne the relation of a whisper to an eruption of Vesuvius. By this time my kindly host, slippered and dressing-gowned, made his appearance in my room, and explained to me at the top of his voice that this abominable din was in the nature of a high compliment, paid to me by my august host of the preceding evening—that it would last for fully an hour and a-half longer—that etiquette required me to remain at my open window throughout the execution of the entire programme, and, finally, that the entertainment would cost me at least ten ducats (nearly five pounds), that being the smallest backshish one so highly favoured by the Pasha could offer to the garrison band. "It is rather unfortunate for you," continued his Excellency with agreeable complacency, "that Ali Riza took such a fancy to you last night at dinner, and that I mentioned to him how fond you are of music. He is a most amiable old gentleman, the very soul of hospitality, and I should not wonder if he were to insist upon sending the band here of a morning, thrice a week or so, to serenade you as long as you remain my guest. You will find it somewhat expensive, I am afraid; perhaps, too, a little Turkish music may go a long way in your case. I am accustomed to it, and rather like it, being uncommonly hard of hearing, though it is now and then a thought louder than I could wish; but I have known people—oddly enough, too, of a musical turn—upon whom it has produced a very painful impression. By the way, you will have to get yourself up *en grand gala* after breakfast, take my carriage, and drive to the fortress to thank the Pasha for his graceful attention, and express your delight with the admirable performance of his musicians. It would gratify the good old man if you could assure him that their strains had struck you as being sweeter than those of the nightingale, and softer than the murmur of a perfumed breeze—something neatly turned in the Oriental manner, you know." So saying, my Amphitryon departed; and I returned to the open casement to "suffer and be strong" for other ninety minutes or so. In due time the backshish was administered to the dusky *chef a'orchestre*, with the noisome effect of eliciting an extra *morceau* from the band, in token of its gratitude. In short, I was made to drink of that bitter cup, even to its very dregs.

Resolved to carry out my instructions, I visited the Pasha early in the afternoon, and found him installed in the "best room" of the *selamlik*, obviously expectant of my call. When I assured him of the gratification I had derived from listening to music " such," I emphatically observed, " as I had never before heard or dreamt of in my life" (which was strictly true), his venerable lineaments positively beamed with delight. "I knew you would like our national airs," he exclaimed; "our friend the Agent told me you were a musician, and as such you could not fail to appreciate them. How much more melodious and beautiful they are than your Western tunes, are they not? Those fellows I sent to you this morning can play all sorts of Occidental music—operatic arrangements, *fantasies* from *Les Huguenots. La Favorite*, que sais-je: all very well in their way, I do not doubt, but they fail to please me. So I told the bandmaster upon no account to play anything to you but real genuine Turkish music; and it seems I did well. You cannot know how it rejoices me that you should appreciate our fine stirring melodies" (stirring was the word, I felt, but not exactly in the sense intended by my interlocutor). "You shall hear one or two of them again, now—this is about the hour at which the band plays to amuse my family and myself—and I will see that you do not lack the music your soul loves whilst you sojourn in Belgrade. Not a word, my dear friend; leave it to me— nothing will rejoice me more, upon awaking at early morn, than the thought that you are enjoying the finest music in the world, which my thrice happy Destiny enables me to place at your disposal." Five minutes later the band was mustered in the *place d'armes* commanded by the Konak windows, and went through its programme of the morning again with punctilious and maddening exactitude. A happier man, the while, than Ali Riza Pasha could not have been discovered within the limits of the Ottoman Empire—nor a more miserable wight than myself. That dire day's experiences and the apprehension of what could not but succeed them, should the Pasha fulfil his promise, considerably abbreviated my stay in the Servian capital. In point of fact I quitted Belgrade the very next morning; and did not return thither until two years later, to witness the evacuation of the fortress by the gallant Turkish garrison, Pasha, band and all—upon which occasion, as Prince Michael rode through the citadel gates upon a priceless charger (the Padishah's gift) to take possession of the stronghold he had so long coveted, I heard for the last time the choice selection of Turkish airs that had driven me out of Servia in the autumn of 1865.

Another curious musical reminiscence of Belgrade dates from the year of the great Servian rebellion (1876), during the greater portion of which it was my duty to abide in the Principality as a chronicler of current events. Whilst in Belgrade, awaiting permission to join the Russo-Servian headquarters at Parachin, I became acquainted with all the members of the Diplomatic Body, which had undergone a complete change of *personnel* since my last previous visit, and was no less surprised than delighted to find amongst them one of the finest amateur pianists and ablest sight-readers in Europe. This was Count Joannini, the chief of the Italian Mission, a pupil and worshipper of Franz Liszt, whose compositions he played with great facility and infinite relish. Upon paying my first visit to this accomplished musician —whom I had hitherto only known by reputation as a particularly well-informed diplomatist — I found him seated at one of two grand-pianos, arranged head and tail in the approved concert "form," in a room the walls of which were lined with bookcases and shelves laden with bound music, whilst every table and chair was profusely littered with "notes" of the newest, printed at Vienna, Leipzig, and Berlin, the leading publishers of which cities, as I afterwards learnt, kept his Excellency supplied, "up to date," with compositions for the P. F. of a certain class. Count Joannini delighted in four-handed playing, and especially in that variety of "morceaux à quatre mains" which is specially written for two clavichords. He was not a little proud of possessing every work of the sort that had ever theretofore been printed, from Mozart's tuneful Sonata in D (Series 16) down to Brahms' complex Variations on a Theme by Haydn (opus 56 B). Several of them, forwarded to him since his appointment to the Mission at Belgrade, he had not even heard in their totality, for the simple reason that there was no one in either the native or foreign local circle of society capable of playing them with him. I have seldom seen anybody look so pleasurably astonished as he did when I mentioned that "il suonare a prima vista" was a favourite musical recreation of mine. Two minutes later we were both "in position," with a thick *cahier* of Liszt's Symphonic Poems facing us; and, before we parted that afternoon, had worked our way through *Tasso*, *Mazeppa*, *Hamlet*, and the *Todtentanz*. He was, indeed—alas! that I should have to speak of him in the past tense—a brilliantly intelligent pianist, gifted with that quick perception of a composer's meaning which is only exhibited by elect musical natures, and deeply versed in all the most approved methods of dealing with technical difficulties. Thenceforth, until the day of my recall from Servia, I spent every hour of my spare time with Joannini at the piano. By the time the great Turkish victory at Djunis had practically put down the rebellion, we had tried every four-handed number in his collection. Shortly afterwards we parted, little thinking we were never to meet again. For four or five years we kept up correspondence, though at long intervals; my last letter to him, however, remained unanswered, and just four years ago, the melancholy tidings reached me that he had perished by his own hand. Partly through brooding over disappointments connected with his career, and partly through self-torment provoked by pecuniary embarrassment, he gradually lapsed into a state of chronic melancholy, forsaking society, and even foregoing his piano; until one morning in March, 1882, finding existence altogether intolerable, he locked himself up in his bedroom and blew out his brains. Thus miserably ended one of the most cultivated musical *dilettanti* it has ever been my good fortune to foregather with—a ripe scholar and gentleman of many " excellent differences," but too sensitive and highly-wrought to bear up against a long run of ill-luck. My saddest Reminiscence of Musicians Abroad is associated with his name.

CHAPTER VI.

INDIAN MUSIC.—ORIENTAL VERSIONS OF THE BRITISH NATIONAL ANTHEM.

THIRTY years ago, when the *peripetia* of the Crimean War were quickening the pulses of Englishmen feverishly, it was by no means an uncommon incident of a stroll through London streets to encounter a lean, shivery foreign person with a complexion the colour of curry-powder, chiefly clad in linen and presenting an appearance, generally speaking, of profound and chronic discomfiture. This saffron-hued alien, when shambling along the pavement of a crowded thoroughfare, was rarely vocal or instrumental; but if you happened to meet him in fashionable or suburban regions, far away from the bustle and roar of the business centres, you invariably found him singing the songs of his native land to the accompaniment of a peculiarly depressing oblong drum, shaped like a rolly-polly pudding, upon either skin-clad end of which he beat incessantly with his knuckles. As an unsophisticated child I remember to have asked those set in authority over me what manner of man this might be, and to have been informed that he was "the poor Indian, whose untutored, &c.," and that the instrument he percutated with such distracting persistency was the tom-tom. At the period I refer to there were a good many of these dingy Oriental soloists about town, to me quite indistinguishable from one another. They all looked exactly alike, and did exactly the same things; things, I am bound to say, almost unbearable to a child afflicted with a musical ear. Their melodies were composed of random notes, alternately howled and moaned to dismal monosyllables, all vowels and liquids, something after this manner: "La-la-lo-na-ma-na-lo-la," and so on *ad infinitum*, with the dub, dub, dub, dub of the rolly-polly drum *obbligato* all the while, as intolerably iterative as the thumping of the pistons in the innermost parts of an ocean steamer struggling along at high pressure against a head wind and a heavy sea—thumps which generate responsive throbs in the temple and qualms in the midriff of the unseaworthy passenger. I remember being incredulous, as a boy, as to these lyrics having any meaning; to me, and I have no doubt to the majority of my cotemporaries, youthful or adult, they sounded like mere gibberish—an idiot's tale, full of sound and fury, signifying nothing. The knowledge of riper years leads me nowadays to surmise that they may have been romantic narratives, such as "The Sports of Krishna," otherwise Samodadamodaro (they sounded very like it); or love-songs of the Sakandkshapundarikaksho class; or haply epithalamia, such as Maninivarnane Chaturachaturbhujo; which, I may remark for the information of concert-room vocalists, is sung to the music Deshîyavarâdî and in the mode Ashtatâlî. Moreover, in the ninth Sarga of the Gîta Govinda, intituled Kalahantaritavarnane Mugdhamukundo, there is a plaintive ditty, the burden of which runs thus: "Mâ kooroo mânini mânamayè" (My proud one, do not indulge in scorn); and this, I feel convinced, the ginger-complexioned songsters of my boyhood's days must have been addicted to yelling, for it lends itself so very aptly to the style of voice-production they particularly affected. According to Jayadeva, the inspired author of the Gîta Govinda, the *refrain* in question should be sung to the music Gurjjarî, and in the mode Yati. If those saffron minstrels complied with his instructions, I can only say that the music of Gurjjarî may have been extremely pleasing to the Raga Megh, a divine fundamental melody, of which, or rather of whom (for the Ragas ranked as deities in the quaint old Hindoo mythology), she, Gurjjarî, was the third wife; but that its effect upon Western organisations lacking, perhaps, the subtlety of sense required for the appreciation of its beauties, was curiously dispiriting.

Edwin Arnold, one of the greatest of English living poets, who has endowed us with an incomparably beautiful version of Jayadeva's masterpiece, the Indian "Song of Songs," tells us that from time immemorial music was always taught orally by the Hindoos, and did not, therefore, pass down through the ages from the old minstrels in any notated form. It is thus that he accounts for the failure of that illustrious Oriental scholar, Sir William Jones, to discover the original music of the Gîta Govinda, notwithstanding the indications afforded by the author, who has prefixed to each of its successive lyrics the name of the "mode" in which it was to be sung. It seems that in the course of his quest after the melodies of the Hindoo Canticle, the Pundits of the South referred Sir William to those of the West, who again referred him to the Northern Brahmins, these latter in their turn declaring that they had no ancient music, but imagined that the notes of the Gîta Govinda must exist, if anywhere, in the land of Jayadeva's birth. Edwin Arnold, however, has ascertained that an elaborate science of melody was familiar to the ancient Indians, who—like the Greeks of yore—understood little or nothing of harmony. According to this paramount authority upon every branch of Oriental art, the distinguishing feature of Hindoo airs still is, as it was in olden times, an extremely fine gradation of notes, which permits the accurate sub-division of the semitone into demi-semitones, on voices and stringed instruments alike, by the native executant. This faculty of sub-division imparts a certain captivating delicacy of *nuances*, recognisable by all cultivated musicians, to the otherwise monotonous temple-singing of India.

Nisikânta Chattopâdhyâya, the author of an instructive treatise on the Yâtrâs, or popular dramas of Bengal—for the most part miracle-plays like the mediæval Christian "Mysteries"—after observing that these dramas consist principally of songs, always provided with their respective melodies and cadences, says that the Hindoos have always been ardent lovers of music. Even in the most ancient period of their literature may be found minute directions how the verses of the Sâma-Veda are to be sung by officiating priests, according to the three different intonations called Udatta, Anudatta and Svarita. "Gânât parataram nahi" (There is nothing superior to song) is an Indian proverb of extraordinary antiquity, and the Hindoo musical literature is very extensive. Dâmodara, a renowned writer upon the Divine Art, in his "Mirror of Song" (Sangîta-Darpanam) describes the Hindoo musical scale as being composed of seven tones, types of natural sound; viz., suruj, the peacock's screech; rikhub, the parrot's cry; gundhur, the bleat of the sheep; muddhun, the crane's call; punchum, the note of the koîl, an Indian bird; dhyvut, the horse's neigh; and nik-had, the trumpeting of the elephant. The notes of the gamut are generally indicated by the first syllables of their designations—su, ri, gu, mu, pu, dhu and ni. Out of these seven primitive tones are formed six Ragas or divine fundamental airs named Bhairava, Mâlakosha, Hindola, Dîpaka, Crîrâga and Megh, each of whom has five wives (Raginîs). Again, each Ragini has borne to her Raga spouse eight melodious children, the Uparâgas, or minor tunes; so that, according to Edwin Arnold, the orthodox repertory of Indian vocal music, or Hindoo "Little Warbler," contains two hundred and forty distinct and individual songs, each having its fixed occasion, subject, and season, all to be reverently observed; as otherwise the deity presiding over each separate lyric was not thought likely to attend and give perfect effect to the music. "These lyric divinities," writes the author of "The Light of Asia," are personified and described in such works as the "Ratnamala:" thus "Gurjjari" (a melodic manner frequently prescribed for use by Jayadeva in the Indian "Song of Songs") "is represented as a feminine minstrel of engaging mien, dressed in a yellow bodice and red *sari* richly bedecked with jewels, and enthroned in a golden swing."

By the Hindoo Pundits of old, musical science was divided into seven branches; surudhyaya, or solfeggio; tal, or time; nrit, or rhythmical dancing; aurth, or poetry; rag, or melody; bhav, or expression; and hust, answering to method, or touch. Endless constructive subtleties characterised these musical terms. "Thus" (I quote again from Arnold's preface to his version of the Gîta Govinda) "tal, or time, is a word made up of the first letters of tand, the dance of Mahados, and las, the dance of his consort Parvati. But these are mere etymological niceties, characteristic of the hard language in which one single word may be written in a hundred and eight ways." According to the erudite Nisikânta Chattopâdhyâya, the same spirit of nice distinctions and minute analysis is manifest in the divisions of the various cadences (Tâlalaya) into which each Raga, Raginî, and Uparâga is appropriately fitted.

Hindoo musical instruments are of four classes—(1) tata, the lute kind; (2) sushira, the flute kind; (3) avanaddha, the drum kind; (4) ghana, the bell kind. Of these, the lute proper, or vînâ, was formerly the national instrument *par excellence*. Sarasvati, the Hindoo goddess of learning and music, and Rishi Nârada, the most popular of Indian saints, are always represented holding a vînâ, and, in the Jajurvedas, Jâjnavalkya is described as the inventor of an instrument of this sort having a hundred strings. The European voice registers are known to the Hindoos by the names udara (bass), mudara (tenor), and tara (soprano). Râgas, Raginîs, and Uparâgas, which may be roughly defined in English as rudimentary airs, melodic methods and perfected popular tunes, must—so says Nisikânta—be carefully adjusted to the divers feelings or states of mind which songs are meant to express, and are invariably so adjusted in the Miracle-Plays, lyrical dramas still so popular in Bengal that they are acted there not only thrice a year, during the three feasts and processions in honour of Krishna, but in all months and seasons upon festive occasions, religious or secular. The Yâtrâ songs are said to be as numerous as the stars, and the list of Hindoo composers, from the tenth century down to the present time, would fill a portly tome. Of cotemporary Indian song-writers, or rather song-setters, Rajah Caurindra Mohan Tagore is at once the most fertile and popular. I have, unfortunately, been unable to get hold of a single specimen of his creative ability as a melodist; but from what I have gathered from Indian acquaintances respecting the character of his compositions, I should imagine that he must be the Jack Hatton of Hindostan.

Not even the great authorities to whom I am indebted for so much valuable information upon the subject of Indian music have been able to find out the name of the *maestro* who composed the music of the Gîta Govinda, probably the most ancient opera in existence; by the way, Nisikânta compares it and other Yâtrâs of equal antiquity to the Pastorals of Tasso and Guarini, in which songs predominated over dialogue, and which, moreover, treated of shepherds and shepherdesses, as did the popular Indian lyrical drama. Edwin Arnold, who has heard all these pieces performed in the best manner by native artists, is of opinion that the special music composed to the "Song of Songs," could it be recovered from the limbo of ages and rendered intelligible to European musicians by the aid of modern notation, would add immensely to the interest of the Sanskrit Canticle. Even at present, he says, any competent inquirer into the existing melodies of India, popular and sacred, might find his research rewarded by many exquisite airs, worthy of study by Western composers and music-lovers. Perhaps the English ear is not quite finely trained enough yet to relish demi-semitones, which appear to constitute the peculiar charm and special attraction of Hindoo songs; but experiments in Indian vocalism would, I have no doubt, be listened to with the greatest interest by London amateurs, were any opportunity of hearing it afforded to them. Where, however, are Indian songs, printed or in manuscript, to be obtained? I have put this question to several "old Indians" in succession, without, however, obtaining anything like a satisfactory answer. One or two have expressed their conviction that Hindoo music cannot be adequately expressed by European notation; and this may be so, if demi-semitones constitute one of its chief integral elements. At any rate, I have failed in all my endeavours to obtain a sight of any Indian musical composition, vocal or instrumental, although Edwin Arnold distinctly states that the Indians of to-day have still their dhoorpuds, or heroic ballads; their kheals, ghuzuls and rekhtahs, love-songs of Mogul derivation; their dadras and nuktahs, serenades of Hindoo origin; the tuppah, hummed by Hindi and Punjabi camel-drivers; the terana, or "song without words;" the palna, or cradle-song; the sohla, or marriage strain; the stooti, or eulogistic chants; and the zikri, which are hymns of morality. It is possible that among these varieties of vocal music, some echoes of the antique melodies to which Jayadeva's admirable lyrics were set, may be preserved; for conservatism in every sort of art is a leading Hindoo characteristic. Perhaps those chilly strangers with the gamboge cheeks and opaline eye-balls, with whom old memories prompt me to associate Indian music, knew how to sing the loves of Radha and Krishna as they were sung by skilled gundharbs or goonees about the time at which Henry II. reigned over England, and could have chanted the demi-semitonic scales with all the accuracy and finish not infrequently displayed by the common or garden cat in practising that description of vocal exercise. Alas! those Asiatic minstrels are no longer perceptible to the naked eye in London streets. The Indian Mutiny put English folk out of conceit with songsters who, independently of the fact that their performances were a very stomach-ache of sound, looked as if they might have been own brothers to the merciless traitors who butchered English women and children at Cawnpore. An unreasonable fancy, very likely; but it certainly knocked the Hindoo vocalist's profession on the head as far as this country was concerned.

At a time when the loyalty of our Indian fellow-subjects is a factor of surpassing importance in the great problem we are called upon to solve—viz., How the British Empire may be preserved in its vast and stately entirety—and when we are being daily assured by Continental friends and foes alike that the populations subjected to our rule in Hindostan are so sick and tired of our selfish and unscrupulous tyranny that they positively yearn to exchange it for the disinterested and conscientious protection of Russia, it may not be inopportune to point out that the natives of British India have of late years manifested an ever-growing disposition to rival Englishmen in their fealty to the Imperial Crown, and more especially in their devotion to the person of our gracious Empress-Queen. To the majority of untravelled Britons, India is still a splendid mystery, the secrets of which they have not even attempted to penetrate, chiefly because the engrossing nature of their bread-earning pursuits in this country hinders them from bestowing serious attention upon matters not immediately concerning their daily life-routine. It may be doubted, for instance, that one Anglo-Saxon in twenty is aware of the fact that " God save the Queen " is every whit as familiar to her Majesty's Indian subjects as it is to the denizens of these isles; that, in short, it is no less the National Anthem of Hindostan than of Great Britain, Canada, and Australia. Yet this is undoubtedly the case. The patriotic emotion—such as it is—of the Berkshire ploughman and Bengali ryot finds vocal expression upon high-days and holidays in one and the same hymn, allowance being made for certain intrinsic and unconquerable differences between the English and Indian idioms and musical figures. For it must be understood that English tune-forms are as unmanageable—I may even say irreproducible—by Indian vocalists and instrumentalists as are the Ragas, Raginîs and Uparâgas of Hindoo music by our own executants. Our plain-sailing melodies, which set forth no narrower interval than a semitone, appear, no doubt, at once intolerably coarse and tame to the Indian ear, trained to relish subtler subdivision of sound; whilst the tunes of the great Asiatic peninsula, abounding as they do in demi-semitones and thirds of notes, untranscribable by our system of notation, seem utterly incoherent and meaningless to European musicians, whose oral receptivity of intervals between note and note is restricted to the capacities of the chromatic scale. Without going so far as to say that it is impossible for a skilled Hindoo vocalist—gundharb or goonee—to sing an English song exactly as it is written, I may confidently assert that he or she would experience great physical difficulty and inconvenience in doing so. No melody, of course, could ever become popular in any country unless it could be sung with perfect ease by the uneducated as well as the cultivated music-lover; wherefore, in order to insure the popularity of "God Save the Queen" throughout our Indian Empire, it was necessary not only to translate the words of the National Anthem into the leading languages of that huge realm, but to fit them with tunes at once singable by Indian vocalists and suitable to Indian taste.

This was no small undertaking; but it was successfully carried out some few years ago by the London National Anthem Committee, a body of gentlemen constituted, if I remember aright, shortly after her Majesty's assumption of the Imperial style and title, with the object of familiarising the natives of British possessions in all parts of the world with "God Save the Queen," by furnishing them with metrical versions of that hymn in their respective tongues, as well as with such musical settings of the translations or paraphrases in question as might meet their views of what an eminently popular lyric ought to be. To achieve this end, as far as British India was concerned, the Committee appealed to a learned Pundit, skilled alike in the arts of poetry and music—Sourindro Mohun Tajore—and persuaded him to undertake the task of rendering the words of the National Anthem into Sanskrit and Bengali, and of setting those words to tunes of a distinctly Indian character. Despite the difficulty of supplying equivalents in either of these languages to English words (such synonyms being only contrivable by ingenious generalisation), and that of writing verse in them which shall conform to the rules of English metre —a difficulty, in the latter case, rendered almost insurmountable by the fact that Bengali and Sanskrit words end for the most part in vowels, whilst English words generally terminate in consonants—Sourindro fulfilled the commission with which he was entrusted, and in such a masterly manner that his musical and metrical versions of "God Save the Queen" have, in an incredibly short space of time, taken as firm root in Indian soil as has the original anthem in its native country. To suit the musical tastes of different Indian races—for it appears that each province of Hindustan has its own melodic method, or, at the very least, manner—Sourindro adapted four native and highly popular tunes to his words, and composed eleven other melodies to which they might be sung, and in which local predilections for this or that sequence of intervals or rhythmical eccentricity have been carefully considered.

It seems that "God Save the Queen," as we know it (and the Germans too, under the title of "Heil Dir im Siegeskranz") bears no inconsiderable resemblance to a famous old Indian melody, hight Luma-Jhijhiti. This latter, therefore, having been submitted to a few slight alternations, requisite in order to make it fit English, Sanskrit, and Bengali words alike, holds the first place in Sourindro's series of adaptations and compositions. It is little less simple than Dr. Bull's tune. The second number of the series is itself a series; that is to say, it consists of the four verses of the anthem, each set to a different variation of the Indian melody Behága, also a tolerably intelligible and unsophisticated strain, though I may observe that it is exclusively made up of natural notes. No. 3 (Ráginí Bibhása) is one of Sourindro's original compositions, chiefly remarkable by the circumstance that, being written in the natural key, it does not contain, or rather use, the subdominant F. In No. 4 (Ráginí Sáranga), also by Sourindro, the notes E and A are conspicuous by their absence from the tune, the intervals of which, here and there, resemble those with which Scotch reels have long since made us familiar. No. 5 (Ráginí Khámbáj), another original Sourindro, is written in the key of F, but concludes in that of C, which would appear to be the predominant key of No. 6 (Ráginí Yoginá), into which, however, Sourindro has introduced B flat and A flat in a haphazard sort of way that produces an exceedingly curious effect upon the ear. His next version

(Ráginí Gauri) is extremely peculiar, from a European musical point of view, and abounds in quaint intervals and uncommon progressions.

In No. 8 (Ráginí Bhairabi), Sourindro Mohun Tajore, whilst professing to maintain the natural key, has indulged in some quite amazing vagaries with the four primary flats; or rather, to speak correctly, he has refrained from modifying the feats in that direction of the composer (whose name is supposed to be hidden behind the veil of extreme antiquity) of the Indian melody Bháiravi, to which our learned Pundit has adapted all three sets of the National Anthem's words. This melody seems to indicate that its author tried to write it in the key of C (about which he was not quite certain), on the vague but accommodating principle of "when in doubt, put in a flat." It is indeed a fearful and wonderful tune, but it is surpassed in all its more surprising characteristics by Ráginí Tori, the air which immediately follows it, respecting which I entertain the double conviction, firstly, that its unlikeness to "God Save the Queen" is an absolute miracle of ingenuity on Sourindro's part; and secondly, that, whatever Hindoo songsters may be able to achieve in the way of tackling it, no English vocalist will ever succeed in doing so. This tune, in which the four flats with which Ráginí Bhairabi is bedevilled are supplemented, as instruments of oral torture, by F sharp, is eminently calculated to enable the Western world to realise exactly why it is that Europeans fail to appreciate the subtle charms of Indian music; and furthermore, how it is that ears trained to take in such hair-raising compositions as Ráginí Tori with grateful rapture are congenitally unreceptive of straightforward Occidental strains.

Before concluding this all too superficial notice of Sourindro's musical versions of our National Anthem, it may be as well to point out, with respect to the nine melodies already referred to, that the first, second, and fifth are generally sung at night; the third, sixth, eighth, and ninth, in the morning; the fourth, at midday; and the seventh in the evening. Why this is so I have not the least idea; but I have the learned man's word for it, and entertain no manner of doubt that the above time distribution of the tunes in question, which involves no change in the words sung to them, is the outcome of some solemn ordinance that carries conviction to the Indian mind.

The tenth of the series before me (Ráginí Sháhaná) is a melody—though I should not have thought so, judging by internal evidence—which was a great favourite in days long past with the Mohammedan Emperors of India. According to Sourindro, it is usually sung on auspicious occasions, and is therefore admirably adapted for "a benedictory song" like the National Anthem. This, I venture to observe, is a matter of opinion. To me it appears to be the sort of tune eminently calculated to produce a lethal effect upon "milky mothers." No. 11, again (Ráginí Surata), "is one of the melodies sung in the rainy season," and was selected by the Pundit—as he modestly states in his luminous introduction to the series —in order to specially commemorate the honour conferred upon him, during that very season of the year, by the National Anthem Society in asking him to undertake

VOL. I. M

"a loyal and grateful task." The twelfth (Ráginí Misra-Deogiri) exhibits rhythmical peculiarities, of which its composer endeavours to convey some notion in the following explanatory sentence. "It has," he writes, "been composed without reference to the number or duration of notes, as observed in the original English piece, and is an adaptation from a style of singing known in India as Nagara-Kirtana, first introduced by Chaitanya Deva, the great religious reformer of Bengal, who flourished about 1498 of the Christian era. The music is religious in character, and is generally intended for singing by a large number of persons in street processions." This version of "God Save the Queen" is an especially interesting illustration of the class of air which, from a Hindoo point of view, is distinctly of a religious character; for, strange to say, it will be pronounced by English musicians to be by far the most cheerful, not to say rollicking, of Sourindro's whole series. For the fitting, or rather misfitting of the English words to this astonishing tune, he alone is responsible. As he has arranged them, they cannot be sung without violating every existing law and custom of metre. Perhaps his Sanskrit and Bengali words go smoothly enough to a wildly incoherent scrabble of notes. Not being able to read them myself, and not having an Indian minstrel at hand to sing them to me, for which circumstance I am humbly grateful, I cannot pronounce any positive opinion upon this point. But I hope they suit Sourindro's music better than do the good old English words, as adapted to that learned Pundit's ingenious adaptations.

CHAPTER VII.

JAPANESE MUSIC.

In all probability my readers, with few exceptions, availed themselves of the opportunities of hearing Japanese vocal and instrumental music that were afforded to Londoners some months ago, before the "devouring element" swallowed up the busy little village, which, while it lasted, was so constantly frequented by the "first flight" of our metropolitan idlers. Without wishing to impugn the intrinsic beauty of the compositions that were performed by the dusky villagers for the delectation of the British public at South Kensington, I venture to assume that the majority of English music-lovers will agree with me, in relation to those compositions, that Japanese music is not altogether intelligible to the European ear, which, moreover, does not derive unmixed gratification from listening to it; that its melodies scarcely realise our preconceived notions of tunefulness; and that its harmonies, possibly owing to their extreme subtlety of contrivance, are to us sources of perplexity, not to say distress, rather than of rapture. Strange as it may seem to the habitués of Richter's Concerts, Monday Pops, and miscellaneous *matinées*, such as the London musical season abounds in, the Japanese relish the works of European composers every whit as little as we appreciate the songs, instrumental *soli* and concerted pieces of Japan. They are of opinion that our physical organisation for the reception of musical impression is far inferior to their own, and therefore incapable of distinguishing, one from another, the exquisitely delicate *finesses* of their tone-gradations and harmonic combinations. Conversing one day with Dr. Mueller, the Oriental historian, on the subject of music and the relative merits of the German and Japanese schools, a noble Japanese, renowned for his proficiency in the fine arts, observed: " Your European compositions can only give pleasure, in Japan, to children, coolies, and women. There lives not a Japanese of good birth, breeding and education who can put up with them for a moment. They are insignificant and dull, lacking alike in invention and variety." The gentleman who pronounced this crushing sentence upon the music of the West had been a sojourner in Berlin and Vienna, where he had heard the symphonies of Beethoven, Mozart and Schubert executed by the best orchestras of Germany and Austria. Those masterpieces impressed him as poor, weak, colourless compositions, unworthy of comparison to the rich, vigorous and brilliant musical works of his native country.

I have no doubt that any distinguished English musical amateur, if asked for his opinion upon Japanese strains, would speak at least as unfavourably of them as the Japanese *dilettante* spoke of the immortal German Masters' sublime productions. To our apprehensions of melody and harmony Japanese airs and concerted pieces appear incoherent and discordant; but, simply because we cannot understand and appreciate it, we are scarcely justified in denouncing the music of Japan as absolutely meaningless. As a matter of fact, the art of music, as it is cultivated and practised in Japan and China, has been for many centuries past an important element of civilisation. It plays a leading part in all public ceremonies of a religious, official, or social character; it is the favourite private recreation of all classes, from prince to peasant; its invention and development are attributed to the gods; and it is organised, as a science, upon a system of such extraordinary complexity and comprehensiveness (being mixed up with astronomy, mathematics, and codes of symbols that have to do with all sorts of objects, animate and inanimate), that our old-established arrangements and rules concerning notation, counterpoint, thorough-bass, &c., when compared with those of Japan, appear to be almost absurdly simple and childlike. Between English and Japanese "theory" there is about as considerable a difference as between simple addition and the extraction of the cube root. It would be unreasonable to deny the value and significance of music having so elaborate a scientific system for its constructive basis, and being, moreover, a national institution of extraordinary antiquity, the pride and delight of a most intelligent and ingenious people. As in the Greek mythology, its origin is ascribed by the sacred historians of Japan to a Deity identified in popular belief with the sun. The Japanese Apollo, however, was a lady, rejoicing in the euphonious title of Amaterasu no Ohongami, and the only daughter of

Izanagi, the leading male divinity of Japan, from whose right eye she issued one fine morning whilst he was bathing in the sea. Ohongami was a lovely creature, but short-tempered and sulky. She took offence, shortly after her birth, at the harmless *badinage* of one or two frivolous young gods of the "masher" type, who chaffed her about her toilette; and all of a sudden shut herself up in a gloomy cavern, the only entrance to which she blocked with a huge boulder, declaring that thenceforth she would have nothing more to do with such rude Deities. These latter, who one and all admired her extremely, held a meeting in the dried-up bed of a river, where they unanimously passed a resolution to the effect that the Radiant Maid must be induced to return to her family and friends by hook or by crook. Accordingly Iskikoridome and Amatsumore, the Japanese Mercury and Vulcan, fabricated a perfect mirror of extraordinary dimensions, and hung it up on a branch of a tall japonica just in front of the rock closing the entrance to the cavern. They then commenced a musical entertainment, specially arranged for the occasion by the celestial hierarchy. The first number was a chorus, performed by several hundred cocks, the heralds of sunrise. As the crowings of these "early birds" failed to produce the desired effect upon the goddess, a female Deity named Ame no Udsume played a solo on the fife, accompanied by several other immortals on bowstrings, at which they plucked with bamboo plectra, and on pieces of sonorous wood, beaten with drumsticks. This *morceau d'ensemble* proving as unsuccessful as the chanticleer part-song to lure Ohongami forth from her subterraneous retreat,

Udsume climbed upon the lid of an enormous round wooden box, and began to dance, singing the while a plaintive lay, the words of which have been preserved to the present day, and are utilised in connection with the Japanese numeral system. They run as follows: "Hito futa miyo, Itsu muyu nano, Ya kokono tari, Momo chi yorodsu;" *anglicé*, "Gods, look at the gate, behold the majestic goddess; Shall not joy fill our hearts? Are not my charms potent?" Hearing these eulogies, presumably addressed to a rival beauty, Ohongami could not resist the temptation to push back the rock a little bit, in order to peep at her competitor, and was heard to mutter, "I thought that my eclipse would plunge Heaven and Japan into darkness and consternation. Why, then, is Udsume dancing on a box-lid, and why do the gods indulge in unseemly merriment?" Udsume replied, "I am dancing and they are in high spirits because we have amongst us a goddess infinitely handsomer and more powerful than yourself." As she spoke, the first-class Divinity Ame no Futadama no Mikoto thrust forward the mirror to the cavern entrance, and Ohongami, fascinated by the reflection of her own charms, issued from her hiding-place. The bearer of the looking-glass at once took her by the hand and implored her, on behalf of himself and friends, to join those present in "a little music," which she complacently agreed to do, and never thereafter manifested any desire to withdraw herself from public attention. In this quaint legend is embodied the Japanese account of the origin of music, to which art, even when illustrated by such primitive instruments as bowstrings and drumsticks, the world lies under at least one paramount obligation, the reappearance of the sun having been brought about by the morning concert given by the denizens of the Japanese Olympus to Amaterasu no Ohongami, the "influential goddess who shines in the heavens."

The influence exercised by Japanese music in its native country does honour to its illustrious extraction, and fulfils the exalted destiny foretold to it by its Divine inventors, one of whom is reported to have spoken of it in the following somewhat highflown terms: "Music has the power of making heaven descend to earth; it inspires human beings with the love of virtue and the practice of duty. Do you wish to know if a kingdom be well governed, and if its morals be good or bad? Enquire what sort of music is current within its frontiers!" In no European country is music so intimately associated with the routine of every-day life as in Japan, where it is regarded as the necessary solace and amusement of mankind. Amongst women the art is so assiduously cultivated that every Japanese matron or maiden is more or less skilled in the manipulation of some musical instrument; and the poorest bride's dowry includes a Sonokoto, or thirteen-stringed lute, and a Samhine, or three-stringed guitar. At every street-corner in Japanese towns minstrels of the *improvisatore* class may be encountered, who chant extempore ballads of inordinate length, accompanying themselves on guitars of different shapes and sizes, every one of which has its own special title and "method." In the Yoshiwara (District of Delights) at Tokio, Mr. Mitford counted nearly four hundred teahouses, in which the well-to-do inhabitants of that city gave their formal dinner-parties and "receptions." Music is a leading feature of these entertainments, and the establishments in question, despite their large number, are all well supplied with executants. So general, indeed, is the demand for music at public places of refreshment in Japan, that even the humblest inns and cabarets are provided with Geshias (female minstrels), who welcome the traveller on his arrival, and amuse him during his repasts with performances upon the Shamiseng, a three-stringed guitar, the body of which is made of mulberry-wood covered with catskin. This instrument, which can be tuned in five different ways, is generally used for accompanying the voice, and is played with a plectrum. The Geshias are farmed out to teahouses, hotels and private persons requiring their services by *impresarii*, who buy them at the age of five or six from their parents, at the rate of from thirty to fifty shillings apiece. Their proprietors have them taught to sing and to play upon two or three instruments; when they have completed their fourteenth year, if they are capable of taking part in concerted music, they are drafted into a tea-house orchestra, and acquire a market value of twenty pounds or so. The charge made for a Geshia's services averages eightpence per hour, besides which she is entitled to a small bonus daily. This she saves up for her dowry; in the course of fifteen years, the term of her bondage, it accumulates until she is finally in possession of a sum which enables her to find a husband. During her professional career she invariably goes by a "stage name;" on retiring into private life she cuts her past adrift, as it might interfere with her matrimonial chances, marries some decent small tradesman or skilled handicraftsman, and makes, for the most part, an excellent wife and mother.

All Japanese musicians belong to corporations of one or another of four classes. The first of these is a highly-dignified and æsthetic body of "swells," called the Gakounine. Its members rank "with and after" the most exalted officers of the State; in former times it was the fashion amongst the Daimios, or great territorial nobles, to belong to the Gakounine, which devotes itself exclusively to the study and performance of sacred music. The "brethren of the Gakounine" are one and all distinguished instrumentalists, profoundly versed in the secrets of musical science. The Mikado's orchestra —the best in Japan—is composed of their picked soloists, and, I need scarcely say, plays nothing but pieces of a religious character and of great antiquity. Its *répertoire* comprehends all the strictly "classical" music of the country. The second corporation, that of the Ghenine, includes all the male performers of profane music, few of whom have penetrated the mysteries of "theory," or are familiar with the elaborate system of notation obtaining in Japan. They rank in the social hierarchy with merchants, and supply executants to the Taicoon's private band. The third corporation, which is divided into two categories, the Kengio and Koto, consists exclusively of blind men, and is restricted to the execution of what the Japanese term "Ordinary Music" —presumably dances and popular ballads. This corporation is a branch of the Boussets-Sato, or Association of the Blind, founded in the twelfth century by Kakigo, a famous Japanese general who, being vanquished and taken prisoner in battle, tore out his own eyes and threw them at the feet of his captor. The members of this association shave their heads, practise all manner of crafts and callings, and pay their wages into the exchequer of the order, which provides for their maintenance. Those amongst them who are unfit for any other trade or profession become musicians, and are chiefly employed in playing at Court, at public fêtes and at noblemen's private parties. The chief of the Boussets-Sato resides at Miako and is invested with absolute authority over all the members of the Association, any one of whom he may condemn to die; his death-sentence, however, must be confirmed by the Minister of Justice before it can be carried into effect.

The fourth corporation or class of musicians—by far the most numerous of all, as well as the least respectable —includes all sorts and conditions of Japanese women who earn their living by taking part in musical performances. To this army of female executants the Geshias contribute the largest contingent, many thousands in number. The fair sex, in Japan, is not permitted to share actively in any performance of sacred music. This prohibition, no doubt, has its origin in a prejudice akin to that which, in Catholic countries, formerly forbade women to participate in the musical services of the Roman Church. Japanese ladies, however, as well as the professional *cantatrici*, learn to sing and to play their own accompaniments upon the Kokiou, a sort of violin, the Ghekine, or guitar, and the Koto, or psaltery, of which instruments, as well as of the Japanese scales, notation, and system of harmony, I shall have something to say further on. But no Japanese woman has hitherto acquired renown as a composer; a circumstance which may partly account for the small consideration in which the fourth musical corporation, or "female division," is held in the realm of the Rising Sun. I may add that, in times long past, the four classes of musicians above described were subdivided into an infinite number of guilds, but that nowadays all the minor distinctions of old have been done away with. Each corporation is ruled by a Grand Master, in whom is vested the right of rewarding special merit by pecuniary recompenses, prizes, or honorific distinctions. It would appear that the distinction most highly valued by executant artists is the privilege of tuning the first string of their violin, guitar, or psaltery an octave higher or lower than the regulation pitch. This honour, though inexpensive, is more rarely conferred than rewards of a more solid character.

The Japanese musical system is identified, constructively as well as traditionally, with the political, religious, and scientific history of Japan. It has to do with the laws of nature, as the Japanese know them, the celestial constellations, the divisions of the year and the articles of the moral code. Notation being symbolical of all these things, a Japanese tune may be a scientific treatise, an astronomical scheme, an almanack, or an essay on ethics. Given a little extra ingenuity in the arrangement of sequences or combinations of notes, it may be all four simultaneously. Five is the cabalistic number of Japan; every system connected with things human or divine is based upon this number, which is invested with a sacred character; in a word, the Pentagon is to the Japanese what the Trinity is to the European, a symbol of perfection, instinct with mysterious significance and power. This being so, I need perhaps scarcely say that Japanese music is pentatonic. It is, in fact, called "The System of Five Sounds," which five sounds are not affected to any special key, but occupy the same positions with relation to one another in all keys. I subjoin their names, with a few of their extra-musical meanings in illustration of the curious connection that, in Japan, exists between notes and all manner of other actualities, terms and ideas :—

Kiou.	First note.	A temple.	A lord.
Shô.	Second note.	Commerce.	A servant.
Kakou.	Third note.	A horn.	A peasant.
Tche.	Fourth note.	A sign.	A material object.
Ou.	Fifth note.	A feather.	An abstract notion.

These five notes constitute a hierarchy of their own, in which Kiou occupies the highest and Ou the lowest rank. They correspond, in their musical order, to the tonic, second, third, fifth and sixth of our diatonic scale; that is to say, assuming them to be parts of the natural key, Kiou is C, Shô D, Kakou E, Tche G, and Ou F. Besides the pentatonic scale there are other notes, also five in number, called "Sounds of Substitution," which make up a sort of chromatic scale, lacking two semitones, however, of the twelve which compose our make-shift P.F. scale, in which true sharps and flats do not exist, but only blendings of them. Though there are only ten notes—at least as far as I have been able to make out the Japanese musical system—there are twelve keys, one for each month of the year, and emblematic of, or rather synonymous with, it. The Japanese believe that the wind prevailing throughout each particular month blows in a certain musical key especial to that month, *e.g.*, that the note Tairiô is preferentially sounded by the breezes during the month Tairiô (January), and so on through the tale of months constituting the full year. Each of the twelve keys has to be dealt with by the composer in a " mode " peculiar to itself, of which, however, the pentatonic scale is the basis; the different "modes" being obtained by substituting semitones for the full tones of the normal, or "astronomic" Japanese scale. One of these " modes " is almost identical with our minor scale. The twelve tonics, or month-notes—made up of the " Five Sounds," the " Sounds of Substitution," also five in number, and two sounds for which I am unable to account by any recorded evidence—form a chromatic scale; and the framework of the system of composition, as well as of the scales used therein, is founded upon successive ascending fifths and descending fourths.

There are several codes of notation in Japan; but only one—that employed in connection with sacred music—is relatively complete. It seems to be chiefly affected to the use of performers upon string and wind instruments; the string to be played upon is indicated by a number placed beside the sign describing the note, a similar contrivance pointing out to the flute-player the hole he must stop with one of his fingers in order to produce a particular sound. The note-sign gives the name of the sound to be produced in relation to the tonic of the key. Accidentals are shown by small accents marked at the sides of the note-signs, and inform the performer that he must slightly raise or lower his finger on the string or hole. A single or double circle, placed on the right or left side of the note-sign, means that the note in question is to be played one or two octaves higher or lower than the normal pitch, which is indicated at the commencement of the piece. The value or duration of each note is shown in two ways—1. By leaving between the note-signs (which succeed one another in vertical order) a space more or less wide, according to the relative value of each note; 2. By placing to the right of the note-sign a circle, semi-circle, or quarter of a circle, imparting a respective value to the note equivalent to our crotchet, quaver, or semi-quaver. Absolute signs or words indicative of time or rhythm are wanting to the Japanese system of notation; but all the tunes, for instruments or voice, that have come under my notice are manifestly composed in common time or in two-four, three beats in a bar being a measure apparently unknown in Japan. The *crescendo* sign is a comma, appended to a long note, and invariably accompanied, in concerted music, by a click of the castanets (Shaku-bioshi). In the notation of secular music, monosyllables (varying according to the character of the instrument for which the part is written) are appended to the note-signs and describe how the note is to be produced—that is, continuously or iteratively. In the case of wind-instruments, for instance, the monosyllable employed is ra; sometimes repeated two or three times, as thus: rara, rarara. Japanese music is written in vertical lines from right to left, beginning at the top of each page. In the case of songs the words are written on the left of the line, and the incidental signs on the right. Singing, in Japan, is regarded as an accessory to a musical performance, not as the principal feature thereof—in fact, as an accompaniment to the leading solo instrument, with which the voice of the singer must always be in unison.

The Japanese orchestra (Baiashi) is generally composed of nine executants, as follows:—Two drummers (Taiko-gata), two flautists (Fuyé-gata), two Pandean-pipers (Shoshi-kiriki), one triangle-player (Kane-gata), and two vocalists (Ootai-gata). Thus constituted, the orchestra is called Koonine-baiashi; when it only comprises one performer of each class it bears the name of Gonine-baiashi. Every piece of music performed by this orchestra is commenced and concluded by the triangle-player, who is followed by the pipers, then by the flautists, and lastly by the drummers. Considering the Kane-gata and the Ootai-gata as *obbligati*, the real orchestral score may be most aptly described as a *sestetto concertante*. There exists an ancient series of paintings on silk descriptive of the festivities formerly held in honour of the mountain-god Shighen. One of these pictures represents a "grand orchestra," to which was assigned an important rôle in the celebrations in question. The paintings consists of two sections, facing one another; that to the right depicts a player on the great Japanese lute (Sono-koto), and a Shoshi-kiriki seated between two performers on the Sho-no-fuyé, a sort of harmonium; that to the left contains two Taiko-gata, two Shoshi-kiriki, two Fuyé-gata, and two more players of the Sho-no-fuyé. The ordinary band engaged for private parties—a Japanese "Bijou Orchestra"—numbers three executants, whose instruments are the Sono-koto, or thirteen-stringed lute; the Shamiseng, or three-stringed guitar; and the Kokiou, a four-stringed fiddle, held across the knees and played with a curved horsehair bow. The belly of this quaint instrument is made of catskin, stretched very tightly and glued to the sides of the frame. Finally, the theatrical orchestra of Japan is composed of the following instruments: the Girine, a two-stringed fiddle, with a back of sycamore wood and a belly of serpent-skin, the sounds elicited from which bear no inconsiderable resemblance to the eldritch screech emitted by a cart-wheel turning on a rusty axle; the Pokpan and Hiongpan, two varieties of castanets; the Seng-tian, an oboe with eight ventages; the Poong-koo, a small drum, upon which the conductor beats time with his bâton; the Soulá, a brass tom-tom, or gong; and the Taakan, a psalterion with twenty-eight wires, which the player strikes with two small bamboo plectra. The Soulá is tuned in accordance with the system of the "Five Sounds," and has a compass of three octaves and a note, commencing with G, first line of the bass clef, and terminating with A above the line, treble clef.

This orchestra, which is very nearly identical with that of the Chinese national theatre, has been heard in London, not altogether with unmixed pleasure. A special education of the ear, such as the performances of Occidental music do not afford, is requisite to ensure appreciation of the profound science that orders all its combinations and methods; whilst its bearing upon astronomy, meteorology, physics, and morality is necessarily lost upon persons unacquainted with the elaborate symbolism that underlies the Japanese musical system. From an English point of view—or rather, of hearing—the effects produced by the Japanese theatrical band proved little short of distracting. Its *ensemble* yielded, so to speak, a *macédoine* of incoherent and dissonant sounds, made up of tinkling, tootling, clashing, screeching, clicking and booming, in which no organic tune could be detected, and no constructive scheme was perceptible. It appeared to us a sort of orchestra that, consisting of *succubi* and fiends of a low class, might have been specially engaged to perform dance-music at a Witches' Sabbath on the 1st of May in the upper regions of the Brocken. I have known men of approved courage—men capable of mounting "the imminent deadly breach" with cheerful alacrity—to flee, pallid and terror-stricken, from the appalling sounds emitted by a Japanese full band, which I had reason to believe was regarded in its native country as a vehicle of entrancing melody and sublime harmony. To me, I admit, its musical achievements appeared to be about on a par with those of the marrowbone and cleaver artists, who were wont to perform at butchers' weddings in days long past, and to whose *morceaux d'ensemble* I have, when a child, listened with mingled amazement and consternation; or with the scarcely less surprising cacophonic feats of certain Turkish provincial bands, veritable volcanoes of noise, with whose stirring strains I have been regaled whilst sojourning with old-fashioned country pashas, delighting in what they were pleased to denominate "the inimitable music of the Crescent." To the best of my belief there is no crescent in London—no, not even in the suburbs, that would put up with it for as much as half-a-minute at a time; but my Mohammedan friends undoubtedly preferred it to the dance-music of Strauss, or to the selections from the operas of Verdi, Rossini, and Meyerbeer, which their instrumentalists were sometimes instructed to "interpret" in special compliment to myself. There must, after all, be some decided merit in music that pleases millions of people. That other millions fail to appreciate that merit is surely nothing to the purpose. Who shall decide whether or not Japanese civilisation—including art-culture, of course—be of a higher and finer kind than ours, or *vice versâ?* Only those who are equally versed in both; and it may be doubted that such a human being exists. For my part, I cannot take upon myself to say, or even think, that an art so elaborately systematised and assiduously studied—not to mention its extraordinary local popularity—as Japanese music, can be altogether irrational, vicious, and abominable. I do not understand or like it; I never shall; but beauty it must possess, for the simple reason that it is beautiful to one of the most intelligent and artistic races in the world.

The musical instruments of Japan, like those of Western countries, belong to three classes; stringed instruments, played with the bow, the plectrum, or the finger; wind instruments; and instruments *à percussion,* from which sound is elicited by blows. But they would not be Japanese if they did not differ from Occidental instruments in many important respects. Imprimis, they are told off by hallowed custom into two grand categories—instruments of purity and instruments of impurity. The former (Gakkooki) are specially affected to the performance of sacred music; the latter, of which I forget the class-name, to that of profane airs, the words of which are not infrequently of an erotic character. Several, however, of the instruments appertaining to the category of purity, slightly modified in construction, are to be found in the impure class. In this respect a hard and fast line is laid down in theory, but is not kept up in practice. For the execution of religious compositions of purely Japanese origin the following instruments are used: the Kagoora-fuyé, a six-holed flute; the Yamato-koto, a six-stringed psaltery; and the Shakoo-bioshi, wooden castanets. But when the sacred music to be performed happens to be of Chinese or Corean extraction, it is the correct thing to play it on the Shono-fuyé, a sort of accordion; the Hitshiriki, a small flageolet; the Koma-fuyé, a four-holed flute; the Fuyé proper, a seven-holed flute; the Kinnokoto, a seven-stringed psaltery; the Biva, a large four-stringed guitar; the Taiko, or big drum; the Joko and Kakko, two small flat drums; and the Shoko, or gong.

In Japan the standard of pitch is not given by a tuning-fork, but by a reed, or set of reeds, expressing the twelve fundamental notes of the Japanese tonality, their sounds being produced by aspiration instead of expiration. A set of these pitch-pipes, twelve in number, contained in a dainty-lacquered box, lined with silk, is called Shoshi; one of six, each tube being two-sounded, bears the name of Shoshi-buyé; one of three, only emitting the six sounds most commonly used in musical composition (namely, Osho, D natural; Kosho, E flat; Taisoku, F natural; Kiosho, G flat; Kossen, G natural; and Tshurio, A flat), is called Mitzshioshi; and there is, besides, a single bamboo-tube, pierced with twelve holes, each hole being lined with ivory and provided with an explanatory Japanese character, indicating the note of which it is warranted to give the true pitch under pressure of inspiration.

The most important variety of wind instrument in the realm of the Rising Sun is the flute, designated indifferently Fuyé or Teki, and subdivided into two classes, the Koowan-teki, or flutes held horizontally; and Siyuteki, or flutes held vertically, as the clarionet and oboe are with us. Of the former class, the original Japanese flute (Fuyé), a bamboo tube pierced with seven holes, was invented at Tangool, whence it passed into China about a century and a-half before the commencement of the Christian era. The Chinese, however, assert that the first Fuyé was made in China, *anno* 143 B.C., by a musical genius named Kiou-Kong. According to the Sinico-Japanese Encyclopædia, all musical sounds, vocal and instrumental, are based upon the seven notes produced by the ancient Fuyé. Flutes of the Fuyé class were formerly made of thigh-bones of a large sort of ape, and yielded a much fuller, rounder tone than the more modern bamboo-flute. Apropos of these monkey tibias, and their power of discoursing sweet music, a story is told of one Shiogen, a celebrated Fuyé player of antiquity, who—at one period of his career a fugitive from justice—was compelled to take refuge from his pursuers in a dismal cavern, popularly credited with being the regular dwelling-place of an enormous anthropophagian serpent. Shiogen knew all about this snake; and the notion that it might put forward some conclusive objection to his intrusion made him very uncomfortable. But what was he to do? From the myrmidons of the law, as enforced in Japan, he could expect no mercy; whereas, as he sagaciously reasoned, perhaps the serpent might be out visiting, or asleep, or not hungry, in any of which cases he would be safer in the cave than out of it. So he lay down, and was composing himself to sleep when something glided up to him, which, upon inspection, turned out to be a python, with a lion's head, fiery eyes, and a forked tongue, three feet long, hanging from its red and gaping jaws. As this creature manifested a disposition to swallow the trespasser whole, Shiogen made up his mind that his last hour was come, and, picking up his beloved flute, began to "play himself out" with a favourite air of the period. He had scarcely tootled a bar when the monster—so says the legend—cocked its head on one side in a sentimental way, and listened. Gradually tears of pleasure extinguished the flames that had hitherto flashed from its eyes; it kept time to Shiogen's melody by waving its tongue to and fro like the pendulum of a Maelzel's metronome; as the tune got more and more intricate it positively slobbered with enjoyment, and even tried to grunt a sort of fundamental bass to the *bel canto* of the seven-holed Fuyé. Presently, unable to bear such continuous rapture any longer, it undulated gently away, leaving Shiogen sole and undisputed tenant of the cavern, which he inhabited for some time thereafter, secure of the absolute privacy which its unfavourable reputation in the neighbourhood could not fail to assure to its occupant. From my own experience of Japanese airs I should incline to the belief that the unfortunate python, aware of its visitor and entering its cave " on hospitable thoughts intent," was paralysed with wonder and consternation by the hideous sounds with which Shiogen assailed its ears, and—after a brief interval of agonised endurance—turned and fled precipitately from what, in its uninstructed simplicity of mind, it probably took to be the actual presence of the leading Japanese Devil. Anyway, from the above-quoted legend is derived the popular belief, still prevalent in Shiogen's native land, that the tones of the Fuyé are specially endowed with power to drive away serpents and other venomous reptiles. However this may be, it is certain that a little of the Fuyé goes a long way with most Europeans, and is apt to hasten their departure from any spot near which that remarkable instrument may happen to be played by a skilled Japanese soloist.

The simplest in construction of the Siyu-teki, or vertical flutes, is the Seuno-fuyé, a set of Pandean pipes twelve in number, made of bamboo, fixed in a frame and adorned with golden dragons on a ground of red lacquer. The twelve tubes produce the twelve fundamental sounds of the Japanese scale. Another variety, the Mine-teki, is an eight-holed clarionet, emitting the notes that constitute our diatonic scale of B major. Then there is the Shak-haci, twenty inches long and pierced with five holes, which was introduced into Japan from China during the reign of the Emperor Ming-hwang (713—742); the Toshio, also a five-holed clarionet, two feet five inches in length, which dates from the seventh century; the Hitoyo-kiri, a much shorter instrument, the tone of which is exceptionally mellow, upon which account it is chiefly used for accompanying the human voice; the Hitshiniki, an oboe producing a curiously shrill and rasping tone, unendurable to the Western ear (this is one of the "instruments of purity," and is eminently calculated to drive those condemned to hear its eldritch screeches to wallow in crime); the Ka, an oboe which is always used in Chinese theatrical bands, and seldom out of them; the Shiono-fuyé, a box of whistles, which may be played either by blowing into or sucking at a mouth-piece inserted in one end of the box; and, finally, the Rapakai, a huge sea-shell, into the point of which an *embouchure* is fitted. This primitive instrument is utilised in war-time for signalling purposes, and is also sounded with soul-subduing effect during certain religious ceremonies. Blown with vigour, it gives out a sound that hits off the happy mean between a moan and a roar—a sort of sublime bray, such as might be uttered by a canonised donkey suffering from rheumatism. Those who hear the Rapakai for the first time seldom linger long with the exclusive object of dwelling upon its strains. They are soon visible to the naked eye in some other neighbourhood, and may be observed to pant from the speed with which they have changed their place of temporary sojourn.

The strings of Japanese fiddles, guitars, etc., are made

of waxed silk; those used for instruments upon which sacred music is played are manufactured exclusively at Kioto, and are extremely expensive, whilst "profane" strings are made at Yedo, and are cheap. They are sold in sets, according to the key in which the instrument for which they are destined is to be played, and each complete set is known by the name of its original inventor, or by the number of its thickest string. The king of Japanese stringed instruments, hight Kokiou, has already been mentioned in a preceding paragraph; so have the Girine and Shamiseng, the most popular instruments of the street-corner Japanese band. But I omitted to describe the bow upon which the Japanese fiddler plays with his Kokiou—the Japanese method being precisely the converse of ours, which prescribes playing on the fiddle with the bow. This latter, in Japan, is three feet four inches in length, made of sandalwood and horsehair. The stick is flat on one side and round on the other, the hair being stretched along its rounded side, and is in two pieces, connected by a metal ring when the bow is in use. It is held firmly in a horizontal position by one hand, whilst the other grasping the Kokiou rubs its strings backwards and forwards against the bow. This method of playing obtains with the Girine, the Kokoon, a fiddle of Corean origin, and the Niyisene, a handsome two-stringed violin, the back of which is made of black lacquer, ornamented with arabesque gilding, whilst the belly and sides are of wood covered with young gazelle skin, and the neck terminates in a gilt dragon's head.

Psalteries play a more important part in Japanese

music than fiddles; their class-name is Koto, and their varieties are more numerous than even those of the Fuyé. The simplest in form is the Soomakoto, a board about three feet six inches long and thicker in the middle than at either end, one of which is square and the other round in shape. It has only one string, which the player strikes with a bone plectrum fitted like a thimble to the tip of his fore-finger, and looking like an elongated nail, whilst he makes the note required by pressing the string with a small bamboo cylinder at the intervals where frets indicate the different tones, or where white lines painted on the string itself serve the same purpose. The Soomakoto is said to have been invented by a mournful Japanese swell in exile, who strove to banish melancholy by stretching a piece of whipcord across the top of his hat and playing on it with a chicken-bone. By reason of its patrician origin, this instrument is still a favourite in Japanese aristocratic circles. The Yakoomo-koto and Atzooma-koto are varieties of the Sooma-koto, provided with two and three strings respectively. The Gokkine, another psaltery, has five, three of which are dyed yellow, the fourth violet, and the fifth blue; in lieu of frets, the names of the notes to be produced by pressure on the string are inscribed on the finger board at the due intervals. The Yamato-koto, of historical renown as having figured prominently in the legend of the Sun-Goddess, narrated in the second paragraph of this chapter, is a six-stringed psaltery of celestial origin, exclusively used for the performance of sacred music. A gracefully-formed and most elaborately decorated instrument of this class is the Soghé-koto (nine strings), which is specially affected to the delectation of the concubines belonging to the chief of the Japanese Government for the time being. Perhaps the most symbolical of stringed instruments is a small harp called the Kiuno-koto, to which is attributed the power of checking vicious desires and purifying the soul. In length it is three feet, six inches, and six lines, representing the 366 days of the Bissextile year. It is six inches broad at either end, because there are six cardinal points in Japan—north, south, east, west, zenith, and nadir. In its centre its breadth is four inches, which stand for the four seasons. It is a little broader at top than at bottom, as a hint that lofty things are superior to grovelling things. Its belly is convex, for the heavens are so; its back is flat, that being the shape of the earth, according to Japanese beliefs. Besides being almost oppressively emblematical, it is highly ornate, being overlaid with black lacquer and gold, and lavishly inlaid with ivory, mother-of-pearl and tortoiseshell in devices of great artistic beauty. The Gindaï, a thirteen-stringed harp, enjoys the proud privilege of being only played upon by members of the aristocracy. One must be indisputably "born," in the German sense of the word, to while away the lagging moments by dallying with the strings of the Gindaï. A plebeian dares not even play a pentatonic scale upon that august appanage of hereditary nobility. Less exclusive harps are the Tsooma-koto, trapezoidal in shape; the Kakoognoto, a square instrument with twenty-five strings; the Nishine, a round harp with a metal tongue in its inside, which vibrates with a buzzing sound when the strings are twanged by the plectrum; the Nighenkine and Sankine, small Kotos which have fallen into desuetude; and, finally, the Sono-koto, or great Japanese lute, a magnificent instrument, six feet in length, fitted with thirteen strings, and so richly inlaid as to be, for the most part, a very marvel of *marqueterie* and decorative ingenuity. It is played with three pointed ivory thimbles, worn on the tips of the thumb, first and second fingers.

First in rank of Japanese guitars is the Koo, an Imperial instrument, the whole surface of which is embellished with arabesques and figures of animals painted in pure gold on a ground of dark lacquer. It is four-stringed, and circular in shape, with a neck eighteen inches long, and nine frets. Then come the Shunga, the Ghekine, the Shighene, all four-stringed; the Kirisiene, three-stringed, and played with a tortoise-shell plectrum; the Kaotari, three-stringed, elaborately ornamented and partly covered with gilt leather, on which the Imperial dragon is painted in several colours; the Taisene, Samhine, Shamiseng (of which there are several beautiful varieties) and the Biva, which dates from the year 851, and was formerly played on horseback. It is now a drawing-room instrument, much in vogue amongst the "upper ten" of Japanese society. Before closing this rough sketch of the leading Japanese stringed instruments, I must not omit to mention the Taakan, a psaltery with twenty-eight metal wires, bearing a strong family resemblance to the Hungarian ciombolan. It is extremely effective in orchestral music, and may be heard in every Japanese and Chinese theatre.

Of the Japanese instruments *à percussion* the most

formidable is the Taiko, a colossal version of our big drum; the trunk of a tree hollowed out and covered at either end with thick deer-skin. There is an elegant little drum called the Tassoomi, which Japanese dancers hang round their necks and strike with their finger-tips whilst performing the Butterfly-dance. The Doo, or gong, is extremely popular in Japan; some of its varieties are quaintly shaped, and *repoussé*, so as to present all manner of surface irregularities. In the Buddhist temples the Nihoihagi—huge bronze cymbals—are always on hand during Divine service; they are also freely utilised in military bands. Clusters of bells, resembling sledge-bells, are attached to a short stick and rattled during the performance of sacred and profane music alike. They are called Soodsoo, and serve to mark the *tempi* of concerted pieces very effectually. Castanets (Shakou-bioshi) of different sizes, and a sort of Xylophone (Mokkine), consisting of thirteen slips of wood set loosely in a frame, and played upon with two metal-topped wands, like tiny drumsticks, complete this category of Japanese instruments. In conclusion, I can wish my readers no better fortune than that they may be preserved from hearing any of the extraordinary performances achieved by Japanese orchestras composed of the above executant elements. That way madness lies!

CHAPTER VIII.

PIANOFORTE-PLAYING.

It is, no doubt, chiefly owing to the extraordinary mechanical developments undergone by the pianoforte in the course of the last three or four decades, that pianoforte-playing, professional and dilettantine, is by no means what it used to be thirty years ago. It is a good deal more, unquestionably, in some respects; in others it is a good deal less—at least, so it appears to me, who have passed my life amongst performers upon the clavichord and was most assiduously taught to play upon that instrument before I could express myself with intelligible distinctness in my mother-tongue. The desirability of producing tone-colour from a colourless keyboard may have been deeply felt in those days; but it was not regarded by executants as "the one thing needful," nor, as a matter of fact, was it a standing subject of discussion in musical circles, as it has been of late years. The chief objects sought to be attained by the school of pianoforte-playing that was prevalent on this side of the Channel in the "forties" were evenness and, if I may say so, silkiness of touch, exquisite finish with respect to the details of execution, flexibility of hand and wrist, independence of each individual finger, a certain rigidity of arm as far as attitude was concerned, and extreme discretion—not to say self-restraint—in the use of the forte-pedal. The pianists of my childhood's days were not in the habit of smiting or browbeating their instruments; they tickled them tenderly, and coaxed them into discoursing most excellent music. Even the disciples of Sigismund Thalberg, whose operatic medleys about that time suggested a number of new and startling effects to drawing-room *dilettanti*, treated the piano on the whole as a willing and plastic soloist, not as a reluctant potential orchestra, to be forcibly coerced into the performance of unnumbered polyphonic tricks. Nobody attempted to wrest from it the tones of the horn, bassoon, or violoncello, or even to make it mimic the human voice—for Mendelssohn's wordless songs had not then achieved the extraordinary popularity they were destined to attain in this country. In a word, more was not expected from the pianoforte than it was capable of yielding. Composers as well as executants took it for what it really was, and dealt with it accordingly. The great innovator, Franz Liszt, and all his works were objects of wonder, rather than of admiration, to the average British pianist, whose deeply-rooted objections to revolutionise his or her fingers and style proved difficult to eradicate. Calm, neat, technically accurate playing was the rule in cultivated musical society; emotional "renderings" and sensational "interpretation" the exception.

When, nearly forty years ago—having been severely trained by an unflinching classicist in the Wohltemperirtes Klavier, Chromatische Fantasie and French and

English Suites of John Sebastian Bach—it fell to my lot to be taken about a good deal to public concerts and private musical parties in green velvet, cut-steel buttons, and a lace collar, airs with variations were all the vogue on the platform and in the *salon*. Compositions of this class by Henri Herz, Cramer, Chaulieu, Czerny, Kalkbrenner, Moscheles, Kuhlau, Osborne, and many others of less note, were played everywhere with amazing perseverance and relish. Amongst the works of a more serious and original character which found favour with the concert-room public were the P.F. concertas and sonatas of Hummel and Field, teeming with intricate execution and levying no inconsiderable tax upon the intellectual as well as physical resources of the player. Doehler, Praeger, Burgmueller, Huenten, Ravina, Beyer, Salaman, and Dreyschock, if I remember aright, came with a rush to the front a little later. I had given up green velvet and taken to broadcloth when all the musical world and his daughters were playing Doehler's Nocturne in 5 flats, Salaman's admirable Saltarello, and Osborne's "Pluie des Perles"—which last-mentioned *morceau de salon* as well as its social successor, Lefébure-Wély's "Cloche du Monastère," laid hold of the British public with quite exceptional tenacity. Thalberg's reign, at first stoutly disputed by critics and classicists, endured for fully ten years after being firmly established by society. It weighed heavily upon the schoolroom, and caused countless keyboards to be bedewed with angry and sorrowful tears. His arrangements, with their airs perplexingly divided between the player's thumbs, whilst the fingers were engaged in letting off fireworks and discharging cascades all over the upper and lower registers of the instrument, were very different enterprises for the daughters of Albion to tackle from Kotzwara's "Battle of Prague," Dussek's Rondos and Sonatinas, Clementi's Studies, or even such tests of digital dexterity as Haendel's "Harmonious Blacksmith," and P.F. Suites. The "rigid attitude," so carefully fostered by inflexible schoolmistresses and deportment-inculcating governesses forty years ago — arms gracefully curved, elbows gently rounded, and the like—had to be foregone in favour of calisthenic gestures worthy of a German *Turner-Verein*. A "show-piece" painfully prepared for society by Anna Maria in the schoolroom—poor girl, how she laboured over and hated it!—became a lively sudorific to the performer, and no small trial to the audience. Thalberg, moreover, led to Liszt, a still more dire revolutionist of style and *Technik*; not to any great extent, for a long time, in English private society addicted to music, but sufficiently, in the way of mere experiment, to inflict a great deal of unmerited suffering upon the then rising generation of amateur pianists. Fortunately, about the time I refer to, Mendelssohn's *Lieder ohne Worte* struck a firm root in hundreds of London *salons*, and succeeded in not only holding their own against the Thalbergian tricks and *tours de force*, but in living them down by dint of sheer intrinsic superiority. Who, amongst average pianoforte *dilettanti*, plays Thalberg's "Home, Sweet Home," "Mosé in Egitto," or "Com' é gentil" nowadays? and who, on the contrary—leaving fanatical Wagnerians out of the account—does not take and give pleasure by rendering on the piano the genial inspirations that flowed from Mendelssohn's musical nature as spontaneously and copiously as limpid water from a mountain spring? The creator's works have survived him, and bid fair to achieve immortality; the great arranger survived his works, which are practically unknown to the pianists of the present day.

My earliest remembrances of remarkable pianoforte-playing are connected with Madame Dulcken, Cipriani Potter, Mendelssohn, Thalberg, W. H. Holmes, Sterndale Bennett, Lindsay Sloper and Alexander Dreyschock. I give the names as nearly as I can in the order in which memory recalls them to me in connection with performances that were at once sources of joy and despair to a musical and ambitious child, still wrestling with the technical difficulties of the keyboard. All the artists above-mentioned were, from my point of view, distractingly, overwhelmingly, crushingly excellent; but the one who most deeply and enduringly impressed me was Mendelssohn, whom I had the supreme good fortune to hear and see extemporise at great length in the house of a gifted friend—alas! long since dead; being privileged to stand the while by the piano and watch the magician's fingers casting their spells upon the subjugated and responsive keys. From that moment—although I only saw and heard him once again, in the organ-loft of St. Paul's, when the rapidity of his pedal-playing well-nigh unsettled my reason—he became my idol and ideal, and remained so for years. It is certainly not too much to say that I worshipped him *dans mon for intérieur* with all the ardour that was in me. His bright, glowing eyes, and sweet benevolent smile, exercised an irresistible fascination upon me; to my boyish apprehensions he seemed endowed with supernatural powers— one to whom naught was impossible and nothing could be refused. On the occasion first referred to, the theme given to him for improvisation was the "Blue Bells of Scotland," with which he dealt in unconventional ways I had never dreamt of, one grand treatment *alla fuga* culminating in a cadence that exhausted the resources of execution, as far as they were then known to me. Another incident, *haud obliviscari*, took place that evening. He made me play a Bach prelude to him, with cold perspiration running down my back and in such an agony of nervousness as I have never since been called upon to fight against—I was only nine years old and extremely sensitive—and, when my terrible ordeal had come to an end, patted my head, kissed me between the eyes, and said: "Little fellow, you were born a musician, and will play the piano some day." I doubt whether that night there was another so happy and proud a boy as I within the confines of Her Most Gracious Majesty's realms.

Madame Dulcken's playing, I remember, struck me as extraordinarily brilliant and forcible. So did Cipriani Potter's, whose twelve masterly P.F. studies had made my small fingers ache many a time and oft. Thalberg astonished and discouraged me; the inconceivable smoothness and featness of his execution, combined with the surprising intricacy of the passages that seemed to glide off his fingers, carried conviction to my soul that it was utterly useless for me to go on trying to learn to play, as I could certainly never hope to attain anything like Thalbergian facility. A scarcely less depressing effect was produced upon me by the wonders wrought by Dreyschock's phenomenal left hand. They were in reality only clever tricks, perfected with infinite pains; but they seemed much more to me at that time. Sloper's sparkling warmth and Holmes's classical coldness created impressions, when I first heard those eminent musicians play in public, which are still fresh in my memory, associated, incongruously enough, with the Chartist Riots of April, 1848, from which circumstance I am led to believe that I must have become cognisant by ear of these famous English executants in that year and month. But —next to the inimitable Mendelssohn—of all the pianists I listened to with more or less rapture and envy before completing my tenth year, Sterndale Bennett was the one who most thoroughly fulfilled my boyish ideal of what playing ought to be. For finish, delicacy of expression, accuracy of phrasing, and a certain gentle grace of style that imparted an indefinable charm to his interpretations of classical works, I have never listened to anybody *quite* his equal. The late Sir George Smart, who delighted in contriving musical treats for me during my green velvet period, once took me to call upon Sterndale Bennett, promising me that " the great man" should play expressly for my delectation. This promise having been explained to Bennett with due representation of my precocious passion for music, he smilingly turned to me, saying, " Well; what shall I play for you?" For the moment I could think of none of the names of my favourite *chevaux-de-bataille*, and nervously blurted out, " Would you mind playing through the full scales with both hands?" He replied, "Not at all; nor is it half a bad test of pianoforte-playing. In fact, I consider it a high compliment to be asked to play my scales;" with which he sate down to the piano and played them so incomparably as to afford me a delightful revelation with respect to the effects that may be elicited from the piano by the simplest forms of execution, expounded by fingers of paramount skilfulness. Perhaps the term "accomplished" was of all others the most justly applicable to him as composer and executant alike. His music and playing were respectively the complement of one another—interchangeable expressions of his exact mind and elegant taste. Hence the chief difficulty of his P.F. compositions to the tolerably proficient amateur. They are not only intolerant but prohibitory of slovenliness and "free individual interpretation." They must be played precisely as they are written, or not at all; they exact completeness of understanding and appreciation from the performer, as well as an unusual degree of manual dexterity.

I think it was during the season of 1853 that I first heard Arabella Goddard, who came before the public as a slight, quiet-looking girl of fifteen, with works at her fingers' ends that had—at least, so it was said at the time—never theretofore been performed in a London concert-room. In Beethoven's greater and later sonatas, then only partly intelligible to me and all but unknown to the English musical public, she was note-perfect, and, moreover, had committed more than one of them to memory—an extraordinary feat for a mere child, such as she was three-and-thirty years ago. According to Sir George Grove, she made her *début* at a concert of the Quartet Association on April 14, 1853, in the sonata, opus 106, which she played by heart; and I am under the impression that a few weeks later I heard her play the Posthumous Sonata without book. Her *tempi* and execution were as a rule faultless, even then—too faultless, perhaps; for over-conscientious attention to the countless details of such colossal compositions as those above referred to, left her no spare intellectual force wherewith to investigate the Master's true meaning. It could hardly have been otherwise, at her age. Endowed by nature with an abnormal capacity for taking pains, she had it in her to overcome the most appalling technical difficulties, and to render them with absolute but passionless accuracy. There was nothing she could not play, if she made up her mind to master it; but her interpretations of great imaginative works, though they might satisfy the intellect, could not content the soul. Romantic music did not appear to move her; she could play Chopin's notes exactly, but not his thoughts. On the other hand, inestimable pleasure was to be derived from listening to her renderings, at once forcible, solid, and crisp, of Bach's Preludes and Fugues, in which it always struck me that her special executive capacities and strong musical individuality found their highest expression. Hers was a fine, firm, even touch; it lacked variety, however, and never conscientiously lent itself to the production of "tone-colour." But she was a great and good pianist in the days of the Crimean War, when she won imperishable laurels in Germany; and, I have no doubt, still is so. The last time I heard her was in the year of Grace, 1856, when I left England for a foreign service that endured throughout twenty-two years, and brought me into personal contact, at one time or another, with all the eminent continental pianists who have successfully aided in accomplishing the revolution in school, style, and manner of pianoforte-playing which has accrued within that period. When I returned definitively to my native country in the winter of 1878-9, I found the pianism—*sit venia verbo!*—of my early youth dead and forgotten—or, at least, only remembered as anything more than a lifeless tradition by a comparatively small number of old musical fogies like myself.

I have endeavoured to indicate the leading features of the important changes undergone some thirty odd years ago by the method of pianoforte-playing generally adopted in this country, referring with unavoidable superficiality to the eminent executants through whose example and influence those changes were mainly brought about. Whether the innovations in composition for and manipulation of the pianoforte called forth the surprising developments of that instrument's resources invented by its manufacturers or were themselves the offspring of those developments, is a question scarcely less difficult to answer conclusively than the antique "poser" respecting the priority of the hen or the egg. In all probability the mechanical contrivances by which the clavichord acquired greater force and breadth of tone, as well as other qualities and capacities that may be said to have revolutionised its special instrumental character, were nearly coeval with the transformation effected by Thalberg and Liszt in the method of playing theretofore prevalent, each innovation being the natural complement of the other. One thing is certain; namely, that, as far as the satisfactory rendering of chamber music is concerned, the improvements achieved in the construction of pianofortes were productive of dire results. They overthrew the balance of power that had been established by the greatest composers of such music between certain stringed instruments and the pianoforte, imparting to—nay, almost enforcing upon the latter an undue and undesirable tone-predominance over the former. Admitting the exercise of an almost superhuman discretion, in connection with the use of the pedal or the employment of physical vigour, on the part of the contemporary pianist, the very instrument he plays upon incapacitates him from producing the effects, in connection with the violin or violoncello, that were contemplated by Beethoven, when he wrote his violin and pianoforte sonatas, or by Mozart whilst deftly fashioning seven of his admirable trios. The combinations of tone aimed at in the composition of these works were necessarily dependent upon the thin quality of the sound then yielded by the clavichord at the summons of a touch far lighter than that of the modern executant. Moreover, the tone of stringed instruments has lost, rather than gained, in force, owing to the heightening of concert pitch by nearly a semitone within the last half century—an innovation that has led to the employment of strings, for the *instruments à cordes*, slightly thinner than those in use at the time when Beethoven established his so-called "classical pitch." The pianoforte of to-day, therefore—chiefly by reason of its own increment of tone-power, and, in a lesser degree, through the loss of such power suffered by the stringed instruments—dominates its associates in chamber music so considerably as to frustrate the arrangements of composite sound put together with such consummate skill by the paramount trinity of trio-writers, Beethoven, Mozart, and Haydn. The chamber music of these great *maestri* is so enchantingly beautiful that its present rendering at the hands of our best executants fills us with profound and lively delight; but we never hear it as its composers meant it to be heard, nor ever shall, while Steinway and Chickering continue to rule the concert-room and sway the *salon*.

It was not until eight years had elapsed after I quitted England, having accepted service under a foreign Government, that I fully realised the radical change that had meanwhile been taking place in pianoforte-playing. I had passed the intervening time in more or less obscure country quarters—towns of the old world sort, in which pianism and pianists were socially at a discount, art-culture of any kind was undreamt of by the well-to-do classes, and music was regarded as an accidental and unimportant relief to the monotony of every-day existence—a sort of frill, ornamental but frivolous, attached to the stiffly starched shirt-front of local society. In one of these retreats—a prosperous trading provincial centre—the only professional pianist was a crabbed elderly gentleman, who kept a small music shop, taught what he had been led to believe was the art of playing to a few dull children of unambitious *bourgeois* parents, and eked out his slender earnings by periodically tuning two or three score instruments, by courtesy styled pianofortes, of the sort which breed grave doubts in the mind of the sensitive musician whether the invention of the clavichord should be appraised as a blessing or a curse to mankind. When any transitory executant star of from the seventh to the fifteenth magnitude condescended to shed a passing ray upon C——, this sour old fellow, being the unique musical institution of his native place, always contrived to get himself "called in" by the authorities as a professional adviser with respect to the arrangement of a concert programme, in which the *bénéficiaire* of the moment sometimes permitted him to figure as a P.F. soloist; and although the deeds he did upon these occasions had as little in common with pianoforte-playing, from an artistic point of view, as screeving has with painting or a Catnach ballad with poetry, they were always sympathetically greeted by audiences familiar with his incapacities "as long as they remembered anything," and who experienced the same sort of passive regard for him that they felt for the town pump, the discordant peal of bells in the tower of their grey old church, or the licensed municipal idiot—a more popular person on the whole, I incline to believe, among his fellow townsmen, than their "only jig-maker." I may parenthetically remark that I incurred the latter's high displeasure shortly after my arrival at C—— by getting up a social agitation in favour of founding a Musical Association and by volunteering to play in public two or three times for the benefit of local charities. With the Association—which took root and flourished exceedingly for some years—he scornfully refused to have anything to do, although courteously solicited to assist in its organisation; and of my performances on the pianoforte he spoke in terms which they very probably merited, but which were certainly the reverse of complimentary. Poor old W——! the easiest of Mendelssohn's P.F. works were far beyond his powers—Beethoven was but a name to him, and of Chopin, Schumann, Liszt, I verily believe he had never heard. Brimful of the romantic school as I was at that time, I must have been a terrible thorn in his side; and I well remember how, whenever he encountered me by chance in concert-room or street, he would conspicuously look another way with an indignant sniff, muttering protests against my existence in language which can scarcely have promoted the welfare of his immortal part. My sojourn at C—— unsettled the established order of things upon which his physical equilibrium had hitherto been kept up, and, as I have since regretfully learnt, he did not long survive my departure from that town, in which, to his apprehensions, I had represented the spirit of revolution and promulgated the doctrines of anarchy. Peace be to his manes!

My next abiding-place was Vienna, whither I was sent on a special mission in the early spring of 1865. There the new school of pianoforte-playing revealed itself to me in its full force and eager striving after variety of tone-colour. Soon after I had settled down in the Kaiserstadt, fully believing that I should live the remainder of my days within its precincts, I became an assiduous frequenter of public and private musical entertainments, and was most generously admitted to the penetralia of the chief Viennese musical organisations by the great artists who directed them. One of my early experiences of "virtuosity" on the piano, illustrating an aggravated phase of its novel departure, was gained at a *matinée* given in a concert-room attached to the Imperial Palace by the Chevalier Antoine de Kontski, surnamed by his admiring countrymen "The Lion of Poland." This title of honour, I am bound to say, was not altogether lacking in appropriateness; indeed it was to a considerable extent justified by his method of dealing with any luckless instrument that fell into his hands professionally. Thus might a vivacious monarch of the desert, with spirits unsubdued and sinews unrelaxed by bondage, play on or with the pianoforte, if that way disposed by nature or accidental impulse. Blows from a playful leonine paw could scarcely, I should think, strike a larger number of notes simultaneously or with greater force of impact than did the vigorous hands of the Sarmatian Lion to whom I listened twenty years ago, for the first time, in a daze of mingled wonder and consternation. One of the pieces he played on the occasion referred to, I remember, had been intituled in such sort as to explain its special function and aim with laudable directness. It was called "Le Réveil de la Pologne," and was eminently qualified, as rendered by M. de Kontski, to awaken the dead, let alone slothful patriots of the Polish or any other persuasion. An eminent Viennese critic wrote a panic-stricken notice of the *matinée* alluded to, on the morrow of the performance, concluding his remarks with the following impressive words: "From battle, murder, and from sudden death, and from the Lion of Poland's pianforte-playing, good Lord, deliver us!"

Shortly after the alarming experience above recorded, I was sent on a brief mission to Berlin, where a young Austrian diplomatist, himself an amateur pianist of the very first order, and one of Carl Tausig's favourite pupils, introduced me to that truly great teacher and executant, then in the zenith of his influence, which swayed the leading circles of musical society in the Prussian capital, even including the "advanced" clique that took its cue, in all questions connected with the divine art, from Frau von Schleinitz, the wife of the Minister of the Household —a lady of great musical attainments, who suffered no P.F. compositions save those of Liszt's, and no "réductions pour le piano" of any works but Wagner's, to be played in her *salon*, the rendezvous every Tuesday evening of many distinguished professional and *dilettanti* musicians. Tausig was good enough to play to me several times, at his own apartments and in the Bechstein repository of pianofortes, where some of the finest instruments in Europe were always at the disposal of masters of the craft. But that his playing lacked inner warmth—whilst teeming with superficial fire and sparkle —I should incline to rank Tausig as one of the three greatest pianists to whose marvellous achievements I have ever listened; placing him immediately after Liszt, and just a little to the front of Rubinstein. His renderings, however—irreproachable in *technique, tempi,* and observance of the composer's markings—were so intrinsically chilly that they never attained the topmost heights of interpretative greatness. He seemed to me always to be playing critically, even when executing the most intricate passages at a speed I have never since heard equalled, save by Alfred Gruenfeld. When I say that he played his own compositions to perfection, and without apparent effort, any one acquainted with those works will readily apprehend that his mastery over technical difficulties was absolute and exhaustive. His memory for details of emphasis and ornament expressed itself in a meticulous accuracy of reproduction that was positively aggravating; so much so, that more than once, whilst listening to his photographic renderings of Bach and Scarlatti, I caught myself wishing that some momentary derangement would prompt him to take a liberty, however slight and venial, with the composer. But he never did, nor would he tolerate any "frivolities" of the kind—that was his term for what dear old Cipriani Potter used to call "the pardonable license of an intelligent interpreter"—in his pupils. It was not in Tausig's nature, though a more musical musician never lived than he, to play anything (including his own works) otherwise than he saw it in black and white. Far from disdaining "effects," even those of a sensational character, to the production of which the resources of the modern pianoforte lend themselves so temptingly, he was extraordinarily skilled in the achievement of such contrivances. But they had to be distinctly indicated by the composer; nothing would induce him to supply them on his own responsibility, no matter how forcibly they might be suggested by the character of the composition. As a necessary consequence of the almost painful conscientiousness by which he regulated his own unexceptionable playing, he was the severest of teachers, never objurgatory, like Kuellak, or pettish, like Taubert, but gravely and witheringly critical. Irony, of a peculiarly saturnine and scathing sort, lurked in his admonitions and imparted a stinging smart to his reproofs. On one occasion, when he acceded to my request that I might be present whilst he was giving class-lessons to a few of his advanced pupils of both sexes, I saw one or two young pianists of high merit—at least, from my point of view—actually wince under the lash of his solemn, unimpassioned satire. Yet all his acolytes loved him, for he was in reality the most amiable of men and kindest of masters, indefatigable in his endeavours to stimulate the sluggish, encourage the nervous, and develop special capacities in the intelligent. He would not have anything to do with unmusical natures. As soon as he convinced himself that any one of his pupils was really deficient in musicality he gave that pupil up, on the ground that he (Tausig) could not consent to receive remuneration for an undertaking he felt himself unequal to. But where he happened to light upon genuine talent allied with poverty—too often the case in North Germany, where the average of well-being amongst the highly educated classes is much lower than in this country—he would bestow the utmost pains upon gratuitous instruction, and even supply out of his own pocket the means of living, whilst pursuing their studies, to his more indigent *alumni*. In private life he was a delightful companion to those privileged to enjoy his intimacy; for his memory was richly stored with anecdote, and his powers of narration were of no ordinary calibre. Being the soul of honour, truth, and uprightness, everything vulgar or trivial was repugnant to him, and licensed jesters, renowned for the salacious coarseness that so strongly flavours German conversational humour, curbed their tongues in his presence. In a word, Tausig was one of the elect of mankind. He did great good whilst he lived, and his premature death was a heavy, I might almost venture to say an irreparable loss to the modern school of pianoforte-playing, upon which his inflexible sobriety of method exercised a restraining and most salutary influence. Reverting for a moment to his characteristics as a performer, I may add that he produced a broader tone than any other Berlin pianist of his day —that his lightness of touch in rendering the fanciful and elaborate ornamentations of Chopin and Liszt was simply exquisite, and that he was especially remarkable for the *verve* and *ton* with which he executed those amazing *tours de force*, invented by himself as well as by the mighty Hungarian ecclesiastic, which are the terror of ninety-nine expert pianists in every hundred. No one who ever listened to his feats in this direction will be likely to forget what a wealth of sound and complexity of combinations his deft fingers extracted from the key-board. In him were combined the more salient excellences of the old and new schools of pianism. It is pleasant to know that his admirable method has been faithfully adhered to by a few of his surviving pupils, amongst whom may be reckoned some of the most distinguished musicians of Northern Germany.

At the close of the 1866 campaign in Bohemia I

returned to Vienna with the fixed intention—which in due time, I need scarcely say, proved as untenable as the majority of human resolves—of making that delightful city my dwelling-place for the remaining term of my natural life. The Kaiserstadt was then, as it still is, the most musical capital in Europe; I felt that my lines were cast in a pleasant place, and, as soon as I had made arrangements for a prolonged sojourn in the second floor of a huge palace in the Freyung, I addressed myself to the agreeable task of obtaining admission to the leading circles of professional and amateur musicians. This undertaking was rendered an easy one by the aid of a few cordial letters from masters of the craft in London and Paris, introducing me to eminent Viennese executants who had reaped abundant laurel crops at different times in English and French concert-rooms; and, as soon as the kindly recipients of my credentials discovered that I was not altogether "a profane," they made me free, frankly and unreservedly, of the inmost arcana of Vienna musical society. During the ensuing three years no production—I may almost say no preparation—of any importance connected with the divine art took place in the Kaiserstadt at which I did not assist, and I still look back to the experiences of that period as the most interesting and instructive of my whole life. Eighteen years ago the Vienna school of pianoforte-playing was entering a stage of transition from the calm, accurate, classical method to the fiery, careless, enthusiastic style it adopted early in the seventies, and has since, as I am assured, adhered to. The *crème de la crème* of Viennese musical society was stricken by wonder, rather than filled with admiration, by Rubinstein's innovations, both in "reading" and tone-production; purists, whose name was legion, took strong exception to Brahms' roughness and technical *laisser-aller*, as well as to the startling liberties he frequently took with classical texts. His following at that time was a small one, compared to what it became in later years under the energetic leadership of Dr. Edward Hanslick; but it was a compact, resolute, and profoundly convinced phalanx, counting in its ranks some of the most able teachers and accomplished *dilettanti* in the Austrian capital. Brahms' playing, however, —rarely heard, and always severely criticised by two or three of the eminent writers who formed, or at least guided, public opinion with respect to matters musical— was not highly esteemed even by those who lauded his compositions to the skies. His renderings of these latter were objected to, as manifesting a reckless disdain of mere executant detail that detracted from their general effect, presenting them to the audience as dashing sketches, instead of as finished pictures. The music-lovers who thronged the Conservatoire or the smaller Redouten-Saal to hear Johannes Brahms play his own music whenever he came up from Pesth to introduce a new trio or P.F. sonata to the public, felt slighted in that he apparently took but slender pains to gratify their fondness for technical exactitude, and grudged him the license he often granted to himself of "vamping" difficult passages he had not taken the trouble to master, or even extemporising, in their place, others more convenient to his fingers. The critics—with one or two distinguished exceptions—eagerly pointed out these shortcomings, apparently unmindful of the fact (which Brahms himself never hesitated to admit) that perfection of *technique*, pure and simple, was, in his estimation, a matter of small moment compared to the purpose he had always kept steadfastly in view—viz., to convey the true meaning of his musical ideas and poetical conceptions to his hearers. To me his playing was always intensely interesting. Its inaccuracy and slovenliness vexed my ear; but its descriptiveness and, still more, its suggestiveness were fruitful in exercise for the intelligence. One of the strongest impressions it made upon me—leaving, of course, its vigorous and subtle intellectuality out of the question—was that the great Hamburg composer never thoroughly studied any work selected by him for performance in public, but contented himself with mastering its plan and intention, as he understood them, and with imparting his view thereof to his hearers. This he succeeded in doing, as far as my experience of his playing enables me to pronounce an opinion, in a highly forcible and intelligible manner. Brahms never left any doubt upon a musician's mind as to the meaning of the composer whose work he happened to be dealing with; or rather as to what he (Brahms) was convinced the composer in question meant. His readings of Beethoven, for instance, often differed in essential respects from those of other great contemporary pianists, notably from those of Rubinstein, whose interpretation of the later P.F. sonatas, in particular, had little in common with that of Brahms, save the actual note-text, and not always even that. But I incline to believe that Brahms is endowed with a clearer and truer insight into Beethoven's musical conceptions than even the illustrious Moldavian, whose lineaments and facial expression bear so striking a resemblance to the portraits of the immortal Master. Making due allowance for inferiority of *technique*—Beethoven's execution is said to have been faultless—and for the developments in tone-producing power effected in modern pianofortes, I can fancy that Brahms plays Beethoven's concertos and sonatas very much as Beethoven himself played them. The influence of Beethoven is so unmistakably manifested in Brahms' orchestral works, and even in some of his songs, that Brahms may reasonably be credited with an exceptional capacity for entering into the spirit of Beethoven's compositions. For my part, I am convinced that he is possessed of the capacity in question, and it is by reason of this especial gift that his renderings of the later sonatas—which in the hands of Von Buelow appear to me mere bloodless, colourless problems—are, to my mind, the most satisfactory I have ever listened to, despite their many technical imperfections. It is probably the result of one of those inexplicable anomalies which so often characterise artistic natures that one who, as a pianist, seems so indifferent to the attractions of adroit execution should, as a composer, set tasks of such inordinate difficulty to the pianoforte-player as those contained in Brahms' P.F. works, some of which exact an almost superhuman flexibility and endurance on the part of their performer. It is just possible that Brahms himself could play them as they ought to be played, if he would take the trouble to practise them. This, however, he does not do—or did not when I was privileged to meet and hear him—and there are but few pianists living who combine the physical strength, manual skill, and intellectual quickness that may enable a performer *hors ligne* to overcome the formidable difficulties with which the works above alluded to teem. To sum up Brahms' pianoforte-playing in a few words, it belongs neither to the old nor to the new school; it is not coldly classical, nor ardently emotional; it lacks some of the qualities that constitute executant greatness of the first order; but it is original, and instinct with a genius that is reproductive as well as creative.

The leading pianist of Vienna during my residence in that city from 1866 to 1869 was Julius Epstein, one of the most careful and conscientious artists in Europe, and almost the last representative of clear, cold, crisp classicality who found favour with the impulsive and somewhat fickle Viennese public. Epstein fulfilled functions of inestimable utility to the music-lovers of the Kaiserstadt, although his intrinsic merits as a performer were relative rather than positive. He was, so to speak, the backbone of chamber music, whilst Joseph Hellmesberger was its right arm. He could be, and was, relied upon to play the P.F. part in any concerto, trio, or duo that concert-givers might deem it expedient to include in their programmes, no matter at how short notice, and to play it, moreover, with a mechanical accuracy above all praise. Excepting when stars of the pianist persuasion were available to the directors of the Conservatorium or of the "Gesellschaft der Musikfreunde"—a frequent occurrence in a city which, during the winter months particularly, is the favourite rendezvous of all the most eminent European soloists—Epstein's name was always to be seen on the "bills" of those institutions, carrying with it the foreknowledge that whatever works he was engaged to play would be rendered with irreproachable correctness. His appearance was in perfect keeping with his style and execution as a pianist. Julius Epstein, when I first made his acquaintance, was thirty-four years of age, tall, slight, and of a sallow complexion, with raven black hair, moustache, and whiskers, as carefully attended to as those of the most dandified "plunger" in the Vienna garrison. His clothes, always dark in colour, were admirably cut by Ebenstein, the prince of Austrian tailors, and fitted him to a nicety. His linen was of unspotted and dazzling whiteness; his pale lavender gloves triumphantly exemplified the supreme fitness of things; his patent-leather boots were lustrous black mirrors. Being somewhat short-sighted, he wore glasses, which enhanced the frigid and precise gravity of his expression. When he was seated at the piano his body never swayed or swerved in the least, even whilst his long white fingers were achieving marvels of agility, but preserved the rigidity and severe *tenue* of a model drill-sergeant under inspection. That such a type of deportment should be frugal in his dealings with the pedals was a natural consequence of the imperturbable sobriety characterising his every action. Tausig himself was not more chary of "effects," other than those produced by the finger, than Epstein; whilst Sterndale Bennett had not a more silky and even touch, the result (as he once solemnly informed me) of indefatigable scale-playing for two hours a day throughout some twenty years of his life. In one respect his playing was always a treat; in another, a disappointment. It was as nearly faultless as anything done by human hands could be; but it never made the least apparent effort to awaken the sympathies of the audience for the composer, or to place the performer *en rapport* with those around him. That Epstein would play every note of the music assigned to him, exactly in conformity with all the author's indications touching time, accent, and emphasis, was a foregone conclusion to all *habitués* of Vienna concert-rooms; but it was no less certain that his faithful rendering of what he saw, and nothing more, would be absolutely devoid of enthusiasm, warmth, or sensibility. He did not blame, or even deprecate, in others what he abstained from himself—more, I have reason to believe, through constitutional reserve than through lack of feeling or incapacity to express what he felt. Rubinstein's wildest extravagances, such as that impulsive artist would indulge in when playing *en petit comité* to a dozen or so of double-dyed musicians, never stirred Epstein to the utterance of a word of protest or condemnation; but neither did the tremendous success of such *tours de force*—I mean, in the way of tone-production as well as of execution—ever tempt him to introduce effects of that class into his own performances. Liszts might come, and Rubinsteins might go; but Epstein went on for ever (and, I sincerely trust, still continues to do so) in the calm, impassive, immaculate style that stamped his playing with the hallmark of surpassing respectability; defied reproach, ignored emotion, exalted propriety to the rank of a first-class virtue, and, by inference, relegated sensationalism to the limbo of unpardonable vices. Such was the pianoforte-playing of Julius Epstein, the most accurate and least interesting of all the eminent pianists with whom I was brought into contact during my sojourn on the banks of the "beautiful blue Danube."

It was in the year 1868 that I first became acquainted with Anton Rubinstein at the chambers of my friend Hofkapellmeister Joseph Hellmesberger, on the topmost floor of a cruelly lofty house in the Tuchlauben, nearly opposite the Conservatorium of those days; a very different sort of building to the gorgeous edifice behind the Hôtel Imperial in which the *alumni* of the Viennese Hochschule der Musik are now taught how to write fugues, read orchestral scores at sight, and play every instrument under the sun. I was exceptionally lucky in hearing the gifted Moldavian play almost daily for several weeks in succession, in private as well as in public. For the first time the new school of pianism was revealed to me in the fulness of its splendid sensationalism. It had not theretofore been my good fortune to encounter Franz Liszt, its illustrious founder, at the piano, or even to hear any of his greater P.F. works performed by executants of his own training. Rubinstein's orchestral effects and variety of tone-production on my favourite instrument, therefore, surprised no less than they delighted me. During his sojourn in Vienna he played —more particularly at the houses of his musical friends, where I most frequently met him—music of every period and description; a great deal of his own, more freely, but less carefully, than that of others; the majority of Beethoven's P.F. sonatas, in the interpretation of which, to my mind, he excelled nearly every other pianist of the day; many of Chopin's and Schumann's most difficult works (his renderings of the 5th Impromptu and the *Kreisleriana* can never be forgotten by any who heard them played by him one night after supper at Johann Herbeck's to an audience after his own heart—pianists of a certain force, every man and woman of them); gems of contrivance and constructive ingenuity by Henselt, Tchaikovski, Heller, and several other modern masters; suites by Bach, scraps of Scarlatti, Rameau and Couperin, studies by Hummel and Moscheles, one and all with extraordinary alternations of vigour and delicacy, and, above all, with an ever-present subtle suggestiveness of the player's own distinct individuality. This latter circumstance struck me as all the more singular—when I had become sufficiently familiar with his playing to note its peculiarities—because his compositions had always appeared to me to receive their immediate inspiration, either in subject or style, from some composer other than himself. Thus, anomalous as it may seem, my view of him as an executant and writer may be most aptly expressed as follows: he plays the music of others as though it were his own, and composes his own music as though it were that of other people. Admitting this view to be correct, it would point to the logical deduction that Rubinstein's originality—genius is perhaps the more appropriate term to apply to so remarkable a musician—finds expression rather in his playing than in his compositions; and I really believe that this is so. His is an essentially impressionable and receptive nature, always—probably quite unconsciously

—under the influence of some individuality stronger than its own. Most of his earlier works afford internal evidence of having been suggested by Mendelssohn's elegant melodic forms and graceful methods of treatment. Later ones have obviously been written by Rubinstein whilst he was under the spell of Robert Schumann's imaginative enchantments. Others might have been improvised by a robust Chopin. A very few are Beethovenesque, although in manner rather than in substance, displaying subjects of noble simplicity, broadly and massively handled. In all likelihood, whilst studying the compositions of these and other *maestri* at different periods of his own musical development, with a view to making himself master of their every detail, he has become impregnated with the special characteristics of each great composer successively, and has been constrained by his own sympathetic and plastic disposition to reproduce those characteristics in whatsoever compositions he himself may have given birth to at the time.

But to return to his playing, in which his vigorous individuality has always made itself manifest. Opinions may, and do, differ about his readings of the musical classics, about his *tempi*, and, above all, about his passion for striking contrasts and sensational effects, which prompts him over frequently to endeavour to make the pianoforte do more than it is capable of doing. But I do not think that any experienced pianist, professional or amateur, will deny that Anton Rubinstein is one of the greatest performers on the clavichord whom the last quarter of a century has produced. With respect to touch, flexibility, power, and endurance, his is exhaustive playing. It is, perhaps, absurd to speak of his touch as though it were a special capability; for he is possessed of every imaginable sort of touch, from the deep and clinging, which has the faculty of extracting the maximum breadth and length of tone from a tense wire, to the light and feathery, such as notes might be expected to yield were the keyboard tripped over by fairy feet or brushed by butterflies' wings. His flexibility is the more amazing that the physical aspect of his fingers, which are short, thick, and blunt, affords no promise of pliancy, but rather the contrary. I have observed, however, in the cases of other admirable pianists, *e.g.*, Wilhelm Taubert, Ferdinand Hiller, Carl Reinecke, Alfred Jaell, Johannes Brahms, Leonhard Bach, and Joséffy, that fingers of the above description, properly trained, are every whit as supple as the long, slender digits of such players as Epstein, Hallé, or Kuhe. Rubinstein's exceptional power and endurance as a pianist are doubtless attributable to his great bodily strength and to a muscular development unusual in pianists. Broad-shouldered, deep-chested and thick-set, any professional pugilist would at a glance pronounce him an ugly customer; and his hand-grip, if he likes you, is something to be remembered with feelings of a not altogether pleasurable nature. Thanks to these corporeal gifts and to the indefatigable industry with which, as a youth, he applied himself to surmounting the mechanical obstacles that bristle so formidably in every earnest P.F. student's path, Anton Rubinstein (like the greatest of all pianists, living or dead, Franz Lizst) arrived long ago at that advanced stage of proficiency in which mere technical difficulties, howsoever complex and intricate, cease to be a cause of trouble, or even of momentary perplexity, to the player, whose fingers are become capable of carrying out without hesitation, and almost without effort, any instructions conveyed to them by his will, the immediate mandatory and interpreter of his intelligence. The indices of the telegraph dial do not obey the dictates of the "operator" more instantaneously, or with more inevitable exactitude than the fingers of such players as Liszt and Rubinstein unravel the tangles of a skein of musical contrivances at their owner's behest. Nothing short of the absolute subordination of the finger to the brain enables great instrumentalists to execute the astounding feats of sight-reading, and more especially of transposition at sight, that seem to be mere matters of course—all in the day's work, as one would fancy from the ease with which they are accomplished—to Rubinstein. Is it possible to conceive a more surprising display of combined intellectual and physical force than the playing at sight of a difficult piece of music in a key other than that in which it is presented to the performer's eye? Leaving out of the question the elaborate unconscious cerebration that must take place during such an achievement, the change of key necessitates alteration in every mechanical detail of the fingering, and this alteration has to be thought out and put into execution simultaneously by the player, who must, at one and the same time, take into his mind a musical phrase (possibly three or four bars in length), its meaning, accents, &c., and the exact notes of which it is composed, *in two keys,* ordering his fingers by an effort of volition in such sort that they shall express that phrase upon the keyboard, not as he sees it with his fleshly eyes upon the printed page before him, but as his spiritual sight informs him it must be at a continuous interval of so or so many notes higher or lower in the scale than the original. I know of no more tremendous achievement—of no exercise of the human intelligence bringing as many faculties of the brain to bear collectively, instantaneously, and simultaneously upon one complex purpose. Of all living pianists, to the best of my belief, Anton Rubinstein is the most infallible reader and transposer *a prima vista*. I have stood behind him, scarcely crediting the evidence of my own senses, whilst he has rendered a manuscript orchestral score, in sixteen parts, on the piano with all the freedom and apposite expression of a first-class pianist who should be playing a P.F. composition with which he was tolerably familiar. I have heard him transpose one of the most heart-breaking fugues (heart-breaking, of course, only from a mechanical point of view) of the " forty-eight " from a flat key into a sharp key, the latter not even being one of his own selection, but chosen by a fellow-pianist whom I shrewdly suspected at the time to be guilty of intending to set Rubinstein an impossible task. He played the fugue in question—which I had only too good reason to know by heart—without missing a note or omitting an emphasis. When it was over, I noticed that the perspiration was standing out in great beads upon his massive forehead, from which unwonted symptom of fatigue I drew the inference that he had put a heavy strain upon his powers. But that he had performed this astonishing feat, at unforeseen request and without a minute's hesitation, others can testify besides myself. Of those who were present on that memorable occasion, I regret to say, four eminent musicians are no longer living—Kapellmeister Johann von Herbeck; Dr. Edward Schelle, the erudite critic, then wielding his mighty pen in the service of the Vienna "Presse;" Count Laurencin, also an eminent writer upon musical subjects, and through his near connection with the Imperial family (he was a natural son of the late Emperor Ferdinand) a highly influential personage in the art circles of the Kaiserstadt; and Roever, the accomplished 'cellist of Hellmesberger's unrivalled Quartet-party, which is still an honoured and flourishing institution of the Austrian capital. But the Hellmesbergers themselves, father and son—the two "Pepis" who have played such leading parts in the musical life of Vienna for a score of years past—are still alive and hearty, well able to bear witness to the deeds above alluded to, and to many others, scarcely less marvellous, achieved by Anton Rubinstein some sixteen years ago in their presence and mine. So are Gruen, Hoffmann, Epstein, Robert Fuchs, and several more, good musicians and true, at that time constant frequenters of the elder Hellmesberger's "mansion in the skies," where celestial music always rewarded the assiduous climber for an ascent which—did patient and persevering athleticism meet with its deserts —should assuredly have qualified Hellmesberger's more intimate friends for membership of the Alpine Club.

Rubinstein's playing has always impressed me as being, in certain important respects, unique; for instance, in its fiery impetuosity, its inexhaustible capacity for varying its productions of tone-colour, and—last, though not least remarkable—its extraordinary *pianissimi;* mere instrumental whispers, but perfectly articulate and free from indistinctness. There is more than one eminent performer of the present day who can " sing " upon the piano quite as sweetly and intelligently as Rubinstein, and who is fully his equal in the execution of individual *tours de force;* but I know of no other whose forces manifestly increase, instead of diminishing, with the vanquishing of each successive difficulty that presents itself to him, and who, at the end of a long programme, can play its last number—generally a terrible exposition of some paramount technical difficulty or difficulties— more brightly, crisply, and vigorously than he played its first. Rubinstein compels the pianoforte to yield up and give out its utmost tone-power, not by thrashing it as though it were an hereditary foe with whom it is his purpose to settle an account of offence that has been running for several centuries, but by applying to its keyboard the exact sort of pressure which is bound to bring it to compliance. It may be said that pianofortes find the discipline they receive at his hands extremely trying—more so, even, than some of them can bear without breaking down under their trials. But, on the other hand, a good master chastens the servant whom he loves —of course, for that servant's good—and no pianist alive, I will be bound to say, is more deeply attached to the instrument upon which he plays than is Anton Rubinstein, that fine musician, magnificent executant, and prince of good fellows to boot.

It is with extreme diffidence that I attempt to record my impressions of the pianoforte-playing of the greatest and most lavishly-gifted performer upon that instrument whose executant feats have heretofore come under my personal cognizance. He who essays to describe the audible outcome of Franz Liszt's genius, as expressed by that transcendent artist's fingers upon the keyboard, should be a combination of Berlioz and Ruskin—a musical and literary capacity of the very first water. For Liszt was universal in his playing, equally a master of all schools and styles, including his own; which latter —from physical as well as intellectual disabilities—other pianists experience great difficulty in mastering. The Canon of Albano was an elderly man when I heard him play most frequently during the Œcumenical winter in Rome, between sixteen and seventeen years ago, and later on lost the inimitable force and flexibility which then characterised his execution; but at that time his normal powers were unimpaired (at least, so I was assured by musicians who had heard him in his prime), and the miracles he worked upon the clavichord were at once so astounding and so beautiful that, by comparison with them, all I had thitherto experienced in the way of accomplished pianism appeared to me as naught. In what I will venture to designate as "orchestral playing," the extraordinary length and elasticity of his fingers enabled him to surpass all other performers. To him tenths were intervals as easily compassed as octaves are to pianists whose extremities are cast in the ordinary mould; he could play them in rapid sequence, with as many intermediate notes as he had fingers to fit to them.

As to his execution, he seemed to plunge his hands into the keyboard and withdraw them thence teeming with passages of the most amazing difficulty, which he scattered abroad without the least manifest effort.

It was my good fortune at different times, in Vienna and Rome, to hear him play a few of the great masterpieces of Beethoven, as well as a good many of his own original compositions and inimitable "transcriptions;" moreover, he extemporised twice in my presence—the first time at great length upon Schubert's exquisite Serenade (Staendchen), and the second, more briefly, but with surprising elaboration, upon "Batti, batti." I have therefore been able to appreciate his various qualities as a performer in their three principal developments; and in all three I found him not only unrivalled, but unapproachable. His interpretation of Beethoven, whilst distinguished from that of almost every other great cotemporary pianist by a devout fidelity to the *tempi* and worded or marked instructions of the composer, was at once dignified, romantic, and passionate. All the secrets of the great master's conceptions were revealed and explained by Liszt's magic touch. Although I had played the notes of the "Appassionata" and the "Adieu" times innumerable, and listened to many more or less intelligent renderings of those sublime works, I had never felt their full grandeur or understood their exalted significance until Franz Liszt's genius expounded them to me, upon an instrument such as Louis von Beethoven knew not when he wrote his ineffable P.F. sonatas. The living player merged his own remarkable individuality in that of the dead composer; or else the spirit of Beethoven moved his interpreter for the time being; at any rate, the result of either psychical process was one never to be forgotten.

To hear him play his own compositions or arrangements in private was almost to hear him extemporise. When performing them in public, I believe he usually adhered to their printed text; but in the *salon* or clubroom (as when I listened to him during a *soirée* given by the German Club at Rome, in December, 1869), surrounded by intimate friends or approved musicians, he could seldom resist the temptation of trying experiments in the way of treatments or cadences, and especially delighted in surprising those familiar with his pianoforte works, by interpolating therein new episodes or novel effects. I particularly remember hearing him dealing in this irreverent and startling way with his admirable transcriptions of *Faust* and *The Flying Dutchman*, to the rapturous astonishment of all the pianists present, who were "note-perfect" in those *chefs-d'œuvre* of mechanical contrivance. Upon the occasion referred to, Cardinal Haynald, Liszt's dearest friend and the companion of his boyhood—himself, moreover, an excellent pianist—who, like myself, was standing close to the piano, threw his arms round his illustrious fellow-countryman's neck, kissed him on both cheeks, and then, turning to the electrified group of listeners, exclaimed, "Was there ever such a God-gifted creature, so fertile in invention, so strangely enabled to realise in sound the beautiful thoughts that incessantly surge up from the depths of his soul to its surface? We must all reverence as well as love this great man, recognising in him an elect recipient of Divine favour, grace, and inspiration!" Indifferent as Liszt had become—and how could it be otherwise, looking back to his interminable list of public triumphs —to plaudits and social worship, he was visibly touched by the heartfelt words of his old friend, and gave vent to his emotion in an outburst of Hungarian melody, harmonised and embellished with the utmost richness and elegance. That night was an ambrosial one, ever to be gratefully remembered by those who were privileged to participate in its delights.

It was, however, when avowedly improvising, that Liszt "let himself go," giving full rein to his fancy or humour of the moment, and indulging, to the top of his bent, in the exaggeration of technical difficulty. At such times, stimulated by strong excitement, he would put forth to their utmost executive limits the exceptional physical forces with which nature had gifted him, and would achieve what, to any other pianist, had been impossible. Practice and will had so disciplined his fingers and accustomed them to fulfil infallibly the orders transmitted to them from his brain, that, in all probability, the word "difficulty" (in connection with *technique*) had ceased to possess any exact significance, as far as Liszt the executant was concerned. Nobody who has heard him improvise can doubt that, absolutely free from any kind of pre-occupation as to the ability of his hands to execute whatever he may call upon them to do, he gives play to the creative and constructive faculties of his intellect without troubling himself in the least about the mere mechanical instruments attached to his wrists. However unexampled the sequences or complicated the groups of notes suggested by his imagination, he unhesitatingly gives them expression, being certain that his executant machinery can and will carry them out faultlessly in obedience to an unconscious exercise of volition on his part. This has always seemed to me one of the most extraordinary powers ever acquired and wielded by a human being. Within my remembrance only three pianists have possessed it—Liszt, Mendelssohn and Rubinstein, the first-named in a far higher degree of development than the other two. To be able, without an instant's warning or preparation—for, in these cases, execution is absolutely simultaneous with conception—to reproduce in organised combinations or successions of sounds the fantasies of genius or problems of science is a faculty so seemingly superhuman to those who have it not that I can conceive it to be utterly incomprehensible, and even incredible to the vast majority of mankind. Were the phenomena of Liszt's improvising feats, for instance, recounted in cold blood to any unmusical person of fair average intellect, it would scarcely be surprising should his only comment upon the statement be, "I do not believe a word of it, because it is impossible!" Extemporisation of this class—like transposition at sight, or those all but instantaneous feats of mental arithmetic with which George Bidder used to dumbfound the ablest ready-reckoners of his schoolboy days—is and must ever remain a more than Eleusinian mystery to the children of men in general.

As it is universally admitted by members of the craft that Liszt has been, for at least fifty years of his life, pre-eminent amongst pianoforte players in interpretation, execution and improvisation alike, there is, I think, abundant justification for the belief I have entertained ever since I first heard him perform—namely, that he is in all respects the greatest pianist who ever lived. This, moreover, was Richard Wagner's opinion of him. Wagner, who was not given to hero-worship, and whose capacity for enthusiasm was always kept under control by his critical faculty, frequently confessed that words failed him to express his wondering admiration of the gift that enabled Liszt to invest himself with the personality of whatsoever composer whose works he might be engaged in rendering. On one occasion he wrote, in relation to this speciality of his illustrious father-in-law: "He who has enjoyed frequent opportunities, particularly in a small intimate circle, of hearing Liszt play—Beethoven's music, for example—must have realised the fact that the playing in question was not mere reproduction, but actual production. The real boundary-line between these two achievements is not so easily settled as most people believe; but this I have ascertained beyond dispute—that in order to reproduce Beethoven, one must be able to produce with him. It would be impossible to make this comprehensible to those who, as long as they have lived, have heard nothing but ordinary performances and professional renderings of Beethoven's pianoforte works.. In the course of time I have gained so melancholy an insight into the evolution and essence of such renderings that I had rather not wound anybody's feelings by expressing myself more clearly with regard to them. On the other hand I would ask all musicians who have, for instance, heard Beethoven's

Op. 106 or 111 played by Liszt to friends in private, what they previously knew about those compositions, and what they learned of them upon those occasions? If this was reproduction, assuredly it was worth much more than all the sonatas reproducing Beethoven which are 'produced' by our pianoforte composers in imitation of those imperfectly comprehended works. The peculiarity of Liszt's development as a musician was simply this— that he did at the piano what others do with pen and ink; and it is undeniable that even the most original composer, during his first period, does nothing but reproduce. .... At Weimar once, during the very day upon which I became certain that my personal safety was endangered" (he was compelled to quit Germany, being under prosecution for political offences), "I saw Liszt conducting a rehearsal of my opera *Tannhaeuser*, and was wonder-stricken in recognising in him my second self. What I had felt in composing that music, he felt in performing it; what I wanted to express when I wrote it down, he actually expressed in giving it sound. It was strange that, at the moment when I was about to become homeless, I should gain, through the appreciation and adaptability of this inestimable friend, a real home for my art, which home I had theretofore invariably longed and sought for in the wrong place. .... At the close of my last sojourn in Paris, when I sate brooding over my sad fate, ill, wretched, and desperate, my glance fell upon the score of *Lohengrin*, and all of a sudden I felt a piteous grief that this music should never be transferred to sound from the surface of the pallid note-paper. At once I wrote a few words to Liszt; he replied that preparations for the performance of the opera were even then being made on the largest scale that Weimar's restricted resources would allow. Everything that men and means could do to make the work intelligible was done; but errors and misconceptions impeded the wished-for success. What was to be done to supply the lacking elements, to bring about a true understanding between all those who engaged in the production, and to ensure the ultimate triumph of the opera? Liszt saw it at once, and *did it!* He it was who gave to the public his own impression of the work in a manner, the irrefutable eloquence and overwhelming efficiency of which remain unequalled to the present day."

During Liszt's second visit to St. Petersburg, the Czar Nicholas invited him to a *soirée* at the Winter Palace, and in the course of the evening personally asked him to play. An imperial request being equivalent to a command, Liszt sate down to the piano and commenced one of his brilliant Hungarian Rhapsodies. The Czar, instead of bestowing that exclusive attention upon the performance to which Liszt was accustomed, and which, in fact, he exacted from his audiences in private as well as in public—no matter of what exalted elements they might happen to be composed—entered into an animated conversation with one of his generals, talking in his usual and by no means subdued tone of voice. Liszt went on playing for a minute or so, at the expiration of which time, seeing that the Emperor was not listening to him, he suddenly came to a full stop, and rose from his seat at the instrument. Tableau! Although he had paid no heed to Liszt's performance, Nicholas Alexandreivich missed the sound of the piano, and sent one of his chamberlains to ask the artist why he had ceased playing—whether he was indisposed or the piano had not been properly tuned. Liszt's steely grey eyes flashed with righteous indignation as he replied: "The Czar well knows that whilst he is speaking every other voice—even that of music—is bound to be mute!" So saying, he turned his back on the astounded official, and abruptly left the room. Everybody present expected that the *maestro* would receive his passport the first thing on the following morning, with the peremptory order on the part of the Minister of Police to quit Russian territory within four-and-twenty hours. To the surprise of the Court, however, Czar Nicholas took in good part the severe reproof administered to him by the fearless pianist, to whom he sent a costly gift the next day; and ever after, when Liszt's name was mentioned in his presence, spoke of him with cordial admiration as a musician who not only respected himself but had the courage to insist upon respect being paid to his art, "even" (as the Czar was wont to observe) " by ignorant persons like myself, who know so little about music that they do not deserve that great artists should waste their time and talents in trying to amuse them."

Having told some part of what I personally know and feel about the playing of the giants of pianism, I will crave permission to say a few words respecting a few of the younger executants of the day, with whose performances I have had occasion to become conversant. They are four in number; two Germans and two Slavs; all excellent artists, deservedly holding high rank in their profession, firmly established in popular favour throughout Central and Eastern Europe, and, being comparatively speaking young men, entitled to look forward confidently to long, brilliant and remunerative careers. Three of them are men of unusually small stature, thick-set and short-fingered; in every physical respect the converse of the ideal pianist, who, as I have been given to understand by musical ladies of my acquaintance, should be tall, narrow-shouldered, long-necked and haired, endowed with slender white talons, and generally (to borrow an epithet from my fair informants) "romantic-looking." It is odd how few of the really great pianists I have met fulfilled these conditions. Franz Liszt and my genial friend Moritz Moszkowski are the only two I can call to mind who realised them exhaustively. Amongst first-class executants little burly men are decidedly in the majority, and long emaciated ones in the minority. To the former category most indisputably belong Joséffy, De Pachmann, and Leonhard Emil Bach, three of the best young performers on the clavichord now before the public. Alfred Gruenfeld, to whom I venture to assign the very first place in the category above alluded to, is an uncommonly good-looking fellow, neither short nor tall, well-built and as muscular as a professional athlete. His appearance and bearing are rather those of an Austrian hussar in mufti than of a pianist. Even when seated at his instrument he is apt to look round him with a gay and somewhat defiant glance, as though he were settling down in the saddle on a favourite charger prior to performing some risky feat of the *manège*, instead of on a music-stool, with a view to rendering a Chopin Polonaise or a Schumann Novelette.

When Alfred Gruenfeld was in London during the season of 1879, he was only three-and-twenty, but had so thoroughly mastered the technical difficulties of his art that—at least in that particular direction—he had nothing to learn. He was, even then, an admirable sight-reader, and gifted in no small measure with the rare faculty of felicitous improvisation. Many of my readers doubtless remember what a sensation he created at a monster concert in the Floral or St. James's Hall (I forget which) by an extempore treatment of the leading themes in *Lohengrin*, which he played as an encore. His capacity for imitating the styles and methods of living and dead composers amounted to little short of genius. He would take some ordinary familiar tune—the simpler, and even the more common-place, the better for his purpose—and deal with it successively in the manners of Mozart, Haydn, Bach, Beethoven, Mendelssohn, Chopin, Schumann, Wagner, Offenbach, Strauss, and a dozen more, so absolutely merging his own individuality in that of the composer whose peculiarities he was reproducing for the time being, as, *au premier abord*, to deceive the most practised ear. His *tours de force*, in the way of mere execution, were no less surprising than his versatility with respect to touch and tone-production. I have, for instance, repeatedly heard him play Chopin's well-known waltz in D flat—the right-hand part, of course—in octaves at full speed, without omitting a single ornament. Every pianist will admit that this, in its way, is an incomparable feat. With such marvels of dexterity, however, he was never weary of regaling his friends, and would play to them all day and all night long, if they wished it, without exhibiting the least sign of fatigue. I never, before or since, encountered such an indefatigable performer. One night, at the German Club in Mortimer Street, upon some special occasion when "high jinks" had been going on all the evening, he dropped in at about half-past eleven (having been already playing at a concert and a couple of parties), "took the piano," in obedience to an unanimous call on the part of the members present and their guests, and kept it, barring brief intervals devoted to refreshment, until five o'clock the following morning. During the interim he gave us specimens of all the leading P.F. composers' works, and extemporised half-a-dozen times upon themes suggested by one or another of his hearers. Like Rubinstein, he believed firmly in the inspiration of tobacco, and never played so well as when a cigar was smouldering in a corner of his mouth. Gruenfeld was, perhaps, too out-and-out a Bohemian—though of the most harmless, genial, and cheery sort—to succeed in London. When I last saw him he told me that he had been grievously disappointed by his reception here, in private as well as in public, and that, in all probability, he should not repeat his visit to this metropolis. For the last five years his time has been chiefly spent "on tour" in Germany, Russia, Scandinavia, Hungary, Poland, Roumania, and the United States, where he has won laurels without number, and, I rejoice to say, has made a good deal of money.

It is so seldom that a high honorific distinction is bestowed upon mere executant musicians in Russia, that the recent conferment of the Stanislas Order upon Alfred Gruenfeld by Czar Alexander III. has made a considerable sensation in German musical circles, as well as at the Court of St. Petersburg itself. The Czars, like the Sultans, have distinguished themselves during the present century by their munificence to pianists "on tour;" but Imperial recognition, in such cases, has for the most part assumed the form of gifts of money or jewels, not of crosses and ribands. Alfred Gruenfeld, however, appears to have carried all before him at Gatchina and the Winter Palace. Princess Woronzoff's palace, on the Moïka Canal, is the chief temple in which aristocratic music-worship is celebrated in St. Petersburg. It appears that Gruenfeld, during his sojourn on the banks of Neva, officiated as high-priest of the temple in question, and performed musical rites almost daily within its walls. Amongst the "congregation" were to be found the Czar's brothers and sisters-in-law, and many of the great Russian Boyars. There are some excellent musical amateurs, vocal as well as instrumental, amongst the ladies of the Imperial Court. The Duchess of Leuchtenberg, a sister of the late General Skobeleff, is an admirable soprano singer; so is Princess Bieloselska; whilst Madame de Scheremetieff holds a post of honour in the foremost rank of Latter-Day "orchestral pianists." Through the influence of the veteran composer, Adolf Henselt, who is inspector-general of the colleges for young ladies of noble birth throughout Russia proper, Gruenfeld was engaged to give concerts in two or three of those educational institutions, the inmates of which lead a strictly conventual life as a rule, and played his very best to highly sympathetic audiences of from seven to eight hundred damsels, all dressed alike in snow-white uniforms. Several excellent pianists, amongst them Woelffl, Luetschg and Van Ark, are attached to the St. Petersburg Conservatoire, their present chief being Madame Sophie Menter, who not long ago succeeded the lamented Louis Brassin as principal Professor of pianism at the Imperial High School, and, like her predecessor, has as much teaching as she can do at two guineas per half-hour lesson. More than one eminent teacher of music in the Russian capital, besides Henselt, derives a large income from some office or employment altogether foreign to the musical profession. Charles Davidoff, for instance, first of living violoncellists, is not only Director of the Imperial Academy of Music, but financial manager of Prince Danischeff's enormous ironworks, with a salary equal to the pay and allowances of two full generals of the Russian army. It appears that Davidoff was an assiduous student of mathematics and physics as a youth, a circumstance which accidentally reached the wealthy ironmaster's ears (Danischeff, it should be mentioned, is *fanatico per la musica*), and suggested to him the "happy thought" of conferring upon the eminent soloist an appointment that should make him comfortable for life, independently of concerts and teaching. It was a kindly expedient, and worthy of imitation in countries which pride themselves on being a long way ahead of Russia in civilisation and "art-culture."

Joséffy is a strange but highly gifted being, to whom even his best friends—and he has been the pet, at one time or another, of nearly every eminent musician of Germany and Austria—do not hesitate to apply the epithet *mauvais sujet*. For some years after I had first made his acquaintance he was hardly ever out of a scrape; and his adventures in the way of overrunning the constable would fill a highly entertaining volume. In appearance he is a rough-hewn replica of Algernon Swinburne, less the delicacy of complexion and fineness of "points" characterising that fleshliest of poets. To the best of my remembrance he has not as yet played in this country; which should be a source of regret to all English music-lovers, to whom his renderings of works belonging to the romantic school—Chopin, Liszt, and Schumann in particular—could not have failed to give the keenest delight. In the matter of *technique* Joséffy is one of the world's wonders. Nothing but the exceptional shortness of his fingers prevents him from equalling the great Canon of Albano himself, as far as mere execution is concerned. He has a way of combining, or rather intermingling the digits of both hands in a certain class of extremely intricate passages that must be seen to be realised and believed in. The last time I met him was in poor Johann von Herbeck's sky-parlour, where he kept a large party of musical critics and executants up till daybreak by a very remarkable prodigality of his *répertoire's* apparently inexhaustible resources. At the conclusion of this entertainment, his hearers being fairly worn out with the high tension at which he had kept their nerves for several hours, nothing would satisfy him but that I should play him a match of "Kegel" billiards at a café of his predilection, which enjoyed the distinction of being permitted to keep open all night long, and—like the Maison Dorée of old—had not been closed to its customers for many a year. The stake, he insisted, should not be money, but a bowl of a curiously deadly potion, compounded of rum, tea, eggs, sugar, cinnamon, nutmeg, and lemon. That was his notion of rational enjoyment—skittle-billiards and hot egg-nog at four o'clock of a summer morning, after a spell of music in the course of which he himself had played from thirty to forty of the most difficult works ever written for the pianoforte. I have not seen him since that memorable orgy, but have been in constant expectation of hearing that he had succumbed to some one of his many amiable eccentricities. Only the other day, however, the far more agreeable intelligence reached me that he had remitted home thirty thousand dollars from San Francisco, in which city he had wound up a triumphant starring tour through the United States. That Joséffy, having earned such a comfortable sum of money, should have kept it, I look upon as one of the most amazing incidents of cotemporary history.

Vladimir de Pachmann has of late been so frequently heard in English concert-rooms and salons, and, during the past season, has achieved so unequivocal a status here as a popular favourite, that I may confine my remarks upon his pianism within a very brief space. As an interpreter of Chopin he is probably unrivalled at the present time. Since the death of that composer, no executant—except, perhaps, the inimitable Princess Czartoryska, who was taught by Chopin himself—has made the true meaning and sentiment of his works so vividly manifest to the public as his compatriot, M. de Pachmann. It was, I think, Fétis who said, "Pour comprendre et faire comprendre Chopin il faut avoir du sang sclave dans les veines;" and the shrewdest of French musical critics was right. All the finest Chopin players I have ever heard have been Poles or Russians; and the best of these latter is De Pachmann. His *répertoire* is comprehensive, and he plays all manner of music with excellent taste, delicacy, and finish; but Chopin is distinctly his speciality. For endurance he is entitled to rank on an equal footing with Rubinstein and Joséffy — " les deux inépuisables," as Madame de Schleinitz once aptly styled them. As a matter of fact, this accomplished artist is as familiar with the creations of Dussek, Field, Hummel, Moscheles, Scarlatti, Rameau, and Couperin, as he is with those of Chopin, Liszt, and Schumann.

Leonhard Emil Bach has for some two years past been frequently and conspicuously before the London public, which has signified its delight in his admirable performances by ample tribute of the applause they have so richly merited. The Chevalier Bach, who holds an honorary position at the German Court as pianist to the Emperor, is a type of the most advanced school of Teutonic pianoforte *virtuosi*, who are trained to credit the clavichord with the possession of a larger stock of expressive resources than it really possesses, but who, at least, successfully compel it to yield up all the sounds and effects of producing which it is susceptible. Under the hands of Leonhard Bach—who has profited largely by the instruction he was fortunate enough to receive from his illustrious master, Franz Liszt—the piano not only discourses most excellent music, but, at times, assumes an orchestral character. I first met Bach at the Abd-deen Palace in Cairo, where he and his fellow-traveller—for the nonce, Ole Bull—were the instrumental stars of a state concert given by Ismail Khedive, then in the zenith of his viceregal splendour. At that time (February, 1876) Bach was a mere stripling, and had but recently terminated his studies. His playing, however, struck me as uncommonly vigorous and intelligent; and he scored heavily in the diplomatic salons of the Egyptian capital, in which music held its own manfully and womanfully ten years ago. Later on I repeatedly heard him play at Berlin and Vienna, in both of which critical cities he took a high position among the younger apostles of sensational pianism. Since that time his style has ripened, and his production of tone is become far mellower than it was during his "storm and strain" period. Bach, I am glad to say, has transferred his household gods from Berlin to London *en permanence*. He will supply a want that has been keenly felt for some years past in metropolitan musical circles—that of a really first-class pianoforte-player, resident amongst us, and always available for the higher musical requirements of the British public.

That such a want as this—and it is undeniable—should exist in so enormous a city as London, which may, moreover, justly advance considerable pretensions to musical taste and culture, is a fact at once extremely regrettable and difficult to account for satisfactorily. Why is this metropolis mainly dependent upon foreign and non-resident talent for pianoforte-playing of unexceptionable quality? How is it that our musical educational institutions have hitherto failed to produce pianists of either sex who may be classed in the same category of executants as any of the great performers referred to in this chapter, or as Madame Schumann, Mademoiselle Janotha, and half-a-dozen other gifted ladies of alien birth who from time to time visit these shores? Is our system of teaching at such establishments defective? or are English men and women lacking in the highest sort of executant ability, as far as pianoforte-playing is concerned? These are questions to which, possibly, answers may be supplied by musical writers of greater knowledge and courage than myself. All I can say is that it seems to me passing strange, considering how extensively the pianoforte is studied in this country, and how numerous are the English-born professional pianists who have learnt all that our Academies and Schools of Music have been able to teach them, that season after season should pass away without bringing to the front a single pure-bred British performer on the most popular of musical instruments, comparable—otherwise than disadvantageously—to any one of the more eminent Continental pianists. Why this is so, I would rather not surmise in this place. But it is so. " 'Tis true, 'tis pity ; pity 'tis, 'tis true !"

CHAPTER IX.

ADELINA PATTI AT HOME.

THE Rock of the Night, at the base of which the Queen of Song has built her home-nest, is a blunt Welsh hill with a strongly-marked brow and an obtuse profile; greener than most of its neighbours, seamed here and there with rudely constructed stone walls, and sparsely studded on its lower slopes with a few sturdy trees, now clad—it is the third week of October, and the Rock faces the window by which I am writing these lines—in all the golden and russet glories of autumn. Craig-y-Nos is one of a long double line of high hills, many of which are thickly wooded, whilst a few present the aspect of tawny, barren moorland; they stretch away inland for some thirty miles from Swansea Bay into the heart of Brecknockshire, where they join the renowned Brecon Beacons. Between these hills winds the Swansea Valley, watered by the Tawe and its tributary mountain streams, whose name is legion; the Valley of the Usk and one or two other picturesque vales, the titles of which are ingeniously compounded of liquid consonants, the sixth vowel and the compound letter w, branch out of this fine valley, along which runs a single line of railway, frequently at an elevation of several hundred feet above the bright river hurrying seawards and babbling as it flows, so loudly that its incessant voice can be distinctly heard from the summit of the Night-Rock. The whole region surrounding Adelina Patti's country-seat for many a mile is of a singularly romantic character; for the most part wild and weird, abounding in verdant fairy nooks and broad expanses of waste-land, over which one would scarcely be surprised, in the grey gloaming, to see giants stalking from cairn to cairn, or cave to cave. The dusky hill-sides and shadowy valleys wear a legendary look during the mystic hours of early morn and late afternoon, as though they must, in some remote age, have been the chosen haunts of elves and sprites, wood-demons and water-nymphs. When the sun shines upon them in the fulness of his power, they glow with fine deep yellows, rich browns and dark lush greens; but "between the lights" they are overcast by sullen shades, from grey to black, that impart to them a strangely grave and forbidding aspect.

On a shelf, or natural plateau, of Craig-y-Nos stands the castle, offering the most striking contrast imaginable to the primitive, old-world region in which it is situate; for it is, so to speak, an epitome of all the comforts and luxuries with which the more recent developments of science and art have enabled Fortune's favourites to solace and embellish their every-day lives. It is a castellated building of great breadth and depth, constructed of reddish-grey limestone, which composes admirably with the prevailing tints of the surrounding landscape. Besides the central turret, from the breezy platform of which waves the "house-flag" of its gifted owner, a massive clock-tower flanks the eastern wing of Craig-y-Nos Castle, and its bells, which faithfully reproduce the Westminster Chimes so familiar to a Londoner's ears, record the progress of Old Time every quarter of an hour throughout the day and night. The Castle, which takes its name from the huge rock beetling high above it to the westward and sheltering it from the fierce Atlantic gales that now and anon sweep up the Swansea Valley, was by no means what it now is, when Madame Patti purchased it from its original owner, one of the "old ancient Powells, look you" whose patronymic is identified with the history of Glamorganshire. At that time it consisted simply of the *corps de logis*, a solid square building to which she has added two spacious wings, and which stood gloomily by itself in the centre of a picturesque wilderness of long cover and pasture land overlooking the Tawe and the opposite side of the valley, the Castle itself standing on a broad slab of rock about a hundred feet above the river-bed. The slope trending downwards from the house to the waterside has been converted into a series of turfed terraces, resembling a wide staircase of giant's steps covered with green velvet. These terraces are skirted at either end by winding gravelled paths with easy gradients, and are, moreover, traversed by one flight of steepish steps hewn out of the hill-side. The lowest terrace of all is merged in a beautiful lawn, level with the river-bank and studded here and there with flower-beds. A light iron bridge spans the river, and connects the castle grounds with a fine young plantation belonging to Madame Patti and bordered by a carefully rolled gravel-walk that follows the course of the swift stream for some hundreds of yards. A similar walk fringes the opposite river-bank, and leads past a long walled enclosure (containing kitchen-gardens, kennels, and a plantation or two of sapling Scotch firs) to a circular lake, well stocked with fish and fed by one of the many crystal brooks that flow into the Tawe hereabouts. This lovely walk, with the river—which just here forms two cascades, distant from one another about fifty yards—on its right, and the gleaming, glassy lake on its left, commands a supremely impressive view of the great valley, walled in on either side by round-topped hills, and seemingly blocked at its eastern end by one of the huge frowning Beacons.

The castle stands back about a hundred feet from the high road connecting Swansea with Brecon. From this thoroughfare it is separated by a pretty garden, square in shape and centred by a circular drive; all this portion of the grounds being enclosed in high stone walls, partly covered by creeper roses, jasmines, and ivy. As you pass through the massive arched gateway facing the main portal, the lodge and entrance to the stables are on your right hand, and on your left is a broad path leading to a large shrubbery and a pheasantry. Entering the house and ascending a double flight of stone steps you come to a hall running the whole length of the old *corps de logis*, luxuriously fitted up, and ornamented with oil-paintings, faïences, and cases of stuffed salmon and trout. Exactly opposite the entrance is the drawing-room door, flanked on either side by two masterpieces of wood-carving, representing a Florentine youth and maiden in fifteenth-century costume. To the right is the dining-room, built upon a lower level than that of the hall, and communicating at its further end with the superb wintergarden, of which more anon. To the left lie the billiard-rooms and music-gallery, Madame Patti's boudoir, a cosy little writing-room and the grand staircase leading to the upper part of the house, where those who happen to be but sparsely endowed with the organ of locality may readily lose their way amongst the successive corridors and quaint little round-the-corner stairs that meander hither and thither, amid suites of guest-chambers, in the distracting way peculiar to old country houses. Madame Patti's bedroom and dressing-room overlook the valley and are situate in the older portion of the castle. They deserve special mention and shall have it; meanwhile, before quitting generalities for details in this word-sketch of the Diva's home, I may mention that the house is lighted throughout with gas, manufactured on the estate, and that all the reception-rooms, including the winter-garden, are brilliantly illuminated by Swann and Edison's electric lamps, yielding a rich, soft, yellow radiance that never fatigues the eyes, whilst it shows off the beautiful furniture, art-decorations, pictures, and bric-à-brac to perfection. The force producing this delightful light is generated in an outbuilding divided from the conservatories, graperies, and peach-houses by a huge kitchen garden; the process is effected by the aid of a steam-engine of six-horse power consuming from six to seven tons of fuel per month. The castle is moreover warmed from basement to roof with hot air, by means of which an average temperature of from 60° to 65° Fahrenheit is maintained in all the corridors and passages as well as the residential rooms, each of which latter, however, is fitted with a powerful *calorifére*, intended to act as a substitute for the hot-air system, should the latter come to grief by any untoward mishap during the cold weather.

All the reception-rooms teem with *objets d'art* presented to Madame Patti by august and distinguished personages, as well as by her faithful and grateful friend, the public of Europe and America, during her long artistic career of triumphs unexampled and unparalleled. But the drawing-room and boudoir of Craig-y-Nos Castle are very museums of souvenirs personal to herself—of precious tributes of homage paid to her inimitable talent, of the affection inspired by her singular sweetness of nature, and of gratitude for the exquisite pleasure her unrivalled singing has afforded to millions of her fellow-creatures during a full third of the present century; for Adelina Patti has been a public singer since her eighth year, and her vocalisation was scarcely less marvellous, in its floridness, accuracy, and finish thirty-three years ago than it is at the present moment. In a bow-window recess of the drawing-room stands a magnificent bronze bust, hight "Time is Money," supported on either side by an elegant bronze vase of elaborate workmanship, presented to the *châtelaine* of Craig-y-Nos by admiring friends of New York. Ranged in glass cases set upon the mantel-shelf are a gorgeous laurel wreath, executed in massive gold, with a large star of brilliants as a pendant, a San Francisco offering; jewelled silvern goblets and huge loving cups in the precious metals, further tribute from the free-handed Pacific State; a horseshoe, splendidly mounted, which Madame Patti picked up on the shore of Salt Lake; and a golden olive-branch, two feet in length, upon each leaf of which is graven the title of an opera belonging to her *répertoire*. The priceless Italian and French cabinets that adorn the walls of this stately salon (the furniture of which, with the exception of some gorgeous presentation chairs, worked by the hands of *grandes dames de par le monde*, might be described in Whistlerian parlance as "a symphony in blue and silver") contain golden and silvern wreaths, offered by the publics of Paris, Vienna, Hamburg, Moscow, Florence and Milan; inimitable knick-knacks of all sorts, such as jewelled *étuis*, smelling-bottles, *nécessaires*, *châtelaines*, comfit-boxes, and ornaments for the head, neck, and waist. In the centre of the room, opposite an admirable *pastel* of Madame Patti, recently executed by the renowned Grispini, and standing by itself on a tall rosewood easel, is placed the colossal concert-grand piano, specially manufactured for and presented to Madame Patti by Steinway. It is the largest instrument of its class in the world, and unquestionably the finest upon which I have ever yet played. The huge table near it is heavily laden with photographic albums, filled with autographic portraits of all the more recent composers and executants, vocal and instrumental, whose names are household words to every musician throughout the wide world. No *maestro*, from Rossini down to Délibes, is missing from this collection, unique of its kind, and one of the Diva's most highly prized possessions. Her boudoir (pink and steel-grey) contains presentation portraits of the venerable German Emperor, the Czar and Czarina, the Princess of Wales, the late Duke of Albany, King Kalakaua, the King and Queen of Spain, Doña Ysobel de Borbon, and one or two of the Infantas, as well as of several other Imperial, Royal and Serene Highnesses. Some of these " counterfeit presentments" are set up in stands on a buhl cabinet crammed with golden and silvern wreaths—Madame Patti has received thirty of these costly offerings, and I may parenthetically remark that one who is poor though honest would rejoice with exceeding fervour were he endowed with her " portable property" in this particular direction *pour tout potage*—dainty Sévres and Dresden china, gemmed and hand-painted fans, each a *chef d'œuvre* of art, and countless other precious trifles, having no object in existence save to be beautiful, rare, and for the most part, worth a good deal more than their weight in gold.

Through the dining-room, the chief adornment of which is a three-quarter portrait of Madame Patti by Winterhalter, we pass into the winter-garden, a long range of lofty glass-houses fringing and overlapping the western wing of the castle, and affording a sufficient promenade for its denizens during wet weather, which occurs not infrequently in the Swansea Valley. This noble crystal gallery and the suite of conservatories adjoining it are *tapissés* with climbing exotics, amongst them several curious varieties of Labigeria, with their fancifully patterned leaves and great glowing scentless blossoms. From amongst this wealth of tropical foliage the electric lamps gleam forth here and there after dark like dazzling flowers, and light up the deep valley below, making Tawe's waters flash again as they ripple impetuously along. Words fail me to do justice to the magical effect produced by this glass reservoir of lambent light upon the wild scene of rock, wood, and water that faces Craig-y-Nos. It must be seen to be realised—once seen, it can never be forgotten. In the eastern wing of the castle are situate two vast billiard-rooms, communicating with one another, the first containing—besides a full-sized English table fitted with automatic bell-markers—a gigantic Geneva orchestrion, which plays fifty-two operatic overtures and selections with a spirit, force, and delicacy of expression that do infinite credit to its fabricators. At one end of the further billiard-room, the centre of which is occupied by an absolutely perfect French table, a broad music-gallery has been erected, in which stands an Erard full-grand of exceptionally fine tone and touch. Another interesting feature of this splendid room is a complete phonographic apparatus, into the ear of which Madame Patti sometimes warbles a sparkling roulade or crisp staccato; whereupon, a handle being rapidly turned, a weird, fairy voice, the miniature reproduction of her own wondrous organ, pipes out her *fiorture*, note for note and inflection for inflection, with truly surprising exactitude. It has been my privilege to inspect some of the art-treasures gathered together in Madame Patti's rooms on the first floor of the castle; they include a genuine Raffaelle, "The Virgin and Child," painted on panel; an ancient and singularly beautiful Russian Ikon, representing the head of Our Saviour; and an admirable *replica* of the immortal Madonna della Sedia. The *suite* itself is furnished throughout with tasteful elegance in pale blue satin and delicate lace. A mighty iron safe is let into the masonry of the thick stone wall fronting the grounds and river. In this fire-proof receptacle, within a few feet of her bedside, Madame Patti keeps such of her jewels, Imperial and Royal decorations, etc., as are not deposited with her London bankers. I have no idea how many *parures* of brilliants, emeralds, rubies, sapphires, pearls, and turquoises she possesses; perhaps she herself could scarcely tell without the aid of her faithful Caroline, who has charge of jewels equivalent in value to several princes' ransoms; but I know that, day after day, when she comes down to dinner, her throat, ears, and fingers are adorned by new splendours, and that every imaginable combination of precious stones would appear to have found a place in her collection of ornaments. Huge diamond butterflies and birds, presented to her by Emperors and Kings, Empresses and Queens, sparkle on her breast; enormous brilliant solitaires glitter with a thousand varied lights as they dangle from her dainty ears; great square emeralds and round sapphires, encircled by lustrous diamonds, glow upon her fair arms. Decked in these precious gauds and in the cunningest fabrics of the needle and the loom, herself far more bright and beautiful than them all, she looks like a Fairy Queen; and such, indeed, is the "Lady of the Castle," as the villagers for many a mile eastwards and westwards are wont to style her—the Good Fairy of the wild Welsh valley in which she has fixed her abode, and in which she has brought comfort and well-being to many a humble fireside, where, before her happy advent to the Rock of Night, poverty and privation sojourned *en permanence*.

The Queen of Song's castle on the Rock of Night is rather a large establishment for a nightingale's nest. During her annual term of residence—roughly speaking, six months of the twelve—Madame Patti keeps up a staff of servants forty-two in number, including three keepers, five gardeners, and two skilled mechanics, whose special charge is the generation of gas and electric light. This small host of dependants is governed by her two lieutenants, William Heck and Caroline Baumeister, both of German nationality and largely gifted with the many-sidedness that is a special characteristic of the middle-class Teuton. Heck doubles the part of bailiff with that of major-domo. He is an able agronome, accountant, and mechanician. He has all the complicated arrangements for lighting, heating, ventilating and sanitating Craig-y-Nos at his fingers' ends; he conducts the business correspondence of the estate and house. Three years ago Madame Patti purchased the superb orchestrion which she has christened " L'âme du château," and for which, I may mention, she paid three thousand guineas. It is an extremely intricate piece of machinery, and requires constant attention, being constructed with such extraordinary ingenuity that its capacity for getting out of order would appear to be unlimited. Heck, however, has mastered its innermost details so exhaustively that he is perfectly competent to treat any of its minor complaints with a thorough knowledge of their nature and the remedies they call for. Caroline Baumeister has charge of Madame Patti's wardrobe and jewels, keeps her accounts, and rules the female department at Craig-y-Nos with a firm and intelligent hand. She, as well as her colleague and compatriot, Heck, is absolutely devoted to the accomplished mistress of the castle, for whom, I am convinced, she would lay down her life at any moment, were she called upon to do so. As much may be said, and as truthfully, of another member of Madame Patti's household—a young Cuban woman named Patrocinia del Castillo, who has for some years past been attached to the Diva's person, and is likely to remain so as long as they both live. No sojourner under Madame Patti's roof can fail to observe with pleasure how devotedly she is served by all her dependants. On her part she treats them more like friends than like mere domestics. Their "ordinary" is as plentiful and succulent as her own; good sound claret is supplied to them *à discretion* during every week-day dinner, and champagne on Sundays. Honest and loyal service is generously acknowledged at Craig-y-Nos, so that all the elder members of the household have prospered exceedingly. I have heard it whispered that "Fraeulein Caro's" savings amount to something very comfortable, and that any one who should purchase her personal jewellery for a thousand guineas would make at least 50 per cent. profit by his bargain.

Throughout three months of the year—from the commencement of August to the end of October—the guest-chambers of Craig-y-Nos are seldom untenanted for more than twenty-four hours at a stretch. From the scenes of Madame Patti's past triumphs on the Continent and beyond seas broader than the British Channel—from

New York, Chicago and far San Francisco—from London and from our great provincial cities, her friends, old and new, succeed one another continuously in voyages of discovery having her hospitable castle for their goal. For the place is not altogether easy to get at, being respectively five and seven miles distant from the two railway stations nearest to it, both situate on the Swansea Valley line, a single, outlying thread of the South Wales network of iron roads. One of these stations, Ystelafera by name, may be most conveniently reached from Swansea, the western terminus of the line in question; the other, yclept Cray, is readily approachable from Brecon Junction on the Midland line. In the whole region intervening between these stations—mere sheds, tenanted by solitary officials, cumulative as regard their functions—and Craig-y-Nos no vehicular means of transport exists, save and except the carriages of the castle; wherefore Madame Patti's visitors are absolutely dependent upon her for the wherewithal to reach or quit her home among the mountains. A level piece of road in the Swansea valley is about as rare as an Alp in the Mark Brandenburg; consequently, the Craig-y-Nos horses find it but a sorry jest to convey batches of guests and mountains of luggage backwards and forwards over the hilly highways, ever being mended but never in thorough repair, that connect the Rock of Night with the slender streaks of steel tapering off Swansea-wards to the west and Brecon-wards to the east. Once arrived at the Rock, however, after eighty minutes' drive by either route through a country whose strange wildness and gloom I have already endeavoured to describe, the difficulty of attaining that haven of rest is speedily forgotten in a sense of luxurious comfort, and in admiration of the intelligence and good-taste that have so judiciously applied great wealth to the creation of a sort of fairy palace in the very heart of a desolate Welsh vale, seventeen miles from a newspaper or a fishmonger's shop, and half that distance from the nearest country-seat—a circumstance, by the way, which all but cuts off Madame Patti from social intercourse with her country neighbours, owing to the steep gradients and generally heavy character of the roads. Her visitors, for the most part, come to her from the remote world of art, literature, and intellectual activity, with the thoughts and sympathies of which the simple valley-folk amongst whom she lives her holiday-life are as profoundly unacquainted as though they were inhabitants of Georgium Sidus.

Daily existence at Craig-y-Nos Castle is a practical refutation of the familiar French axiom "Les jours se suivent et ne se ressemblent pas." Such, at least, has been my experience of more than one sojourn within its walls. My visits, however, have always been paid late in the autumn, when the days are short and the evenings shivery. In sultry August, doubtless "truly rural" resources of pastime are more available than in chill October. But the routine of the castle, when I have been staying there, has invariably been as follows. Madame Patti's guests are served with their first breakfast in their own apartments, and at what hour they may please to indicate. She herself passes her mornings in her special snuggery overlooking the Tawe and Pen-y-Bwlth, a copse-girdled, bald-browed hill that faces the Rock of Night from the opposite side of the valley. It is during these forenoon hours, and then only, that she exercises her voice, chiefly with chromatic scales and *staccati;* at other times she does not sing in her own house, though she may often be heard dashing off a *roulade* or warbling a *trillo* in her incomparable fashion as she trips about the corridors. Executant music, indeed—always excepting that performed by the gigantic orchestrion every evening—is not *à la mode* at Craig-y-Nos; for the *châtelaine* hears more than enough of it, of her own and of other artists' making, during the eight months of the year which she devotes to professional work. Who can wonder that she should seek respite and nepenthe from her memories of operas and concerts in an annual holiday, exempt, or nearly so, from vocalisation and pianism? There are four pianos at Craig-y-Nos, each a *chef d'œuvre* in its kind; but, even when Madame Patti's guests have included as many first-class performers as the instruments she owns, I have known day after day pass without one of the latter being opened. This *par parenthèse*. At noon precisely—up to which hour their time is unrestrictedly at their own disposal—all the Diva's guests are expected to assemble in the huge glass *annexe* adjoining the dining-room, where "breakfast at the fork," artistically prepared by M. Justin, the *cordon-bleu* of the castle, is served in princely style. To partake of perfectly cooked food and *premiers crus* in a lofty crystal hall, thoroughly warmed, perfumed by exotic flowers, and commanding a superb panorama of mountain, valley, wood and water, is a circumstance productive of highly pleasurable sensations. It promotes cheerfulness of spirit, and a fine indifference to the quality of the weather outside. The one daily delivery of letters and newspapers comes off when coffee and liqueurs are brought in at the close of this superlative meal; and a soothing hour is passed with the aid of cigarettes, small-talk, and the latest London and Paris news. At two precisely a string of landaus, phaetons and dog-carts makes its appearance on the broad, curved sweep of gravel fronting the grand entrance; and the whole party of guests, told off into *côteries* of three or four and led by their hostess in her pony-carriage, is whirled away to some romantic spot, a dozen miles or so distant, where all alight and take a "constitutional" on the Queen's highway whilst the horses are rested and baited. Refreshment for man, as well as for beast, accompanies these afternoon expeditions in the shape of biscuits, fruits, and pleasing liquids of various descriptions. At five o'clock the *cortège* again draws up before the castle doors, and everybody retires to his or her room—where tea is served—until dinner-time, sharp seven, when the electric light is turned on, and the great mansion assumes a highly festive aspect. Madame Patti's boudoir, adjacent to the English billiard-room, is the place of general rendezvous in which her friends assemble punctually as the second gong is sounded. To them she descends, arrayed in a ravishing toilette—I have never yet seen her twice in the same dress—and adorned with gleaming jewels, which set off her dark beauty to admiration. Dinner at Craig-y-Nos is the sort of meal that would have secured the approval of Lucullus, when that accomplished epicure dined with himself. Again a cheerful frame of mind becomes manifest in the *convives* gathered round Madame Patti's table. Coffee is served in the French billiard-room, whither all hands repair at the close of this ineffable repast; for men do not sit over their wine, telling highly-flavoured stories, at Craig-y-Nos, *modo anglicano*, but "take out their ladies" *à la française* in the same processional order as that observed during the previous transit from boudoir to dining-room. Whilst the post-prandial cigar is aglow, "the soul of the castle" (as Madame Patti has nicknamed her mighty orchestrion) plays overtures, operatic selections and dance-music for an hour or so; after which the great event of the evening—a "sport" called Ladies' Pool—comes off on the fine match-table in the English billiard-room. This game is a novel and, for persons of the sterner sex, somewhat tantalising version of pyramids. As its name denotes, it has been devised for the exclusive diversion of "ministering angels." The exhilarating privilege of pocketing a ball or balls is reserved for those who double our joys and halve our sorrows. Lovely woman has it all her own way, as usual; but something more conspicuously than is her wont. No male player may make a winning hazard; or, if he be so ill-advised as to commit that offence, the ball he has holed is ignominiously replaced upon the upper spot, and he is severely reprimanded for having retarded the progress of the game. His only legitimate, though distinctly humiliating function—one which, if he be a true pool-player at heart, fills his soul with rage and mortification every time he makes a stroke—is to leave his object-ball in the very jaws of some pocket, so that the lady whose devoted jackal he is for the time being may be enabled to hole it with a minimum of skill and effort. This maddening reversal of the whole purpose and intent of the noble game of pool is apt, I have observed with pain, to conjure a big, big D not infrequently to the lips of the masculine martyrs called upon to put it in practice. Imagine the horror and remorse of an expert whist-player, condemned by some hideous law to trump his partner's best card in the very trick upon which the fate of the rubber depends! No less poignant is the anguish that racks the breast of the male participant in Ladies' Pool every time he complies with the malignant regulations of that abominable game. I played it nightly for a fortnight at Craig-y-Nos, thereby, I shrewdly fear, prejudicing the prospects of my immortal part to no inconsiderable extent. Fortunately, it never lasted long; for the axiom "Early to bed" has the force of a statute in Madame Patti's realm, the denizens of which are expected to retire for the night at eleven P.M. An hour later the gas—and with it the electric light—is turned off at the main, and darkness, save for the glimmer of a stray candle here and there, reigns throughout the castle. One of the parrots—there are three of these fowl on the premises, all "full of excellent differences"—is privileged to have a night-light in his bedroom, it being an idiosyncrasy of this particular bird (Cooky by name) to fall off his perch when asleep. It would appear that he cannot see in the dark, contrary to the custom of his kind; consequently, when he tumbles down, he requires a light to enable him to regain the exact position in his cage which he is accustomed to occupy during his slumbers. He is, moreover, gravely suspected of being afraid of ghosts; so the rule of the castle with respect to the extinction of all lights at midnight is waived in his favour. The other parrots, Jumbo and Charlie, sleep in the dark. They are less nervous birds than Cooky, and seldom suffer from nightmare. Besides, Cooky is Madame Patti's prime favourite. If she thought a whole chandelier-full of lighted wax candles, perfumed with ambergris, would contribute to his bodily ease and mental tranquillity, that article would certainly figure in his sleeping-chamber; whereas her affection for Jumbo and Charlie is of a calmer and less absorbing character. Yet Jumbo is a highly-gifted parrot, gifted with fluent and appropriate speech, and with extraordinary powers of mimicry. He is considerably older and wilier than Cooky, and takes an intensely practical view of life, whilst Cooky is sentimental and impulsive. I regret to say that gluttony is a leading characteristic of the latter bird, who would pawn his birthright for a cold boiled potato, floury to the core. Jumbo also loves this particular dainty well; but his greater self-control prompts him to consume it deliberately and with due observance of social decorum. Charlie is a bird of great beauty. His livery is not sober grey, turned up with scarlet, like that of Cooky and Jumbo; but gorgeous green and gold, shot here and there with blue and red of different shades. Despite this splendid array, he is a gloomy cynic, for the most part brooding over imaginary wrongs, and severely resentful of any delicate attentions in the nature of "Scratch a poll, poor Polly!" I have never met a more saturnine or less sycophantic fowl. All Madame Patti's choicest blandishments fail to soften his rugged nature, or even to unsettle for a moment his sullen imperturbability. He is the Timon of parrots.

This brief word-sketch of the Nightingale's Nest and its inmates would be curiously incomplete and unsatisfactory did it not set forth some details of interest relating to the distinctions and gifts bestowed upon Madame Adelina Patti by those born in purple, as well as to the treasures, artistic and literary, of which Craig-y-Nos Castle is the repository. The name of these treasures is legion; they form a collection, a *catalogue raisonné* of which—such as might be drawn up by a very superior kind of auctioneer with the assistance of the Court Newsman—setting forth all their special attractions would fill many pages of this book. Such mention as I am permitted to make of them here must necessarily be somewhat cursory and incomplete. Craving indulgence for certain unavoidable shortcomings, let me address myself to my task without further preface, animated by that inflexible sense of duty which prompted the immortal Captain Reece, R.N., "commanding of the *Mantlepiece*," to marry his washerwoman.

First and foremost in the estimation of its gifted owner, as well as in its own intrinsic interest, comes Madame Adelina Patti's autographic album—an oblong volume bound in dark leather and fitted with a patent lock, the tiny golden key of which, confided to the keeping of Fraeulein Caro, is only produced from time to time by that functionary, in compliance with special request, for the behoof of those whom her mistress delighteth to honour. The book contains about sixty *souvenirs* of eminent musicians, dead and living, composers and executants; *souvenirs* taking the various forms of stanzas, sonnets, epigrams in verse and prose, and of musical *motivi* or *cadenze*, set down in manuscript notation by the greatest *maestri* of the past quarter of a century. The only name of supreme renown uninscribed on the pages of this interesting album is that of the late Richard Wagner, none of whose fatiguing soprano *rôles* (fortunately for her voice) Madame Patti ever undertook to impersonate, a circumstance which probably accounts for the absence of his autograph from her *recueil* of composers' signatures. On opening the book, the first *paraphe* that meets your eye is that of Emilio Naudin, the famous Parmesan tenor, with whom Adelina Patti sang shortly after her *début* in Europe, and who, as far back as the year 1863, has recorded in black and white his conviction that her vocalisation, when she was only just out of her teens, was inimitable. The next signature, appended to a few lines manifestly dictated by affectionate admiration, is that of the ever to be lamented Mario, Conte di Candia, with whom Madame Patti maintained an unbroken friendship for more than twenty years. Many important contributions were made to the album during the year 1864; for instance, a few bars of the great bravura air from *Il Barbiere*, written by the hand of Gioachino Rossini; an excerpt from the *Pardon de Plöermel*, in the MS. of Jacob Meyerbeer; scraps of music, poetry, and prose, subscribed by the composers Hector Berlioz, Stephen Heller, Michael Costa, Vincent

Wallace, and Michael Balfe, and by the following vocalists of the "first flight"—Giulia Grisi, Marietta Alboni, Theresa Tietjens, Constance Nantier-Didiée, Theodor Wachtel, Antonio Giuglini, Italo Gardoni, Giorgio Ronconi, Tamberlick, Sims Reeves, Charles Santley, and Brignoli. For grace of *tournure* and happiness of thought, the epigram inscribed by Hector Berlioz, in bold, square characters, that contrast so vigorously with the careless caligraphy of many of his fellow-composers, is the literary gem of the year abovementioned. It runs thus:—

"Oportet *pati*."
Les latinistes traduisent cet adage par
"Il faut souffrir;"—
Les moines par
"Apportez le pâté;"
Les amis de la musique par
"Il nous faut Patti."

HECTOR BERLIOZ.

The honoured names of Arabella Goddard and Luigi Arditi are also included in the list of autographs with which 1864 enriched Madame Patti's album. That of Stigelli—Georg Stiegele, the accomplished Wuertemberg tenor and song-writer—is the only one of conspicuous mark contributed during the ensuing year; but 1866 is distinguished by an inscription and musical excerpt under the sign-manual of Maestro Verdi, whose intense appreciation of Madame Patti's talent finds expression in a sentence unmistakably inspired by genuine enthusiasm. Like Rossini before him, he appears to entertain the conviction that Adelina Patti was brought into the world for the express and exclusive purpose of interpreting the creations of his genius to absolute perfection; and I have been told that on one occasion, an *impresario* having written to him asking for the names of the three *cantatrici* who, in his opinion, were best qualified, as actresses and singers alike, to impersonate Violetta (*La Traviata*), he replied laconically: " First, Adelina; second, Adelina; third, Adelina." Beneath his entry in the album, and on the same page, stand autographic tributes of homage and friendship from that gifted artist, Madame Trebelli, and her genial husband, the lyric tenor, Signor Bettini. Next in succession come the signatures of Tamburini, Calzolari, Cotogni, and Bottesini, followed by four inestimable autographs, not one of which, however, is dated. That of Daniel Auber is appended to a few bars of the overture to *Fra Diavolo*, and a line or two of unstinted laudation; Charles Gounod has set down in obvious haste the *motivo* of the garden-duet from *Faust* " to recall himself to the remembrance of inimitable Adelina; " Christine Nilsson records her "devoted friendship for the songstress queen" on the next page, and the lamented Julius Benedict contributes a carefully turned compliment to the *châtelaine* of Craig-y-Nos, written in the album during his last sojourn at the castle, some four or five years ago, when his eyesight was so seriously affected that, for the time being, he was practically blind. I was staying at the house that autumn—it was not very long after his second marriage—and well remember the tender care and absolute devotion lavished upon the septuagenarian *maestro* by his gifted and attractive young wife. The king of oculists, Critchett, subsequently wrought a miracle in his behalf, and restored his sight; but, at the period I allude to, Benedict believed himself doomed to total and life-long blindness, and his straggling, laboured autograph in Madame Patti's album bears touching testimony to the nature and extent of a calamity which he endured with singular fortitude, and even cheerfulness, although it threatened his old age with poverty, and with what appeared to him still more terrible—enforced idleness.

Another interesting screed in the Diva's collection is the opening phrase of the famous *Fledermaus* waltz, jotted down and signed by its composer, Johann Strauss. Braga, too, has written in a dozen bars or so of his "Chanson Valaque," with the 'cello obbligato, which ran through every concert-room in Europe about a decade ago. Two rival "heroic tenors," Niemann and Capoul, outvie each other in offerings of flattering homage—the German in verse, the Frenchman in prose—on successive pages of the album; and hard by their passionate effusions may be found the MS. of an original song, composed at Craig-y-Nos last year, and dedicated to the "Schlossherrin," by Kapellmeister Wilhelm Ganz, one of Madame Patti's most faithful and trusted friends in the musical profession. Besides the souvenirs more particularly mentioned in the foregoing lines, the album contains verses by Spanish, Russian, French, and Italian poets, and a good many autographs of minor interest. Enough, however, has been already said to demonstrate its extraordinary value as a probably unique *recueil* of its kind. Not even the honorific distinctions and costly gems bestowed upon Madame Patti by the rulers of mighty nations bear such incontrovertible testimony to the paramount quality of her executant gifts as do the spontaneous outpourings of the enthusiasm those gifts and their application have aroused in the breasts of such mighty musicians as Berlioz, Verdi, Meyerbeer, Rossini, Gounod, and Auber, who, one and all, have recognised in Adelina Patti the greatest songstress of the past quarter of a century.

As, to the best of my belief, an absolutely complete list of the parts studied and committed to memory by Madame Patti in the course of her career as an operatic singer has never heretofore been brought to public cognizance, it seems to me fairly probable that the following summary of her *répertoire*, which I have taken down from her own lips, will be perused with no inconsiderable interest by my readers. I should, perhaps, premise that I have indicated, by prefixing a star to certain titles of operas in the subjoined list, those *rôles* which Madame Patti has at different times found herself called upon to learn, and even rehearse, but which—owing to one untoward circumstance or another—she has never performed in public:—

Verdi:—*Traviata, Trovatore, Ernani, Rigoletto, Aïda, Luisa Miller, Giovanna d'Arco, *Vespere Siciliane, *Ballo in Maschera.*

Rossini:—*Barbiere di Siviglia, Semiramide, Gazza Ladra, Otello, Mosé in Egitto.*

Donizetti:—*Lucia di Lammermoor, Don Pasquale, L'Elisir d'Amore, Figlia del Reggimento, Linda di Chamouni.*

Meyerbeer:—*Les Huguenots, L'Etoile du Nord, Le Pardon de Plöermel,* **Robert le Diable.*

Bellini:—*La Sonnambula, I Puritani.*

Mozart:—*Nozze di Figaro, Don Giovanni,* **Il Flauto Magico.*

Gounod:—*Faust, Romeo et Juliette, Mireille.*

Auber:—*Les Diamans de la Couronne,* **Fra Diavolo.*

Poniatowski:—*Gelmina, Don Desiderio.*

Bizet:—*Carmen.* Flotow:—*Martha.* Ricci:—*Crispino e la Comare.* Campana:—*Esmeralda,* Lenepveu:—*Velléda.* Cohen:—*Estrella.*

In all forty-seven operas, in the leading parts of which she is "note-perfect," and forty-two in which she has actually appeared upon the operatic stage. Many of the above *rôles* she has sung in French, as well as in Italian, and is fully qualified, were she required to do so, to render them in Spanish, German, or our own vernacular, all which tongues she speaks with remarkable facility and purity of accent.

Amongst the Imperial and Royal decorations and gifts of jewellery, *longum describere*, bestowed upon Madame Patti in acknowledgment of her great acquirements as a vocalist I may mention a few which are invested with special interest in connection with their donors as well as with their recipient. The late Czar Alexander Nicolaievich, of whose kindness to her Madame Patti has innumerable anecdotes to relate, conferred upon her the Russian Gold Medal for Proficiency in the Arts and Sciences, set in magnificent brilliants and suspended by an Imperial Crown in diamonds to the riband of St. Alexander Nevski —an Order of Chivalry corresponding in rank to the

Garter, Golden Fleece, and Annunziata. Madame Patti is also the proud possessor of a somewhat out-of-the-way decoration, as Knightly Orders go—that founded by the Royal Kalakaua, King of the *ci-devant* Cannibal Islands, whose full-length portrait adorns the blue boudoir in Craig-y-Nos Castle. I believe the correct style and title of this Island Potentate's Order to be "Kulia i Kannu," whatever that may mean. It is an eight-pointed cross, executed in crimson enamel and gold, of a somewhat barbaric gorgeousness. A five-pointed star, formed of thirty large brilliants of exceptional whiteness and lustre, which Madame Patti frequently wears when *en grande toilette*, looks as if it ought to be the symbol of some "Exalted" or "Most Illustrious" Order. It is, however, only a token of regard presented to her by the citizens of San Francisco on the occasion of her last visit to California. From Maria Pia, Queen of Portugal and own sister to Humbert of Italy, Madame Patti has received a massive locket, containing Her Majesty's portrait, and enriched by an enormous Oriental pearl encrusted in brilliants; from Queen Victoria a valuable diamond bracelet; from Ysobel de Borbon, whilom Queen of Spain, a huge amethyst *solitaire* set in pearls and diamonds, and a pair of superb ruby earrings. Every imaginable sort of ornament in precious stones has been presented to her by members of the Hohenzollern, Romanoff and Hapsburg Imperial families, quite as much at one in loading her with trinkets as in maintaining the integrity of the Triple Alliance. For the information of the fairer moiety of my readers (those of the sterner sex are requested to skip the remaining lines of this paragraph)

I may add that Madame Adelina Patti's collection of jewels—for the most part consisting of gifts from august personages or testimonials offered to her by the general public—comprises five diadems of brilliants, five *rivières* of brilliants, six complete *parures* (*i.e.* necklace, earrings, bracelets, brooch and ring) executed in (1) brilliants; (2) emeralds and brilliants; (3) rubies and brilliants; (4) sapphires and brilliants; (5) pearls and brilliants; (6) turquoises and brilliants. Of "casual" rings, brooches, bracelets, earrings, and jewelled pins, not forming part of any particular set, she owns scores upon scores. Amongst her miscellaneous ornaments are half-a-dozen gigantic diamond bees, butterflies, and beetles, each one of them worth a good deal more money than the "three acres and a cow" with which Hodge has recently been tempted to essay a new political departure; several parures of pale and deep red Neapolitan coral, of glowing carbuncles, of rococo "arrangements" in gold and gems of many colours, and of antique camei and intagli. To her vast collection of "curios" I have already alluded, omitting, however, to mention a silvern double-barrelled pistol, richly encrusted with precious stones, two sets of rare old golden and *cloisonné* cups from Moscow and Tula, a couple of embossed trowels with which the Diva has on two occasions patted lumps of wet mortar in the process of laying first-stones, golden *medailles d'honneur* by the dozen, and, finally, no end of diplomas, triumphs of calligraphic dexterity cunningly engrossed upon creamy vellum or milk-white parchment, and recording Madame Patti's active or honorary connection with musical institutions in every part of the civilised world. One of these documents, handsomely framed, occupies a post of honour in the castle library, between two excellent likenesses of the *châtelaine* and Signor Nicolini, and over against a fine portrait of Mr. Joseph Bennett, the eminent essayist and musical critic. It is the grand diploma of the Philharmonic Academy of Bologna, certifying that Madame Adelina Patti is the only female member of that illustrious corporation. She is not a little proud of possessing this brevet, unique as regards musicians of her sex ; indeed, she has reason to regard Bologna with especial affection and gratitude, for one of its theatres bears her name, and the date of her first appearance on the stage of the old Œmilian capital is recorded for all time to come on a marble tablet let into one of the walls of the Teatro Comunale, to my mind the best opera-house in all Italy.

If in the foregoing pages I have succeeded in conveying to my readers some idea of those " outward and visible signs" which point to the results actually achieved by the talent, industry, and perseverance of a woman still in the prime of life, who, in the course of her artistic career, has earned over half a million sterling by singing and acting, I have done what I aspired to do when I commenced this chapter, and am content.

CHAPTER X.

MUSIC IN THEATRES AND AL FRESCO.

In no executive branch of the musical art has a more striking and general advancement been achieved in this metropolis within the past quarter of a century than in that portion of theatrical entertainments which consists of orchestral performances, such as may be heard every night in any London theatre, agreeably prefacing the play or plays on the bill of the evening, and, in one or two instances, making the *entr'actes*, or "waits," even more recreative to the audience than the stage business itself. A good band is nowadays well nigh as essential an attraction to a metropolitan playhouse as a good acting company; and the former may be counted upon by the public with even more confidence than the latter, taking one theatre with another. Formerly—let us say from twenty-five to thirty years ago—this was far from being the case. Managers—more especially those of the minor theatres—provided " music " for their patrons, in compliance with a custom even then firmly established in London alone, of all European capitals; but the "music" in question, as a rule, was curiously trivial in character and feeble in execution, when not actually offensive to those among the audience who happened, for their sins, to be endowed with sensitive ears. Operetta, at the time I refer to, had not taken up the high standing in popular favour which it now enjoys, and the demands made upon theatrical orchestras in the matter of accompaniment to the voice were insignificant compared to those of the present day; but even in houses devoted to the performance of extravaganzas, and styling themselves "the home of burlesque," the bands were as a rule at once weak and coarse, scrapy fiddling and obtrusive cornet-blowing being their leading characteristics. The orchestras at the two opera-houses were then the only theatrical bands that could justly claim to be excellent; that of the Princess's (then under the management of Charles Kean, who conscientiously endeavoured to make every item of his programme as good as possible of its kind) was a fairly efficient one, most intelligibly led by Mr. J. L. Hatton, whose incidental music to the Kean revivals and novelties was for several successive years a conspicuous feature of those admirable entertainments. But musicians who remember the wheezy and squeaky debility of the band at the Haymarket when one of the finest companies ever gathered together on London boards was playing Shakespeare at that theatre, or even later, under the Buckstone *régime;* the slovenly roughness of the accompaniments at the Strand, in the palmy days (as far as acting and dancing were concerned) of Marie Wilton and Elise Holt, Clarke and Rogers; the deeds of darkness, from a musical point of view, that were perpetrated with string, wood, and brass at the Olympic, what time the inimitable Robson succeeded for a time in breaking the traditional ill-luck of that dingy little house, and at the Adelphi, during the reign of the king of melodrama, the late Benjamin Webster, whose like we shall not look upon again; those, I repeat, who can still recall to mind the musical accessories to theatrical performances of the period intervening between the Crimean War and the Napoleonic campaign in Lombardy will not hesitate to admit that the artistic progress effected in the training and utilisation of instrumental executants in the minor London theatres is little less than surprising.

As a matter of fact the theatrical bands of this metropolis can stand comparison, favourably to themselves, with those of any Continental city. I venture to make this assertion somewhat confidently, having, in the course of the past twenty years, attended every imaginable sort of theatrical performance in all the countries of Europe, except the Scandinavian kingdoms and the Hellenic realm. There be opera-houses on the other side of the silvery streak, enjoying no inconsiderable reputation as musical institutions, and considered inimitable by their local frequenters, of which the orchestras are, in more than one respect, inferior to those of the "Comedy," the "Empire," or even the "Alhambra," before the last-named theatre reverted to its original condition as a music-hall. Of course bands engaged to play ballet music and the accompaniments of comic opera, operetta, etc., are expected to be of a quality superior to that of the average theatrical orchestra. But the latter, in London at least, has attained so high a standard as to leave little to be desired. The bands at Drury Lane, the Lyceum, Haymarket, Princess's, Gaiety and Criterion discourse excellent music nightly; and the orchestral interludes at the Court, arranged with exquisite taste, and conducted with consummate skill by Carl Armbruster (of whom, three years ago, Hans Richter said to me, "I do not know throughout the length and breadth of Germany a better musician or cleverer conductor") constitute by no means the least attraction of that admirably managed house. Even at theatres of more modest pretensions in the orchestral line, such as the Vaudeville, Adelphi, and Strand, the musical performances are every whit as good as those of the Paris Variétés or Berlin Wallner and Friedrich Wilhelm, although the bands of the latter theatres claim to belong to the specifically operatic category. In short, it is at present as difficult to pick out a thoroughly bad theatrical orchestra in London as it was to discover a thoroughly good one five-and-twenty years ago.

This huge conglomeration of cities, the capital of the most powerful and extensive Empire the world has ever known, covering as much ground as a minor German Principality, and numbering more inhabitants than one or two full-blown kingdoms of my acquaintance, not only lacks a national opera-house, but does not even own a theatre specially affected to the performance of classical tragedy and comedy. Paris has her Théâtre Français, Berlin her Schauspielhaus, Vienna her Burgtheater, in all of which the works of the most eminent dramatists, living and dead, are played in a highly authoritative and complete manner by companies remarkable for their general efficiency rather than for superlative excellence in any of their individual members. London possesses no Thespian temple hallowed thus to the cult of the legitimate drama; even a combination of the Lyceum and Haymarket, as they have functioned for some years past under the Irving and Bancroft managements, would not yield a theatrical concretion equivalent to that afforded by any one of the above-named establishments, in which melodramas such as *The Bells* and *The Lyons Mail*, or nondescript absurdities of the *Lords and Commons* class could not, under existing circumstances, possibly obtain representation. But, whereas music is an integral and indispensable element of recreation, as that commodity is supplied to the London public by theatrical managers, the classical subventioned houses of continental capitals require no "concords of sweet sounds" to round off and relieve the entertainments they provide for their clients. It is held by many persons exercising recognised authority with respect to the "fitness of things" in Germany, as well as in France, that the interruption of a dramatic unity by musical interludes, for the most part irrelevant to the story or fundamental thought (*Grundidee*) of the piece, or whose relevancy thereto, at the best, is disputable and therefore distracting, is a barbarism not to be tolerated by properly trained and justly balanced intelligences; that such interruption breaks the thread of artistic continuity which should run without a hitch or tangle throughout the performance, and is calculated to jerk the spectator's train of thought off the rails; finally, that music in connection with the drama, unless interwoven with the dialogue and made essential to the action by the express intention and will of the author, is an anachronism and incongruity unworthy alike of an æsthetic management and a thoughtful, conscientious public. There is another reason, less high-sounding, but a good deal more to the point than any of the foregoing ones, why the Intendants of the "classical" theatres in Paris, Berlin, Vienna, and other great continental cities taboo music from their programmes. An orchestra is a costly item in a theatrical *menu*, involving an outlay that swallows up the income to be derived from the sale of a goodly number of stalls and dress-circle seats; whereas the three knocks with which the prompter or call-boy announces the proximate "pull up" of the curtain to the audience entail no extra expense whatsoever upon the *impresa*. I apprehend that sagacious thrift has prompted the guiding spirits of the dramatic institutions in question to indoctrinate the public in the theory that, just as good wine needs no bush, so good theatrical performances need not the adventitious aid of music to enhance their attractiveness. Use is second nature; and I doubt not that the habitués of the Français, the Hofburg, and the Schauspielhaus (who differ in many essential respects from the all-round theatre-goers of the French, Austrian and German capitals) would be painfully shocked were so frivolous an innovation as an orchestra adopted by the dramatic establishments in which they are accustomed to pass their evenings with the proud consciousness that they are combining instruction with recreation.

Although our fellow-Europeans on the other side of the Channel, no matter to what variety of the Caucasian race they may happen to belong, persistently refuse to admit that we are a musical people, it is very certain that any London manager who should venture to eliminate incidental music from his entertainments would have good reason to regret so ill-judged an experiment. Whether they pay any attention to the feats of the orchestra or not, English audiences expect to be supplied with some sort of instrumental performance between the acts, and would assuredly resent its omission as an unjustifiable slight. The patrons of melodrama, cispontine as well as transpontine, still cling fondly to the tradition that crime requires to be accompanied on the strings, *tremolando* and *alla sordina*, and that fiddles cannot do less than shiver sympathetically when the gas is turned down in preparation for a deed of blood or a spectral manifestation. We are a sentimental and a sensation-loving people, and delight in any ocular or oral effect that helps to pile up the agony of a powerful "situation." Deferring to the exigencies of this national characteristic, actors of high intellectual culture and keen artistic perception like Henry Irving and Wilson Barrett do not deem it inconsistent with the dignity of dramatic art to emphasise sensational episodes—even in Shakesperian plays—by "mysterious music" compounded according to the most approved recipes for that class of orchestral stimulant. To my mind this is a custom more honoured in the breach than in the observance: but managers should know their own business best, and if men who have served the true interests of the drama, as well as their own, so strenuously and loyally as the lessees of the Lyceum and Princess's theatres deem it necessary, or even expedient, to comply with old-established usage in relation to such anachronistic but trivial details as tremulous chords and subdued stage illumination of any particular hue, doubtless they have good solid reasons for practising these and other cognate tricks of the *ad captandum* kind. The public at large owes them a debt of gratitude for treating its transmitted prejudices with such kindly consideration; and a far larger meed of thankfulness for the increased excellence of the musical fare which they and other enterprising London managers have provided for it " since this old hat was new."

In the matter of open-air music, we Englishmen are heavily handicapped by our perfidious and malignant climate. The seasons, in this country, are jumbled up together anyhow, and cannot in the least be relied upon with relation to any prospective social arrangements. Sometimes our finest weather comes off in the winter months, and summer disgraces itself by playing ghastly practical jokes upon us in the shape of snowfalls, cold winds, hail, rain, and that hurly-burly of meteorological conditions in general which the Germans, in their fine figurative way, are wont to attribute to family differences between the Devil and his Grandmother. Not infrequently May might be January or November; were it not for the young green leaves that tell an undeniable spring story, no little ingenuity would be requisite to divine that a combination of east wind, frigid sleet, lowering skies, and soaking slush, lasting from a fortnight to three weeks, correctly represents the month of transition from Thomson's " ethereal mildness " to Arnold's " lusty June." By reason of the dreadful uncertainty which chronically haunts us respecting the intentions of the weather, we are precluded, even at high summer-tide, from making definite arrangements in connection with out-of-door recreations which do not involve athletic effort or pecuniary speculation. In other lands, as northern as our own, where the seasons display a certain sense of order and decorum, proprietors of public gardens are enabled, year after year, when the buds begin to crack their cases and the birds have done their courting, to advertise *al fresco* instrumental performances at stated intervals throughout the warm months—say, from May 1 to September 30—with a tolerable certainty that they will not be prevented from fulfilling their pledges to their patrons by any untimely marvel in the nature of a transposition of the seasons. In the famous Volksgarten, at Vienna, Edward Strauss's inimitable stringed orchestra, or some scarcely less renowned military band, such as that of the Kœnig von Wuertemberg regiment—equally efficient with strings or brass and wood—plays every evening in the open during the summer, except when a thunderstorm drives musicians and audience alike for shelter into a straggling wood and glass shanty which stands hard by for their accommodation. There are bands on Sundays and holidays—that is, about four times a week throughout the pleasant time of the year—at the three Kaffeehaeuser, or chief refreshment-stations of the Prater, at the Neue Welt in Hietzing, and at cognate establishments in the other great suburbs: good military bands, if you please, not scratch orchestras like those to which one listens with dismay in English watering-places and the minor German Bad-Orte. I am speaking quite within limits when I say that a dozen such bands play for public amusement in Vienna every summer Sunday; and yet the Kaiserstadt can only boast of twelve hundred thousand inhabitants as against London's five millions. At Berlin, similar provision is made for the diversion of the Emperor's lieges, partly by the State and partly by private enterprise. From April to October, the splendid Kapelle of the Guard-Cuirassiers is engaged for Saturday Concerts at the Zoo on the Spree, where thousands of people belonging to the middle and upper classes dine *sub Jove*, to the accompaniment of a most excellent "concourse of sweet sounds." Every afternoon the spacious and romantic Thiergarten resounds with the strains of military music, performed by one or other of the garrison bands in the Hofjaeger-Allée, or—on Corso days, when society airs its high-well-born attractions on horseback and in open carriages—in the stately Kaiser-Allée itself, at the northern end of which the ugliest monument in the world rears its hideous head—the Sieges-Denkmal, or Memorial of Victory, upon which no Frenchman can gaze without feeling that his country's defeats and humiliation are amply avenged. At the Eiskeller, a vast beer-garden in the Dorotheen-Stadt; at the Tivoli Brewery, near the Kreuzberg, a mild sand-hill overlooking the southern suburbs of Berlin; and at half-a-dozen other resorts of a similar character, Saturday and Sunday afternoons and evenings are enlivened by admirable orchestral performances which, I need scarcely say, draw crowds of customers to the establishments in which they take place; for the average German's ideal of enjoyment—a very harmless and reasonable one, as human pleasures go—is to sit in a garden where he can eat and drink at a moderate figure, with dance-music and operatic selections thrown in, "free, gratis and for nothing." The amount of thin, cool beer that he—and she, too—will imbibe in the course of such an *al fresco* concert as any of those above referred to would amaze the majority of untravelled English men and women. I have more than once watched the feats of young girls belonging to the *haute bourgeoisie*—what Mr. Yellowplush might have defined as the "hupper suckles" with singular appropriateness, in subtle allusion to their powers of absorption—wonder-stricken and admiring, whilst they swallowed eight imperial pints of Schwechater, or Tivoli, within an hour-and-a-half, never leaving their parents' side for a minute as long as the band continued to play. Their achievements in the direction of putting away the barley-bree were, of course, far surpassed in quantity by those of their male relatives and admirers, listening to music being, perhaps, the thirstiest pastime of the Fatherland; but I am bound to say that during my many years' residence in Germany and Austria, beer-drinking Empires *par excellence*, I never saw any person of either sex the worse for liquor at an open-air concert, or was a witness to the least misconduct or breach of social decorum on the part of those present at the hundreds of *al fresco* musical performances I attended in the respective capitals of the Hohenzollern and Hapsburg realms.

My experience—an unusually large one for a Briton born and bred—of the vast amount of inoffensive and inexpensive happiness derived by Continental people from orchestral entertainments of the class indicated by the title of this chapter, convinces me that English cities in general, and this gigantic metropolis in particular, would be much pleasanter places to live in if the resources of *al fresco* music available to their inhabitants were at least ten times more copious than they are, or ever have been within my remembrance. London is fortunate in the possession of several parks, leaving nothing to be desired in the way of accommodation capacity, as far as space is concerned. It can also dispose of, at least, half-a-dozen excellent military bands—little enough, considering the *chiffre* of its population, to which, however, the strength of its garrison bears no relation that will stand comparison with the proportion of the military to the civilian element in the chief continental capitals. Thus we have at hand the material for making open-air music, but apparently do not know how to utilise it. It might be organised by the State, or by private enterprise, or by both, either in combination or rivalry. The English climate is its most formidable opponent; the first thing to be done, therefore, is to devise a practical means of protecting people against torrents of rain and bitter blasts, such as are only too apt to impart a peculiarly homicidal character to the London summer. Spacious refuges—like that in the Vienna Volksgarten, to which I have already alluded —should be erected in the immediate vicinity of the open spaces selected for the accommodation of the bands and their audiences, and fitted up with strong common wooden chairs, a central platform for the musicians, and a tea and coffee bar, if alcoholic refreshment be considered objectionable by the authorities. In the public parks these refuges might be run up, solidly but inexpensively, by the Woods and Forests Department, and leased at remunerative rents to private contractors, who would doubtless find them profitable tenements enough. By adopting this expedient the malignity of our national weather might be checkmated, as far as its effect upon open-air concerts is concerned, at least; and a rich vein of harmless amusement might be worked for the benefit of the classes to whom at present Sunday is a day of deadly boredom or sottish indulgence.

Of one thing I am certain, to wit, that we have not nearly as much *al fresco* music in London as is good for us. The reasons why, are numerous, the most difficult to counteract being our climate, as aforesaid, our Sabbatarian prejudices, which hamper every scheme for popular Sunday recreation, our official thrift in relation to small matters, which contrasts so disagreeably with our official wastefulness of enormous sums, and lastly the curious reluctance of our Parliament to authorise expenditure with the object of providing any sort of rational and innocuous amusement for the people. These latter, too, are manifestly apathetic with respect to a question which, after all, possesses only a relative interest for the wealthier classes, who can command musical entertainment of the best quality, as well as every other luxury of life, by paying for it. There is not so much nor such variety of peripatetic out-door music in this metropolis nowadays as there was when I was a boy, from thirty to forty years ago. True, German bands, like the poor, are always with us; even more so than of yore, and of a deadlier character. Likewise there is no very depressing lack of piano-organs, which have entirely replaced the would-be orchestral instruments of torture, dragged along by donkeys, and the merry old tinklers on broomsticks, with fluted silk fronts and green baize jerkins, of my childhood's days. But I miss the violoncello and clarinet soloists, mostly sightless, who used to patrol the streets of the "quiet" neighbourhood in which my early youth was passed, whose rate of progress averaged about one mile in four hours, and who never played any air, so far as my memory serves me, that was not imbued by its nature or their art with a settled and heartrending melancholy. What has become, I would ask, of the Hieland pipers, "braw" in all the faded splendours of eighth-hand sporrans and plaids, kilts and philabegs, with their tartans of clans which they could not name when solicited to do so, and their significant little knives stuck in their stockings, indicating profuse weasand-slitting to the unsophisticated childish mind well primed in Scott's national novels, but really functioning (as observation taught me) in connection with the carving of bread and cheese and the extraction of the reluctant winkle from his curly home? I never see or hear those pipers now, and I am glad of it, for their instrument is one which does not convey unmixed gratification to ears that, like my own, have not undergone a peculiar training in appreciativeness of its musical charms. But they used to be seemingly ubiquitous in London streets about the time I refer to, and compared unfavourably, to my childish apprehensions, with the wooden Highlanders on guard in front of the snuff-shops, who were cleaner and more glossy than their perambulatory compatriots, over whom they had the additional advantage of not giving utterance to a stomach-ache of sound. Where are the bright-eyed Savoyard boys with their sad little hurdy-gurdies, picturesque rags, and white mice that lived inside their waistcoats? Where the shaggy *pifferari*, skilled in evoking unearthly squeaks and wails from hairy bags, tightly squeezed under their left arms? I have not seen a *pifferaro* in London highways or by-ways for at least a quarter of a century. The music they made was not strictly classical; but how suggestive they were of Calabrian forests, brigands' caves, and all the picturesqueness, mystery, and horror of outlaw life in Southern Italy! Whither have vanished the two or three really meritorious stringed bands—one of them used to play every Thursday afternoon in Manchester Square—which performed the overtures to *Zampa*, *Masaniello* and *William Tell* so dashingly? They were, I fancy, chiefly composed of Italians and Frenchmen, and used to take something considerable in silver every time they performed. In common with many other youthful music-lovers, I loved to follow them about for hours at a stretch, and yearned to enlist in their harmonious ranks. I also miss the legitimate artistic successors of the two reduced *Signori* who were formerly wont to execute pleasing feats in concert upon a wiry piano on wheels, harnessed to a duet-proof white horse with un-commonly hirsute fetlocks, and upon a weak violin, which its owner or lessee used to extract from a gloomy-looking black leather case with a tender care that would not have been exaggerated in connection with the handling of a priceless Guarnerius or Amati. Those dejected but able executants used to play, moreover, duos of a class that has long been forgotten in this country—thinly spun-out arrangements of obscure Italian operas by Mercadante and Paesiello, which had never taken root in popular favour on this side of the Channel. Why, I would ask, has so much of this eccentric but eminently entertaining *al fresco* music disappeared from our streets, leaving open-air London so much duller and less eventful than it was between the date of Her Majesty's accession to the Throne and the outbreak of the Crimean war?

CHAPTER XI.

WAGNERIANA—STRAUSSIANA.

It is a no less curious than interesting fact, that in the year of Richard Wagner's birth (1813), when his native city was suffering all the horrors of an energetic siege, a man of letters was living at Dresden who foretold the principles and foresaw the practice of the system of operatic composition which has, for the past thirty years, been identified in general opinion with the great Saxon *maestro*. At the time referred to, Hoffmann, universally known some years later by his extraordinary ghost-stories, had but newly taken to literature as a profession; and it was in 1813 that he wrote an admirable essay, intituled "The Poet and the Composer," which subsequently appeared in his famous work, "The Serapion Brothers." This essay takes the form of a conversation between two friends, who discuss the distinctions existing between poet and composer, and whether or not one and the same person could or should discharge the functions of both. They arrive at the important conclusion that the barriers seemingly separating poet and composer must be swept away, for that poetry and music are so closely allied as to be one in reality. "For," writes Hoffmann, "words and notes receive their highest inspiration from one and the same secret. The only true opera must be that the music of which is the direct and immediate progeny of its text. Is not music the mysterious language of a remote spiritual realm—a language the wondrous accents of which are echoed in our utmost soul, awakening a higher and intenser vitality in it? Shimmering and sparkling, all our passions are stirred to common strife, and subside into one inexpressible longing, which expands our breast. Such is the indescribable effect of instrumental music. But music must deal with life itself and its phenomena ; adorning words and deeds, it must describe definite passions and actions. Can we speak of mean things in noble words? Can music reveal to us aught save the marvels of those regions from which it is transmitted to us? Let the poet equip himself for a bold flight to the distant land of romance ; there will he find the wonders, living and glowing with brilliant colours, which he may import into actual life, so that we may willingly put faith in them ; ay, so that we, as in a hallowing dream, may escape from dry, everyday existence, and wander along the flowery paths of romantic life, fully understanding its language, the words of which are set to music." That these lines, scarcely less than prophetical of Wagner's endeavours to make music and poetry homogeneous, or at least to render each the necessary and irrevocable complement of the other, should have been penned by Hoffmann within a few weeks of the "happy event" that brought the greatest composer of this century into the world, was surely a strange and fortunate coincidence!

A hitherto unpublished letter, written by Richard Wagner, during his "Sturm und Drang" period, explaining his views of operatic potentialities and principles of composition, will certainly be perused with interest. It was addressed to Baron de Biedenfeld at Weimar, bears date January 17, 1849, is in the possession of Major von Donop, one of the Hessian Landgrave's Chamberlains, and runs as follows:—

"I ever strove against the employment of the immeasurable apparatus, comprising action, situation, and plot, supported by the liveliest co-operation of all existing arts—such as painting, plastics, gymnastics, etc.—merely to impress a certain number of taking melodies upon the public memory; I convinced myself that the only object of all this display must be no less than the whole dramatic work, and that opera, in this respect, must stand even higher than the spoken stage-play, because, to all other known methods of expression, it adds that of music, the richest, most various, and most inexhaustible. The Greeks, and perhaps even some of our mediæval dramatists, were able to adapt musical effects to their dramas; but, since in our own times the heroes of absolute music—that is, of music apart from poetry—and in particular Beethoven, have raised the expressive capacity of this art, through the orchestral medium, to an entirely new potency, not previously dreamt of even by Gluck, the influence of music upon the drama has unquestionably acquired importance, inasmuch as music naturally puts forward claims to the development of her rich resources. The drama itself, therefore, would have to augment its expressive faculty;

to disclose and cultivate its corresponding capacity to the wealth of musical expression seemed to me to be only possible to a musician. As I thus exalted the musician to the rank of poet, I could not, of course, permit him to lose sight of the drama's chief aim; for his special art—music—would be called in to fulfil this, the highest of all artistic aims; wherefore it necessarily became my task, whilst cognisant and intimately convinced of the wealth of musical expression, to resolve upon the creation of nothing but drama—that is to say, of such drama as could not be produced without the aid of musical consciousness in its author. To make myself fully intelligible upon this point I must refer to one of the principal scenes in my *Tannhaeuser*, viz., the Minstrel Competition. Obviously, in order that the catastrophe should be brought about by this scene, it was indispensable that the poetical intention should predominate. To allow the singers to compete with one another by performing tricks of vocalisation, ornamental passages and cadences, would have been to represent a concert-room trial of skill, not a dramatic struggle of rival ideas and feelings. On the other hand, however, this poetical contest, in which the whole and full individuality of each man taking part in it was to be displayed, could not be realised save through the agency of the highest and most varied forces of musical expression, as I understand it. To my great satisfaction I have found that this very scene, risky as it is, has secured—whenever it has been performed—the most vivacious and enthusiastic sympathy on the part of the audience; and it was my triumph to lay hold of our opera-public, quite unaccustomed to this method of treatment, by appealing to their intelligence instead of to their sensibility.

"Let me repeat it briefly once more: I have taken my line as a musician, who—starting from his conviction of the inexhaustible resources of music—*wills* to create the highest work of art, namely, the drama. I say *wills*, in order to indicate my endeavour; whether I *can*, or not, I am not able to judge; but should I break down, it will not be for lack of volition, but by reason of my feeble gifts. I shall be much gratified if this succinct communication enable you to obtain some insight into the entity of my compositions; I could impart to you more words upon this subject, but not more meaning. If possible, accord to me your favourable sympathy. Begging you to greet Liszt cordially for me, I remain most respectfully your obedient servant, RICHARD WAGNER."

Another interesting and (until lately) unpublished letter from the pen of the late Richard Wagner, addressed to the Countess Agénor de Gasparin in March, 1861, has been communicated to me. The genesis of this document is accounted for as follows by its possessor. Wagner was highly indignant at the scandalous treatment to which *Tannhaeuser* had been subjected by a cabal of frivolous fops at Paris. He had withdrawn that work from the hands of the Opera-house management, and absolutely refused to permit its repetition, although strongly urged to weather the trumpery storm aroused by its production. The Countess de Gasparin, a fervent admirer of Wagner's genius, had been painfully affected by the accounts of the Jockey Club's barbarous behaviour on the occasion in question—details of which filled columns of the leading Parisian papers at the time—and wrote to the great composer a long letter of condolence and sympathy, in which she poured out all the sorrowful and angry feelings with which her kind heart was overflowing. A few days later she received the answer, which I subjoin in translation:—"Paris, 3, Rue d'Aumale, March 29, 1861.—Honoured Madam,—You cannot for a moment doubt the effect produced upon me by your wonderful letter. You knew that it would bring me the solace of which I stood in need. Accept my heartfelt thanks, and doubt not that I am absolutely incapable of making the least concession to save appearances, so long as the essence of my work fails to obtain recognition. You have assuredly heard ere this that I have withdrawn my opera—I cannot refrain from avowing with what deep inward grief I have done so. The speciality of my artistic conceptions invariably leads me back again to the drama; no means of realising them lie open to me but those connected with the modern theatre; and what sort of an institution that theatre is I need not tell you, for you hold it in no higher estimation than I do. Imagine what my sensations must be when I—emerging, as it were, from the most absolute solitude—find myself compelled to come in contact with this deeply dishonest world, in which everything—ay, even the commonest terms of my craft—hurts me to the very marrow of my bones! Do you now believe me, when I tell you that my longing for death is profound and real? My grateful greetings are yours; grateful, for that I have been permitted to encounter you on the path which else I had been doomed to tread alone! With respectful homage, your most obedient RICHARD WAGNER." It is only too manifest, from the dejected tone of the above remarkable letter, that the writer, when he penned it, had drained the bitter cup of disappointment to the dregs. It was indeed indited at one of the darkest moments of his chequered life, when his gallant spirit was all but broken by a crowning mishap. Happily, Fate had splendid compensations in store for the then unappreciated composer of *Tannhaeuser*.

Curiously and sadly illustrative of the state of pecuniary embarrassment — sometimes nearly approaching destitution — in which the late Richard Wagner was constrained to live during the earlier years of his career as an operatic composer, is a letter written by him forty-one years ago to a Herr Morath, at that time engaged as contra-bassist in the orchestra of the Magdeburg Stadttheater. Wagner, whilst sojourning at Magdeburg, had become indebted to Morath in a sum that was no doubt considerable, at that time, to debtor and creditor alike. The latter eked out the modest wages allotted in the year 1840 to a double-bass player in a provincial German opera-house by copying music, in which occupation he had so distinguished himself by correctness and legibility as to have gained a reputation in musical circles, even beyond the walls of Magdeburg city, that kept him in full and tolerably remunerative employment. As it would appear, he copied out a great deal of manuscript for Wagner, for which service the Saxon *maestro*, then passing through an especially dismal phase of his unappreciated period, was unable to pay the appointed price, or any part of it, and remained so for many months after he had ceased to reside in Magdeburg. It was from Dresden, on January 4, 1843, that Wagner addressed to his patient and long-suffering creditor the following characteristic letter, which has been published for the first time very recently, and is at present in the possession of Jules Bernhardt Schroeder, the well-known Magdeburg pianoforte dealer:—"My best Herr Morath,—I have made you wait a long time, and I must confess that it has pained me in my innermost heart whenever I have thought about you, and yet have found myself so situated that it was absolutely out of my power to pay you. It is only by means of the heaviest sacrifice imaginable that I have been able to open out to myself my present improved prospects; I have been compelled to endure all manner of want and privations in order not to succumb completely. Even now, as far as my external conditions are concerned, I have by no means attained my goal; for my earnings are so small as to be scarcely worth mentioning. However, God will help me on my way; and I will commence, at least, an endeavour to right myself with you, for you have done me good service and ever treated me with all possible consideration. Besides, of all my creditors, assuredly none needs money more urgently than yourself. Pray, therefore, accept herewith the thirty-five thalers you asked for in your last letter. If I can ever serve you in any way, believe me I shall do so with the best will in the world. Receive my heartiest thanks for all your kindness, and the assurance of my profoundest respect.—Your most obedient RICHARD WAGNER." That, in his own great need, he should have mustered up resolution enough to discharge—who knows at what painful inconvenience to himself?—a part of an old-standing obligation to a man in humble circumstances who had first trusted him and then had the magnanimity not to dun him, is a fact sufficiently proving of itself that, under the surface ruggedness of Wagner's character lay rich *strata* of conscientiousness, honour, gratitude, and loving human kindness.

Tristan and Isolde, strange to say, was not produced upon the stage of the Vienna Hofoper until two years and a half ago. The story of this great "tone poem" in connection with Vienna—what the Germans would call its *Vorgeschichte*—is in some respects an odd one. Twenty-three years have elapsed since that opera was accepted by the management of the Hofoper. Scenery was painted, properties and costumes were made for it. Learning that it was about to be put in rehearsal, Wagner came up to Vienna for the special purpose of rendering every assistance in his power to the artists of all categories selected to take part in its performance. Months passed away, during which he spared no pains to render his music intelligible to the leading singers of the Imperial company; but in vain. They studied their parts assiduously, but could not master them; at last they came to him in a body and declared that the opera was quite beyond their powers. One or two of them went even farther, respectfully stating their conviction that it was intrinsically too difficult to be ever performed by any set of merely human artists. Remonstrances availed nothing; *Tristan and Isolde* was dropped by the management, and Wagner had uselessly sacrificed several months of his valuable time, besides having been put to heavy expense when he could ill afford it. The unhappiest weeks of his life, he has often alleged, were those immediately following the abandonment of his favourite work by the Vienna *Intendantur*. One day he left the Kaiserstadt secretly, letting none of his friends there know whither he was going. The consequence of this proceeding was that when, during the following spring (1864), King Louis of Bavaria made inquiries of the Austrian Government, through his Minister at Vienna, respecting the whereabouts of "the great master, whose works he had admired for years, but whom he personally did not know," nobody in Vienna could say where Wagner was to be found, and several weeks elapsed before his hiding-place in Switzerland was discovered. When King Ludwig's summons at length reached him, it raised him from the depths of despondency to a pinnacle of hope he had never theretofore attained. He had, indeed, begun to despair of his works ever being performed at all, and was on the verge of melancholy madness when the Royal Wittelsbach, in taking him by the hand, saved his reason from overthrow and, in all probability, his life to boot. Since that fortunate conjuncture in his career *Tristan and Isolde* has been successfully produced at Munich, Berlin, Leipzig, Weimar and Hamburg—last, though not least, at London, where during the summer of 1882 it drew two of the largest audiences ever gathered together within the walls of Old Drury. But on the first of European operatic stages it was never once performed during Richard Wagner's life; the Vienna Hofoper, having owed him a debt of honour for a score of years, only paid it to his *manes*. *Tristan and Isolde* was set and mounted with the utmost splendour in the spring of 1884; its cast comprised Winkelmann, Scaria and Frau Materna; its "tone-poem" was interpreted by the finest operatic orchestra in the world; but it is a pity that so handsome an *amende honorable* could not have been made but one twelvemonth sooner, to the living Master, instead of to his justly offended shade.

An impression has for many years past been prevalent throughout Europe that Wagner not only believed himself to be the greatest composer the world had ever known, but revelled in the adulation of his disciples, and heartily despised as well as disliked any one who withheld from him the worship he considered his due, or failed to recognise the surpassing merits of his music. Now Franz Muncker, his intimate personal friend and a daily visitor at Wahnfried during Wagner's yearly sojourns in Bayreuth, represents him as "disliking to be regarded as a phenomenal, or even exceptional being. . . . . He was of late years constantly surrounded by eager admirers and fanatical followers, and put up with them (though not always); but they gave him no delight. He preferred to them—sometimes very conspicuously—his friends of independent opinions, and often complained to these latter that he could scarcely ever get up an interesting conversation with the others, because they invariably agreed with everything he said. 'Come and sit by me,' he would whisper to a friend who had views of his own; 'let us get away from these tiresome fellows who are always saying "Yes."' . . . . Nothing annoyed him so much as when his admirers, in their exaggerated homage to his person, happened to misapprehend his wishes and perpetrate some act of silly indiscretion. After the first performance of *Parsifal*, he told the loudly applauding audience that he gratefully accepted their manifestations on behalf of his artists, but begged them not to summon him before the curtain in the usual way with the call of 'Author.' At the next performance, his rabid worshippers strove with all their might, by hissing and groaning, to suppress the general public's manifestations of approval, upon which he angrily exclaimed to my father, 'These Wagnerians are the stupidest people in the world; I should like to break down the theatre doors with their heads. They must be hissing, indeed! It is disgraceful!' And he did not hesitate to tell them so to their faces, later on.

"It was his constant endeavour to cultivate ripe and independent judgment in those of his disciples who were in close personal relation to him. To a musical student, who spoke to him of Mendelssohn's and Schumann's works rather contemptuously, he presented such of their compositions as he happened to possess, with the recommendation to 'thoroughly study the works of those composers and of others spiritually akin to them, before finding fault with them.' . . . . He never would allow himself to be measured against or compared with Mozart and Beethoven. 'I should be the greatest fool alive,' he used to say, 'if I attempted to equal those Masters, or to produce anything like what they have produced. I can only hold my own, after and anywhere near them, by proving my intention to do otherwise than they did.'

Beethoven, in particular, was always esteemed by him as 'the absolutely Unattainable and Inimitable,' whose compositions it was his greatest delight to conduct. I shall never forget Christmas Day, 1878. In celebration of his wife's birthday, Wagner had summoned the Meininger orchestra to Wahnfried, and rehearsed with its members several purely instrumental works, exclusively Beethoven's compositions. Whilst changing the parts, one of the executants happened to let fall a Beethoven book. As he was stooping to pick it up, Wagner jestingly exclaimed, ' Let it lie, it is of no importance. Our turn comes now; Offenbach and I, we only represent true art. What do we want with Beethoven !' His meaning, revealed by his tone and manner as he spoke, was plain enough to most of us; and yet there were those present who jumped to the conclusion that 'Wagner thought and spoke scornfully of Beethoven !'"

"Not only did he, as a general rule, strongly object to be asked to perform his own compositions, but it was particularly disagreeable to him, in mixed society, to be interrogated with respect to his artistic notions. Above all, the catchword *Zukunftsmusik* (Music of the Future) when unintelligently employed in conversation with him, never failed to put him in a violent passion. He himself never questioned anybody—not even his most intimate friends—about their musical professions of faith; indeed, he had friends who, as he was well aware, did not understand a note of his music, and whom he did not love one whit the less on that account. But he did not think it worth his while to discuss, far less to dispute, about the value of his endeavours with persons who had not even an elementary idea of what really were his aims and purposes."

The Town Council of Leipzig, in its capacity as Keeper of the Register in which are entered the real names of authors publishing works in that city anonymously or under pseudonyms, has made official announcement to the effect that the libretto of the four act opera by J. F. Kittl, *Bianca and Giuseppe, or the French before Nice*, published in the year 1852 by Messrs. Breitkopf and Haertel, was exclusively written by Richard Wagner. This fact is worth noting by encyclopædists and compilers of the deceased composer's biography.

The above passing reference to the Wagnerian "Hotspurs," whose extravagant and unreasoning partisanship of his "system" caused the gifted Saxon so much vexation and annoyance during the latter years of his life, calls to mind the absurdities, in the way of "synthetic analysis," perpetrated by one of those fiery factionaries, Edmund von Hagen, the author of an unconsciously humorous work, entitled "Contributions to an Insight into the Being of Wagnerian Art." One of these "Contributions"—an essay containing fifty-three pages of printed matter—is entirely devoted to "The Trumpet-Signal of Freedom" in *Rienzi*, upon the importance of which, musically, æsthetically, and politically, Von Hagen dilates to the top of his bent. The following brief extract, which deals more particularly with the A sounded on the trumpet at the opening of the overture, will serve to exemplify the state of exaltation into which Wagner-worshippers contrive to work themselves up when engaged in explaining the secrets of his "method" to profane outsiders—*i.e.*, the general public. "The note A," writes Von Hagen, "constituting the first bar of the *Rienzi* overture, and blown upon the trumpet, is to me a glorious example of how the physiognomy of a tone-poet may lie quite distinctly stamped upon the surface of a single note, and may unmistakably look us in the face out of that single note. This A—the first tone of Wagner's first published opera—tells us that Wagner is an organically creative artist. At the same time it is of beautiful significance that the trumpet-call in question should also be a summons to freedom. Thus, this one tone, in its form and capacity, contains Wagner *in nuce*. The trumpeter who has to sound the A in question must know this. He must be inwardly conscious of what he is blowing when he blows this note; he must be penetrated through and through with the knowledge that this note belongs to liberty. Should the trumpeter only comprehend this note as a musician, and confine himself to simply sounding it correctly, musically speaking—that is, exactly as it is written—he had better go about his business. Were he even the leading Chamber-Virtuoso in a Court-Orchestra, he is certainly no artist, and is utterly unfit to perform Wagner's music."

Gounod and Verdi were interviewed by Martin Roeder upon the subject of Wagner, shortly before the latter's death. Gounod expressed himself as follows:—"Wagner is the cleverest dramatic musician that ever lived. But he is blind—his followers have robbed him of his sight. If this extraordinary man had pursued the course in which, with *Tannhaeuser* and *Lohengrin*, he captivated the hearts of his countrymen and of the whole educated artistic world, we should have before us a phenomenon of art such as the world had never heretofore beheld. As it is, however, Wagner will perish; and he himself has dug his own grave."

Verdi found fault with Wagner's disciples and so-called "school" far more severely than with the Saxon composer or his compositions. "Highly as I esteem the man and artist, I would strictly forbid any art student, not thoroughly grounded in every branch of simple and double counterpoint, to meddle with a Wagnerian score. All our most gifted young composers—I can count them for you on my fingers—are bent on imitating 'il maestro tedesco.' They cannot get on nowadays without ten trombones and as many horns, with the aid of which they bring forth abortions which only help to heap discredit upon the name of Wagner. Personally I honour Wagner, although he has held me up to scorn; but I have a horror of his school!"

To Mr. William Singer, the well-known musical critic, Gounod has also unbosomed himself with respect to Wagner, àpropos of a treatise he (Gounod) is said to have written upon that composer's character and works. "In reality," said Gounod, "the matter stands thus. Shortly after the publication of my essay upon Mozart, one evening at the house of a friend the conversation turned upon Richard Wagner. My hostess asked me what I thought of that master. I told her; whereupon she observed, "You really ought to put all that down upon paper." Why not? I confess that the notion took my fancy; and I jotted down a few of my ideas. In order to put it out of my power to renounce my project, certain persons circulated the report abroad that I had completed a pamphlet on Wagner, whereas my utmost intention had been to write a magazine article about him. To that intention I still adhere; for I feel absolutely called upon to do justice to Richard Wagner, of whom formerly a great deal too much evil was spoken. Now far too much good is said of him. Doubtless, a man who created such works as his cannot have been an ordinary person. Who would wish to deny that his was a great nature, which rendered important services to music? But between just recognition of his manifold qualities and unbridled, extravagant enthusiasm there is a wide difference. My convictions do not allow me to admit that interminable recitative is endless melody. Endless melody is to be found in Mozart. He always sings. Inexhaustible song bubbles up from every portion of his works. Only listen!" Gounod commenced playing, and then singing, with exquisite finish, Zerlina's air from *Don Juan*, "Vedrai carino," and then broke off into reminiscences from Beethoven's and Haydn's works, regaling Mr. Singer with an admirable pianoforte recital, at the close of which he exclaimed, "That is what I call endless melody; not an eternal straggling onwards, without goal or repose—not everlasting musical sprinklings (*arrosage musicale*)—not continuous tentativeness, regardless of forms—not quavering masses of sound, devoid of definite formulæ. Such methods overstep the boundaries that even the most original artistic individuality is bound to prescribe to itself. They only lead to heresy; and indeed, as far as the majority of his works is concerned, Wagner is no better than a musical heretic. .... If it were only he! But the whole crew of his followers and worshippers—it is they who do him the greatest wrong by tacking their own extravagances on to his, and endeavouring to organise the entire mess into a system! As if Gluck, Mozart, Beethoven, Auber, Meyerbeer had ever thought about 'systems' when they wrote their masterpieces; as if sober classifications ever crossed the mind of a composer during those happy and beneficent moments at which his genius finds expression! This never-ending descriptiveness, this effort to depict the smallest matters in sound, how far it all is from the genuine inspiration that descends, like grace, upon the composer from on high! These people only conceal their poverty of ideas under a clamour of words and notes; as if art consisted of doing very little with abundant means, instead of making a great deal out of small materials. Incapable of constructing a shapely and compact work of art with organic, recognisable and graceful or sublime forms, they bewilder the astounded hearer with noise and false movements. Tap, tap, tap, tap, again and again and again, wallowing in the vast orchestral sauce (in which never a fish can swim) until they are fairly drowned in it. The consequence of this robust struggle to get on somehow is that it becomes impossible for any one to concentrate himself, in order to really become something, instead of only appearing to be something. Hence you find most of our young artists excluding genuine feeling and true art-worship from their music, and making nothing but a noise in art, as well as in life—seeking success in fussy festivities, advertisements, banquets, and public notoriety. Everything from without and nothing from within. Mere show; no real power."

Mr. Singer asked him whether he had entertained any personal relations with Wagner. He replied, "When Wagner lived in Paris, and things were going badly with him, he complained to me that nobody would produce his operas. I advised him to select the most attractive numbers of his works, and to have them performed at a concert. In carrying out this suggestion I assisted him to the best of my ability. The concert turned out a success; and at that time he was grateful to me. You know how he attacked me later on; but, believe me, that did not in the least alter my opinion of him as a musician. It is necessary, in the case of Wagner, to make a distinction between the man and the composer." I ventured to remark that Wagner's music is played nowadays at nearly all the Parisian concerts, and asked Gounod whether he—taking into consideration the character, artistic predilections and tastes of the French people—believed in a future for Wagnerian music in France. "Wagner's compositions are being played here," replied Gounod, "and it is quite right that those of his works which are beautiful and imperishable should be performed. But it is difficult for me to believe that his music will ever find a lasting home in France." He added with solemnity, "On the contrary, I see the time rapidly approaching at which the whole world will become weary of these musical sophists and rhetoricians who unremittingly strive to transform human pleasures and enjoyments into suffering. The object of music is to make people happy, not to sadden them or to increase their griefs and gloominess. Whether Wagner meant it or not, his music has become the tattered umbrella under which Messieurs les Chevaliers de la haute blague—the champion humbugs—try to shelter themselves from a bursting downpour of public discontent. A storm-blast will sweep this thing away, and all that is gay, noble and lovely will then sparkle in brilliant sunshine."

Wagner prided himself above all things upon being a typical German; and undoubtedly he was so in many respects. But he offered a striking contrast to the majority of his countrymen in one regard; *viz.*, in his steadfast aversion to orders of chivalry, medals, and other "outward and visible" honorific distinctions. A greedy worship of these baubles is one of the leading traits of German character; and Wagner's frequently iterated refusals to accept decorations were an inexhaustible source of wonder to the sons of the Fatherland. He had, however, two good and sufficient reasons for rejecting the collars, stars, and crosses offered to him by a score of emperors, kings, and princes. In the first place, he held that "monarchical badges" did not beseem the breast of an "inveterate Republican," as he delighted to style himself; in the second, he appraised his own genius so highly as to deem it far above reward or recognition by symbols of Imperial or Royal grace. Nineteen years ago the Chapter of the Maximilian Order ("Pour le Mérite") solicited its Chief, the King of Bavaria, to confer the Grand Cross of that exalted Order upon Richard Wagner. His Majesty was willing; but the great composer respectfully declined to accept the decoration.

Shortly afterwards the late King Victor Emmanuel sent him the "Soliti Santi" *au cou*—in other words, the Commandery of the venerable Order of SS. Maurice and Lazarus. This high distinction was also "declined with thanks." In 1876, upon the occasion of the great *Nibelung* production, all the German sovereigns, including the King of Prussia—who consented to look over Wagner's democratic proclivities in consideration of his transcendent genius — proffered their emblems of chivalric honour to him, as likewise did the Emperors of Austria and Russia, the Kings of Denmark, Spain, Sweden, etc. One and all were courteously rejected ; and Wagner remained to his dying day the only German composer of any eminence whose button-hole knew not adornment by the least shred of parti-coloured riband.

* * * * * *

There was a genial side to Wagner's masterful character, which found expression in large and generous hospitality, love of good cheer and jollifications, a tendency to indulge in badinage, and, above all, an exquisite tenderness of manner towards his consort's children, as well as his own, that rendered him an object of little less than adoration to them. When he took to wife Cosima Liszt, some time Frau von Buelow, she brought him three step-daughters, the issue of her union with the eminent pianist of that name. To these girls, Daniela, Blandine, and Isolde, he was the tenderest of fathers. Had they been his own flesh and blood, he could not have loved them better, or treated them more kindly. When, however, a son of his very own was born to him, his joy and exultation knew no bounds. He purchased a vast quantity of costly gay-coloured silken stuffs, to make hangings for little Siegfried's nursery, and yards upon yards of rosebuds, sewn together and made up into garlands, with which he decorated the walls of that apartment, and the cradle in which his baby heir reposed. His only weakness in the way of personal embellishment displayed itself in his indoors apparel—gorgeous dressing-gowns, resplendent smoking-caps, many-hued silken socks and "decorative" slippers. In the streets he was almost always to be seen in old clothes, for which he had a clinging and loyal affection. One short overcoat, of a yellowish, bilious tint, he wore in cold weather for nearly thirty years, and could not be induced to give it up. Once his wife, moved to indignation by the dilapidated condition and squalid shabbiness of the garment in question, hid it away from him. As, however, he gave no one in his house any peace whilst his "old friend" was missing, she was fain (with many protests and remonstrances) to restore it to him. He wore it frequently at Bayreuth, during the abominable weather that prevailed whilst *Parsifal* was undergoing rehearsal; and in the course of the winter, the "sopr' abito giallo del gran maestro sassone" got to be as well known in Venice as the Lion of St. Mark itself.

In the year 1869, Wagner was staying at Lucerne, busy with the composition of his famous Tetralogy. His Bavarian Majesty, desiring to give the Saxon Master a birthday treat such as would delight his soul, specially engaged the famous French stringed quartet (Messrs. Maurin, Colblain, Mas, and Chevillard) which at that time enjoyed the reputation of interpreting Beethoven's three last quatuors with supreme intelligence and felicity. Early in the morning of the 22nd May, Wagner's natal day, these executants were introduced into the composer's house, by the connivance of a member of his family, about an hour before he had risen from his bed. They softly tuned their instruments and took up a position in his breakfast-room, awaiting his appearance to strike up. What was his astonishment and pleasure when he came down to breakfast as usual in his duffel dressing-gown, to be received by the strains of a composition for which he entertained profound admiration and reverence—one of the Posthumous Quartets—performed by artists of such surpassing ability! For a few seconds he stood, as though turned to stone, mouth and eyes alike wide open; then, suddenly recognising Maurin, whom he had known and frequently heard in Paris, he rushed up to him with open arms and embraced him, fiddle and all. The French musicians spent the whole day with Wagner, during which they played at least a dozen quartets for his delectation. He, on his part, feasted them right royally, and during dinner proposed two toasts in eloquent language—one to "his Royal benefactor," and the other to "the greatest of French musicians, Camille Saint-Saëns." To the end of his days Richard Wagner retained a lively and grateful remembrance of this particular birthday "surprise." Indeed, only a few weeks before his death he told one of his intimate friends that he had never heard Beethoven's last quartets so satisfactorily played as by the Frenchmen whom the King of Bavaria had sent all the way from Paris to Lucerne to regale him with "the finest music ever composed," on the morning of his birthday anniversary, in the year of grace 1869.

Immediately after the third performance of *Tristan and Isolde* at the Royal Opera House, Munich—namely, on the 19th of June, 1865—Richard Wagner addressed the following characteristic letter to the members of the Bavarian Court Orchestra:—"Dear and honoured gentlemen, my very worthy friends,—It is out of the question that on this day, after the third and (for the present) last performance of *Tristan and Isolde*, I should part from you without addressing to you a few last words of gratitude. In truth, no artist can ever have been animated by a more exhilarating feeling than that which I have experienced throughout my relations with you. Even a mother, rejoicing in the child to which she has given birth with anguish, cannot feel the exquisite satisfaction which pervades my being when I hear the score that has so long lain dumb before me, resounding in my ears with such a warm and rapturous tone-life as you have breathed into it by your marvellously beautiful performance. To attempt, by any praise of mine, the recognition of the inimitable importance of your feat would only be to break in rudely upon your own splendid consciousness of merit. You all know what a feat it has been, and what it means, as far as you yourselves are concerned : your hearts must tell you what you have become to me, through this performance. You must know that I feel as a personal friend towards each one of you ; for nothing short of the most hearty reciprocal friendship could have inspired you with the warmth, passion, and tenderness with which you have revealed my work, nobly and expressively, to the world at large. The hours of our rehearsals in common cleave to my memory as the most agreeable and encouraging of my whole life; the days and years that we, perhaps, are destined to spend together in the future shall bear witness to the exalted significance of those hours of commune. As long as I shall breathe and have my being it will be the inmost vocation of my heart to prove to you how dearly I love you, and how entirely thankful I feel towards you.—Always your faithful and devoted friend, RICHARD WAGNER." The above letter can scarcely fail to be a surprise to those—and they are many, both in England and Germany—who entertain the conviction that Wagner was constitutionally incapable of any feeling akin to gratitude.

On the 15th of October, 1884, a jubilee celebration took place in Vienna at the Wieden Theatre, to commemorate the fortieth anniversary of the day upon which Johann Strauss, the "Walzerkoenig," made his first public appearance in the character of an orchestral conductor. The stalls, boxes, and pit were crowded with the *élite* of Viennese society, fashionable, artistic, and literary—the sort of gathering that may be seen in the great central *allée* of the Prater on May-day, when every other person you encounter on horseback, wheels, or foot has some generally-recognised claim to political or social distinction; Archdukes gossiping with actors, financiers arm-in-arm with journalists, native Ministers and foreign Ambassadors paying eager homage at the shrine of beauty, their worship dedicated with absolute impartiality to ladies of the Court and *belles* of the ballet. It was just such an assemblage that filled all the "numbered" seats at the Wieden on the jubilee night above referred to, whilst the galleries were thronged almost to suffocation by Strauss's most enthusiastic admirers—the true-born Viennese of the lower middle classes. Archduke William—who, being Grand Master of the Order of St. John, seldom shows himself in a theatre—occupied the Imperial Box, whilst King Milan of Servia sate out the whole performance in a ground-tier stage box, signifying his admiration for the *bénéficiaire's* talents and achievements by conferring upon him, towards the close of the evening, the Cross of the Takovo Order. The programme of the occasion consisted of selections from Strauss's operas, conducted by himself. His desk was converted for the nonce into a gorgeous flower-bed of the costliest exotics; and his appearance thereat, bâton in hand, was the signal for a demonstration of affectionate rejoicing on the part of the audience, such as, according to the leading journals of the Kaiserstadt, has never before been witnessed within the walls of a Vienna theatre. He opened the entertainment with his bright little overture to *Indigo*—his first opera, produced at the Wieden Theatre about twenty years ago—which was rapturously re-demanded. Then came the first act of *A Night in Venice*, followed by the immortal *Schoene blaue Donau* during the entr'acte, which inimitable waltz brought down a shower of laurel wreaths upon its composer's head. The second act of *Fledermaus*, with some additions to the dialogue written especially for the occasion, came next, and was succeeded by "musical episodes" from *Spitzentuch, Methusalem, Cagliostro, Der*

Lustige Krieg, and the *Carnival in Rome*, each successive number being supplemented by presentations of addresses, medals, and flowers. Amongst the floral devices offered to the hero of the jubilee were two, in particular, revealing remarkable taste and ingenuity in their designers, viz., the Strauss coat of arms, executed in fresh blossoms of its respective heraldic colours, and a huge silken banner, displaying the titles of all Strauss's operas in letters composed of full-blown white and red roses. Mighty bouquets and costly bâtons, forwarded direct to the theatre by his admirers in Berlin, Dresden, Munich, Pesth, Prague, and a dozen other distant cities of the German and Austrian Empires, were brought upon the stage during the "waits," and presented to him.

The professional career of the delightful composer to whom such splendid and well-merited honour has been paid in the city of his birth—for Johann Strauss first saw the light within the precincts of the Kaiserstadt—was during its earlier years a singularly adventurous one, by no means unfamiliar with mishaps and even privations. His parents wished him to study engineering; but he was not to be diverted from his resolve, adopted in early boyhood, to become a famous musician. To realise this resolve he worked day and night at the instrument of his choice (the violin) and at counterpoint from his twelfth to his eighteenth year, during which period he attained extraordinary proficiency as an executant. When a mere stripling of nineteen, he contrived to get together a scratch orchestra of young players who had sufficient faith in his talent and energy to elect him their leader, and started from

Vienna upon a concert-tour through Transylvania and Roumania. The slender fund with which this joyous company set out on its wild expedition was soon exhausted, and at Pancsova, a small town in the Lower Banat (situate on the left bank of the Danube and famous, of late years, for the excellence of its beer), Strauss and his merry men found themselves one fine morning without a kreuzer in their collective pockets. What was to be done? The band performed a serenade under the mayor's bedroom windows, and its leader succeeded in borrowing from that functionary a sum sufficient to purchase the immediate necessaries of life, but only on condition that the loan should be repaid out of the proceeds of certain concerts to be given in Pancsova itself. To these concerts, however, the Pancsova public so steadfastly refrained from coming, that the Strauss orchestra fell into grave embarrassments, culminating in the seizure of its instruments, at the instance of hard-hearted creditors, by the myrmidons of the law, one evening in the middle of a performance at the Town Hall. Long and animated negotiations ensued between Strauss and the local authorities, resulting in the restitution of the instruments, with permission to their owners to prosecute their professional tour—in charge, however, of the Pancsova chief constable, who was to accompany them at their costs and charges until their debts in the town should be discharged to the last penny. Seated on the box of the van in which their instruments, music-stands, etc., were packed, this official stuck to them for several weeks with unappeasable appetite and insatiable thirst. With him they visited and performed at Semlin, Arad, Temesvar, Grosswardein, Hermannstadt and Kronstadt, *en route* for Bucharest, paying instalments into his hands whenever their receipts exceeded their expenses. At last, on their arrival in the Transylvanian *chef-lieu*, he informed them that, as far as the town of Pancsova was concerned, their liabilities were discharged, and took leave of them with the assurance that he had enjoyed his trip amazingly.

By this time the members of the Strauss orchestra were in an alarmingly dilapidated condition, ragged, dirty, unshaven and wayworn, presenting the outward and visible aspect of incorrigible "rogues and vagabonds." No Kronstadt inn-keeper would accord them food and shelter or allow them to perform within his premises, the view taken of them being that they were highwaymen disguised as wandering musicians. Consequently, although it was the depth of winter, they and their instruments were crammed into an open hay-waggon and conveyed across the Carpathians to the Wallachian frontier under a strong military escort. At the close of this remarkable episode in their tour, the members of the band mutinied against their leader, and vowed they would go no further. Upon this Strauss harangued them in the following terms: "Comrades! We must see this thing out together. One man is as good as another, if not better. Let our watchword be 'One for all and all for one.' We will give a farewell performance in the nearest town, divide the proceeds, and then get back to Vienna the best way we can!" To this proposal they all agreed; but a fresh difficulty arose, the offspring of their fears (in which Strauss himself largely participated) of being attacked by brigands whilst working their way down the Roumanian slopes of the Carpathian pass, at that time infested by more than one predatory band of blood-chilling reputation. It was resolved to purchase weapons at the sacrifice of two violins, in exchange for which they managed to obtain a few old rusty pistols, but no ammunition. These were distributed amongst them by Strauss, who, however, kept three for himself, sticking them in his belt, where they imparted to him a highly impressive air of robber-chieftainship. His trombone-player, one Seidl, a man of exceptional thew and sinew, scornfully rejected the pistol tendered to him, remarking that " he would back himself to settle any ten bandits of the whole neighbourhood with his trombone."

So formidable was the appearance of the Strauss cohort, numbering thirty-four ferocious-looking musicians, that the peasants of the villages on their road fled or hid themselves as they approached, taking them for brigands of the deepest dye; and, between Kympena and Ploesti, a real robber-band which chanced to encounter them took to its heels, panic-stricken, in the full belief that a rival association had come down the mountain-side in overwhelming force for the purpose of putting an end to local enterprise.

Eventually Strauss and his formidable cohort reached Bucharest in safety, where for some time they did extremely well, from a pecuniary point of view. Their conductor's amatory proclivities, however, brought the tour to a premature and somewhat tragical conclusion. A Wallachian lady of rank, who had conceived an irresistible passion for the handsome young Viennese, made a tender appointment with him at the house of her washerwoman, whither, however, she was followed by her husband, an energetic and vindictive Boyar. This much-wronged personage brought half-a-dozen of his man-servants with him, to whose unmerciful hands he committed the luckless musician, whilst he himself beat his wife almost to death with a heavy dog-whip. By the domestics in question—semi-barbarous Wallachian peasants—Strauss was very roughly handled. They drubbed him soundly with thick sticks, tore out the greater part of his hair and beard, and inflicted upon him two severe scalp-wounds, which kept him confined to his bed for two months, and actually endangered his life and reason.

A year later Johann Strauss took his orchestra "on tour" for the first time to Russia, and underwent some uncommonly quaint adventures and experiences in that country. It was odd, for instance, that a railway company should engage him to give a series of concerts in the capital, to attend which entertainments it ran excursion trains from different stations on its line. One day he received the Empress's command to attend with his band at "Tsarkoë-Selo," and to perform before her Majesty in the park of that Imperial summer resort. Upon his arrival there he was informed by the Chamberlain on duty that he would have to rehearse the *morceaux* of his programme thrice before playing them to the Czarina. His amazement at so unprecedented a request found vent in eager inquiries as to its motive; but no explanation was vouchsafed to him. Such were

Her Majesty's orders, and he had nothing to do but to comply with them. Still greater waxed his astonishment when he observed that during the three rehearsals an empty Court carriage was drawn by a pair of horses slowly backwards and forwards in front of his orchestra. During the final performance, however, the meaning of this mysterious proceeding became apparent to him. Owing to a' sharp attack of gout, the Empress was compelled to recline in a carriage, with her foot on a cushion, throughout the concert; and the object of the three rehearsals had been to accustom the horses to the sounds produced by a full string-band, lest, haply, they should take fright and bolt with their Imperial mistress. At the end of the performance an exalted dignitary of the Russian Court bade Strauss follow him to his apartments in the château, where he sate the Kapellmeister down to a splendid grand piano, saying: "Now, be good enough to play me all the newest Vienna dance-music." Though extremely fatigued by his three rehearsals and "State" performance, Strauss deemed it expedient to comply; but after he had played continuously for over an hour, he came to a stop, observing, "I presume that will be sufficient." "I am not at all tired," coolly rejoined his Excellency. "But I am!" replied Strauss, and rose from the instrument. It is said that he came very near being sent to Siberia for "disrespectful behaviour, unprecedented in a person of his condition."

Another ill-timed complication, arising from an *affaire de cœur* in which Strauss became entangled, compelled him to quit Russia—never to return thither—before the completion of his professional tour. He had fallen desperately in love with a young lady belonging to a highly respectable Russian family resident in St. Petersburg, and contrived to obtain access to her in the character of a German pianoforte teacher. Her parents, however, one fine day, made the discovery that he was playing with their daughter's feelings instead of teaching her to play the piano; whereupon they informed him that he must espouse her forthwith, or take the consequences, which promised to be something very disagreeable indeed. He declined to be forced into matrimony and invoked the protection of his patrons at Court; more especially of the Austrian Embassy. The Russian authorities, however, decided that he should marry "the victim of his wiles," or suffer still more unpleasant pains and penalties; they even went so far as to fix his wedding-day. Nothing but desperate measures could save him from the Hymeneal noose; so his friendly Embassy demanded his arrest and consignment to its custody on the very morning appointed for the celebration of his nuptials. Notes were exchanged with unflagging energy between the Austrian Ambassador and Prince Dolgorouki during some six weeks, Strauss remaining a guest of the Embassy all that while, and never once venturing outside its gates. Finally, the matter was arranged *à l'aimable*, and the somewhat too amorous Kapellmeister was permitted to quit the Czar's domains unwedded and otherwise unmolested.

Such were a few of the more emotional *peripetia* of Johann Strauss's early career as an orchestral leader. It seemed likely at the time of his *début* in Vienna, that he would be heavily handicapped by his father's fame as a composer and conductor of dance-music. But his creative and executive talent was so unmistakably first-class that it obtained prompt and unreserved recognition from the Viennese musical critics, whose *doyen*, Johannes Nepomucene Vogl (the poet) wrote in the *Oesterreichisches Morgenblatt*, of October 9, 1844:—" The Vienna dancing-world was as deeply exercised by hopes and fears as though it had been on the eve of a great battle that should decide the fate of thousands; but Strauss junior, round whom all these hopes and fears revolved, made his appearance, and the first stroke of his bow reassured the doubting and confirmed the hopeful. I can bear witness that young Strauss possesses eminent abilities as a conductor, and displays, in composition, the same flow of melody, the same piquant and effective instrumentation that distinguish his father, whose method, however, he does not slavishly imitate."

At nine o'clock on the morning of the jubilee, the Chief Burgomaster of the Austrian capital (like Berlin, Vienna has two Mayors) waited upon Johann Strauss, at the latter's residence in the Igelgasse, to offer him the municipality's congratulations and present him with the freedom of the city. A host of theatrical deputations followed, bearing thank-offerings to the "Waltz-King," and presently his only surviving brother, Edward—for Joseph Strauss, a scarcely less admirable conductor than Johann, drowned himself in the Danube a few years ago, in consequence of a love disappointment—appeared with the entire *personnel* of his orchestra, and serenaded the hero of the day. The gift of the band led by Edward Strauss was a huge cornucopia of roses and camellias, on either side of which passages from Johann's most popular waltzes were notated in hyacinth blossoms and Parma violets. Magnificent vases and oil-paintings arrived from Russia; valuable presents without number from all parts of Germany, Hungary, Poland, Roumania and Switzerland. The Archduke John sent a telegram of cordial felicitation from Linz, regretting that indisposition prevented him from running up to Vienna for the day in order to express his sentiments of regard and admiration *in propriâ personâ* to a great musician whom he was proud to call his countryman. It is agreeable, in these prosaic days, to record such convincing proofs of the gratitude entertained—not only by his own compatriots, but by thousands of persons alien to him in birth and speech—towards a peculiarly genial and fanciful composer who has been the means of sensibly increasing, throughout four decades, the sum total of human happiness. May Johann Strauss live in prosperity and honour to celebrate his Golden Jubilee—the fiftieth anniversary of his first appearance at the conductor's desk!

I hear that Johann Strauss is about to embody the musical reminiscences of his youth in an opera, the leading *motivi* of which are to be revivals of dance-tunes composed by him when he was a lad, studying engineering against his will. His boyhood, as well as that of his brothers Joseph and Edward, was spent under the roof that sheltered his renowned father, whom, however, he seldom saw; for his parents were separated, and for many years lived in different storeys of the same house, the Strauss boys having been judicially assigned to their mother's care. All three developed remarkable musical ability at an early age, and, when still in round jackets, were familiar figures in several musical *salons* of Vienna, where they constantly played their father's compositions, and sometimes their own. Their musical feats of course reached old Strauss's ears, much to his gratification: but he made no sign until, several months having elapsed since he first became aware that they were acquiring celebrity, it struck him one day as absurd and unnatural that he should be about the only musician in the Kaiserstadt who had never heard any of his own son's compositions. Forthwith he sent a message to his wife, who occupied apartments above his own, but two flights higher, to the effect that he would esteem it a favour if she would permit his sons to pay him a visit. His request was granted at once, and the three boys were ushered into their father's presence. But, strange to say, the "Waltz-King" (as the Viennese had christened Strauss the elder) had no pianoforte in his rooms. What was to be done? After some hesitation, he decided upon sending another message upstairs to ask Mamma Strauss to lend him her piano for an hour or two. Presently down came the piano, and the boys began to play—first their father's music, and then their own. The old man's delight was unbounded; he embraced them over and over again, gave them his blessing, and then sent them back to their mother, together with the piano and his "compliments and thanks!"

CHAPTER XII.

MUSICAL AUDIENCES IN AUSTRIA, GERMANY, ITALY, AND OTHER CONTINENTAL COUNTRIES.—ENGLISH FREQUENTERS OF CONCERT-ROOMS, OPERA-HOUSES, AND OTHER PLACES OF MUSICAL ENTERTAINMENT.

Composers and executant artists live by the breath of public favour, and are dependent upon the "many-headed" alike for the bread they eat, and for the approbation that nourishes their immortal part. Remunerative royalties and high salaries are the solid pudding of popularity; applause is the immaterial pabulum upon which the musician's soul regales itself, when it can get it, with unappeasable appetite. It is the way of the world that audiences should all but worship their favourite artists, creative or interpretative, luckily for these latter; whereas the common-sense view of the relations between the composer or singer and the public which does its best to satisfy his physical and psychical needs can hardly fail to suggest that, after all, he lies under a weightier obligation to his patrons than any he can possibly impose upon them. For it can scarcely be doubted that the pleasures of living in a comfortable house, eating and drinking of the best, dressing well, owing nothing to your tradesmen, and keeping up a satisfactory balance at your bankers, are completer and more enduring than those derived from listening to a faultless performance of the finest composition extant. And yet my acquaintanceship with professional musicians—which, for some thirty years past, has been an exceptionally large and varied one—leaves me under the impression that, as a rule, they regard their audiences with feelings from which affectionate gratitude is conspicuous by its absence. I have heard the most eminent composers and the most popular singers speak with disparagement and scorn of the public that loaded them with material and sentimental proofs of its admiration and favour. Of the reflection they thus cast upon their own merits they always appeared sublimely unconscious; although one need not be a logician of the first water to conclude that if an audience be chiefly composed of dunces and dullards it is more likely to applaud a bad composition or performance than a good one. Musicians, however, are a supersensitive folk, peculiarly self-tormenting, greedy of praise, jealous, exacting and fretful. The more cultivated among them, although enthusiastic plaudits never fail to greet their public achievements, growl at audiences for lack of discrimination in their demonstrations of approval, objurgate them for missing "points" of rare delicacy or thoughtfulness, and even go so far as to invoke curses upon their devoted heads for applauding "in the wrong place." The less gifted, for obvious reasons, grumble at them for their coldness, unreasoning favouritism, and perverted judgment. No matter how generously it pays, or how lavishly it applauds, an audience rarely succeeds in satisfying the exigencies of a professional musician, who is apt to look down upon it somewhat contemptuously from a self-erected pinnacle of assumed superior knowledge and finer taste.

It has been justly remarked by a Transatlantic sage that "there is a good deal of human nature in man;" and musical audiences—more correctly, gatherings of persons who desire to listen to music—are, after all, composed of average men and women, having in all probability but one common characteristic; a predilection, more or less pronounced and instructed, for "concords of sweet sounds." Carlyle defined the British nation as so many millions of human beings, "mostly fools;" and if he was right in thus appraising his own compatriots it is scarcely unfair to assume—as these latter are renowned all over the world for their strong common-sense—that the predominance of folly is at least as remarkable in other peoples as it is in ours. An ordinary theatrical or musical audience may be assumed to epitomise, more or less accurately, the nation to which it belongs; therefore silly folk are likely to be more numerous in its ranks than wiseacres. As a matter of fact, it is the preponderance of the silly element throughout all classes of society that enables innumerable incompetent artists to live very comfortably, and even to flourish like the green bay-tree. Pretenders and impostors hang in thick clusters to every branch of the arts—no less abundantly to that of music than to those of poetry, painting, and sculpture—and their prosperity is manifest to the naked eye. They draw largely at sight upon the inexhaustible bank of human folly, which honours their drafts with unfailing punctuality, displaying a liberality for which—no matter what its motive may be—I contend that they ought to be more grateful than I have hitherto found them to be. One of the privileges of genius is to be discontented with everybody and everything; there is always a pea hidden in the mattress upon which Nature's elect lie, and they are distressfully sensible of its presence, like Andersen's Princess, however thick and downy may be the featherbeds of popularity and well-being intervening between their tender skins and the fundamental *paillasse*. Another prerogative of genius is to be more unthankful, and with greater impunity, than is permitted to mere average talent. This is probably as it should be; for extreme susceptibility and absorbing egotism are intrinsic elements of the creative nature. Those musical demi-gods, Beethoven and Wagner, were both extensively worshipped during their lives, as well as after their deaths; but their quarrelsomeness and intense selfishness debarred them from enjoying the pleasures of friendship. Let us, by all means, make allowance for the eccentricities of temperament that render great geniuses so much more agreeable to contemplate from a distance than to know intimately; let us condone their unamiability, and totter along, as best we may, under the burden of the conviction that they despise us. But when sham prophets, or even fairly good capacities of the merely reproductive class, to whom the divine afflatus is wanting, usurp the inborn right of genius to decry the intelligence of average mankind—such, for instance, as supplies an ordinary musical audience with its various component parts—let us mildly observe to them : "These people, upon whom you profess to look down, are in many cases better bred and educated than yourselves, abler far to estimate the exact quality of your performance than you are to appraise their intellectual capacities or taste, and themselves entertaining in a dozen different ways, whereas you are only so, if at all, in one. Besides, do not forget that they could live without you; whereas you would find it a hard matter to live without them. Be, therefore, at the very least, tolerant of the public, whose favour is all in all to you, and do not speak, or even think, despitefully of it."

The musical audiences of different countries resemble one another in a broad and general way. Like other aggregations of men and women, they display national characteristics to the intelligent observer, and afford ample opportunity to him for accurate appraisement of the several standards of musical culture attained by European peoples. One and all, they are made up of technically educated dilettanti; of persons endowed with a natural taste for music; of those to whom musical performances, good, bad, or indifferent, supply an agreeable ear-tickling; of slaves to fashion, who frequent opera-houses and concert-rooms because they deem it "the correct thing" to be seen in such places; and finally of the wealthy idlers of society, whose presence at musical entertainments is simply the outcome of their chronic yearning to consume the leisure that hangs so heavily upon their hands. It is in the respective proportions of these elements that the main distinctions between French and English, German and Italian,

Spanish and Russian audiences make themselves manifest. The minor differences have their rise in local customs and in social habits generated by special climatic conditions. The audiences in Northern Europe are more judgmatical, decorous and, in particular, tolerant of false intonation than those of the south; but less easily moved to demonstrations of enthusiasm for the art, or of sympathy with the artist. The Latin races love music in an unreasoning sort of way; they experience little or no inward call to analyse the sensations it occasions to them, being averse to introspection or any other mental exercise in connection with their amusements. The Teutons also love music, but are prompted by their painstaking, straw-splitting instincts to expend considerable intellectual effort in trying to find out why they like it, and what there is in it logically to justify the pleasure it causes them to experience. In pronouncing praise or condemnation, Italian and Spanish audiences obey their momentary impulse, whereas a German audience is guided by a judicial spirit. What they have in common is a genuine fondness for music, which they express differently—the Latins by outbursts of emotion, the Teutons by concentrated attention. To the true artist the latter is the more satisfactory, although far less exhilarating than the former.

Typical German audiences of the musical variety, are those of Vienna, Berlin, and Munich; the two latter more distinctively so than the former, because the public of the Kaiserstadt on the Danube is by no means exclusively Teutonic, being strongly leavened with Slav, Magyar, and even Italian elements. Viennese society is an epitome of the huge Hapsburg Monarchy, in which four, if not five, nationalities are co-existent and contrive to get on together more or less harmoniously. Their representative men, political, commercial and artistic, naturally gravitate to the capital of the empire; and it may be assumed that non-German Austrians constitute from one-fourth to one-third of the music-lovers who throng the Hofoper and the various concert-rooms of the Residenz whenever any special attraction is offered to them by the managers of those recreative establishments. In no country of Europe is the art of music more generally and assiduously studied, or are musical entertainments more distinctly recognised as an essentially popular class of amusement than in Austria proper and the Kingdom of Bohemia. These two divisions of the "Eastern Realm" furnish the Vienna Conservatoire with nine-tenths of its students, and supply a similar proportion of instrumentalists to the theatrical orchestras and military bands of the empire. Austrian musical audiences resemble savoury broth, the main strength of which lies in its German stock, whilst its appetising odour and high flavour are attributable to a felicitous blending of Slavonic, Hungarian, and Latin ingredients. They are at once appreciative and sympathetic gatherings—critical *avec connoissance de cause*, but of a kindly temper—exacting with respect to small excellences, and tolerant of great defects. As far as instrumental performances are concerned, nothing short of such perfection as it is human to attain will content them. They are accustomed to the very best, and will have it. This rule applies to chamber music as well as to the renderings of orchestral works. The Viennese expect quartets and trios to be played to them no less faultlessly than symphonies and overtures. To the shortcomings of their singers they are amiably forbearing; to those of their instrumentalists they show no mercy. The virtues of the Hofoper orchestra cover a multitude of vocal sins perpetrated nightly in that Imperial establishment.

But Viennese opera-goers and concert-frequenters alike, though constituting in many respects ideal audiences from the artist's point of view, have one extremely unpleasant and objectionable characteristic in common. They become fidgety and fussy shortly after nine o'clock P.M. Up to that hour their demeanour is exemplary. The singer or player, at least, if expert in his function, has no reason to complain of it; for his hearers are attentive, sympathetic, and ever ready to give tongue to their approval at the opportune moment. But, with a few exceptions—the sum total of which does not amount to five per cent. of an average musical audience—they are bond-slaves to a baneful tyrant who rules the middle-class Viennese with an inflexible and undisputed sway. Their bondage begins to weigh upon them with peculiar oppressiveness at the hour I have referred to; they become more and more nervous and uneasy with every minute added by the clock-hand to the record of fleeting time; no spell of music's magic has power to restrain them from making rustling noises, shuffling their feet, and scraping their chairs along the floor, and finally, if the performance be protracted for as much as a quarter of an hour beyond the time-limit in question, from quitting their seats and hurrying out of the theatre or concert-room with a precipitancy that is manifestly prompted by dread of their dire despot. Let me explain.

Broadly speaking, no Viennese has a house to himself or his family alone. Viennese families inhabit flats in enormous buildings, some of which accommodate as many inhabitants as a small country town, and yield incomes of from forty to fifty thousand pounds a year to their proprietors. In one of these houses—the so-called Buerger-Spital—when I resided in Vienna, over three thousand human beings of all social classes lived and had their being. It had thirty distinct entrances and was pierced by eight paved roadways. The "palace" in which I occupied a small third-floor suite of rooms, at a rent of £180, contained a hundred and twenty separate habitations, was six storeys high, and covered as much ground as the green enclosure of Portman Square. These huge edifices are, one and all, in the charge of officials rejoicing in the title of House-Master, which very accurately describes the character and extent of their authority. Police-regulations, framed at the instance of the influential house-owning clique, have invested the House-Master with the right to levy a tax of seven kreuzers (nominally seven, practically ten) upon every inmate of the dwelling controlled by that functionary who demands ingress or egress after ten o'clock in the evening, at which time the main streetdoor is closed and locked, no tenant being allowed to hold a pass-key that will open that general portal. To obtain access to his own domicile, therefore, sixty minutes after the hour at which dramatic and musical entertainments terminate in Vienna, the Kaiserstaedter must pay twopence to his landlord's representative—or more, unless he wishes to suffer a thousand petty annoyances at the hands of that congenitally vengeful person. His habits and amusements are to a great extent regulated by this tyrannical institution. He dines in the middle of the day, goes to his theatre or concert at half-past six, or seven at the latest, and consequently requires supper before retiring to rest. This meal he is accustomed to partake of in a restaurant or beer-hall; he seldom consumes it at home. Hence his mental disquietude and corporeal restlessness at the hour of nine; for his desire not to contribute to the Hausmeister's prosperity is no less keen and ardent than is his yearning to eat and drink at his ease in his favourite supper-room, possibly a mile or so distant from the place in which he has been taking his evening's pleasure, and as far from his residence. He knows that his tyrant is eagerly on the watch for the striking of the hour that entitles him to claim his gate-money, and that the delay of half a minute will have to be expiated by a cash payment, the more vexatious because it is unjustified by any necessary service whatsoever rendered by its recipient. To be the Hausmeister of a large "Palace" in a fashionable quarter of Vienna is to enjoy a lucrative sinecure, the material advantages of which are spiritually supplemented by the ineffable pleasure of being able to torment your social superiors in many several ways, without incurring the least risk of punishment. It is delightful to be largely paid for doing nothing; but how much more so to derive one's remuneration from reluctant persons, whom one is licensed to use despitefully, as well as to mulct them of their substance! During my three years' tenancy of the rooms above referred to in the Hardegg Palais I never failed to comply with the prescriptions of the law, as far as my Hausmeister's fees were concerned, although I never once had a civil word from him, or the least *quid pro quo*, in the way of service, for my periodical payments to him. He never said "Thank you," on receiving his gate-money; for was it not his legal due, and why should he waste politeness on its acknowledgment? As I passed his abode on the ground-floor, I used to hear his two daughters alternately playing Liszt and Chopin on an excellent grand-piano. Subsequently I was informed that they had been taught by one of the best and most fashionable pianists in Vienna; and when they took their walks abroad—as the testimony of my own eyes repeatedly convinced me—Solomon in all his glory was certainly not arrayed like unto either of them. In fact, their magnificent appearance, costly accomplishments and haughty demeanour were, to my apprehension of the fitness of things—shared, I doubt not, by many another overborne and quailing tenant of the Hardegg "Palace"—more than sufficiently demonstrative of the pecuniary productiveness, as well as commanding influence, characterising the high office of house-porter, as exercised by Fortune's favourites in the Austrian capital. I happen to have a somewhat exhaustive acquaintance with European despots, some of whom are kindly, well-meaning people enough in their way. But I know none so arrogant, so greedy, so idle, and so superlatively useless as the

Viennese Hausmeister, the consciousness of whose oppressive yoke blights the sincerest music-lover's relish of a quartet or sonata—after nine P.M.—and converts the rapt attention of a Hofoper or Conservatoire audience into feverish anxiety to be gone from the scene of their artistic enjoyment in time to baulk their remorseless tyrant of his prey.

Vienna is especially fruitful in that variety of musical audience which inclines to combine conviviality with art-worship, and is assiduous in its attendance at the winter *soirées* given by artistic associations, from which ladies are excluded, I suppose by tradition; for nothing can be more harmless or decorous than the entertainments offered by these societies to their subscribers, as well as to a limited number of outsiders fortunate enough to obtain invitations. Many of the members, let us say of the "Hesperus," belong to the "Hilaria," at the same time that they are natives of the "Green Island," worshippers of the "Danube Nymph," votaries of "Euterpe," squatters in the "Damp Wood," and supporters of "Thalia." There is something of the student —the noisy, beer-swilling, cloud-emitting, chorus-chanting, ostrich-stomached, Juchs-loving German student— in the gravest of grown Austrians, be he Hofrath or Primarius, lieutenant-general or linendraper. Jollity, of which the national Gemüthlichkeit is a mitigated form, expresses itself in Vienna in bolting blocks of lukewarm, over-roasted meat, washed down by a flood of pleasant and innocuous beer, and flavoured with a curiously-sickly tobacco smoke, the while pæans to woodland gods or hymns to Amor are being breathed forth harmoniously by tuneful choirs, or occasional poems declaimed by Thespians in mufti. What more innocent or unsophisticate than these recreations, which can do no wrong, save to the over-taxed digestions of the jocund revellers? Can anybody who knows the realm of the Hapsburg imagine a state of being in which an honest Austrian gentleman can be more complacently comfortable, more completely happy, than in a large room filled with inferior smoke, a piled-up plate of dry roast veal and preserved pears before him, a brimming glass mug convenient to his right hand, his half-consumed weed smouldering hard by his bread, a friend on each side of him to whom he can say "Du," and a popular actor in a white neckcloth within hearing, telling how the hard heart of Dionysius the Tyrant was melted?

Of all the convivial societies that sprinkle the long Vienna winter season with "art" evenings, the "Hesperus" was formerly the most hardworking and successful. It numbered amongst its members most of the leading musicians, painters, and poets of the capital, all of whom lent their talents, in turn, to the enlivenment of certain entertainments given by the association to its subscribers. Let me attempt a sketch of the meeting especially consecrated to St. Sylvester, and attended only by the male members of the "Hesperus." Imagine a room about the size and shape of St. James's Hall—a tiny platform on one side, and at the end farthest from the entrance doors a miniature stage; the rest of the apartment being chequered with small supper tables of six-man power, every one of which is surrounded by

Hesperians, eating, drinking, smoking, and talking. It is the correct thing to be in morning dress: only those artists who have volunteered their services for the evening appear in magpie costume. Gathered round a board spread with good things, the committee and their *invités* deserve inspection; for here may be seen the principal literary, musical, and artistic notabilities of the Kaiserstadt, among whom I will venture to say there is more goodfellowship and mutual regard than would be found in a like number of professional caterers for public amusement in any other continental city. One remarkable characteristic of the assembly is the almost total absence of uniforms amongst the guests; the gentlemen of the army are not great lovers of art, or great favourites in the artist world, as yet — we shall see what the stimulus recently applied to their intelligence will do towards facilitating their admission into the society of clever and cultivated men. Nevertheless, if you look carefully round the room, you will detect one or two grey generals, their breasts covered with decorations, seated at a modest little table, out of the way, taking their pleasure meekly, but evidently enjoying the good music as deeply as the longest-haired enthusiast of twenty. Presently, the President of the Society ascends the platform, rings a noisy little bell, and announces that four eminent musicians will play a comic stringed quartet. Did you ever hear one? Well, it is very funny, as well as profoundly scientific—an harmonious lunacy, such as can only emanate from the brain of a German composer. After this, we are regaled with Joan of Arc's celebrated farewell remarks upside down, illustrated by a punning panorama, painted for the occasion by an eminent Viennese artist. As specimens of the pictorial word-plays, I select two of surpassing infamy. "Ihr traulich stillen Thäler" were represented by half-a-dozen plates (Teller) reposing quietly in a plate-rack; and "Ihr Grothen" were typified by three or four fat toads (Kröten) disporting on the brink of a pond. This humorous travesty of Schiller was followed by a four-part cantata, composed by Engelsberger, the subject of which is a journey made by the incredulous St. Thomas to earth, at the request of his Supreme Master, in order to examine into the state of things *là-bas*, Thomas returns with a poor opinion of mundane arrangements, and recommends the Omnipotent to rain gold for a few hours on the terrestrial globe, as the only means of alleviating the paper currency disease from which mortals are suffering. The advice is rejected, on the grounds that as soon as "civilised" people get any more money they spend it on war preparations—a practice highly condemned in heaven; and another remedy for human ills is hinted at—education; but St. Thomas finishes by being a greater sceptic than ever.

Like the citizens of the Kaiserstadt on the "beautiful blue Danube"—a river, by the way, which vies with the Tiber in yellowness—the Berlinese inhabit flats and are addicted to supper. They are, however, ungalled by the yoke of the Hausmeister, which from time immemorial has bowed the necks of the long-suffering Viennese. Life is earnest, however, and hours are early in the Prussian capital. At eleven p.m. the streets of Berlin are for the most part still and void. There are a few exceptions to this rule, of course, such as the Jacobstrasse, in which was formerly situate the Orpheum, one of the most magnificent free-and-easy dancing saloons in Europe, privileged to keep open until the small hours, and imparting an untimely liveliness to the long, narrow thoroughfare above-mentioned. The Friedrichstrasse, too, is unpleasantly animate with bad characters all night long. The criminal classes of Berlin especially affect this handsome street, fully qualified to hold its own in unsavoury competition with that section of Lower Regent Street which begins at the Criterion corner and finishes at Pall Mall. But the Linden Avenue and the Leipzigerstrasse, Berlin's chief arteries of traffic and locomotion; the Wilhelmstrasse, with its princely palaces, foreign embassies and huge financial mansions; the splendid terraces of the Thiergarten region, at once the Hyde Park, Belgravia and South Kensington of Berlin, are all empty, silent and forlorn an hour before midnight. Starting from the Royal Castle on the Koenigsplatz, at that time of night, and walking due westward for an hour at a brisk pace—say, as far as the Zoological Gardens—you seldom meet more than a score of people, exclusive of policemen; unless, indeed, a ball happens to be going on at the Russian or French Embassy, when long strings of carriages block the roadway and phalanges of tall footmen encumber the *trottoir*. The typical Berliner, as a matter of fact, likes to get home betimes, although he is essentially a theatre-going and supper-eating creature. The fashionable dinner-hour in "Modern Athens" is five of the afternoon, but the bourgeoisie dines still earlier. Theatrical and musical performances commence at half-past six or seven, and seldom terminate later than ten, except in the case of such a lengthy Wagnerian work as *Tristan und Isolde* or *Die Meistersinger*, which occupies fully four hours, as given at the Berlin Opera-house. At ten p.m., as a rule, the recreative Berliner sits down to his evening meal; not in his own lodgings, but, if he be a swell, in some restaurant of the Hiller and Evest class, or, if he belong to the bureaucracy or to one of the learned professions, at some respectable Bier-Halle, Kneipe or Austern-Keller—the last-named establishments are frequently subterranean — where he can eat and drink his fill in congenial company for the German equivalent of half-a-crown. Being a rapid, as well as a copious eater, he only requires half-an-hour, or even something less, wherein to put away his food; after which he lights a cheapish cigar (those at seven for threepence, if an army officer), absorbs a final libation of amber-hued Tivoli, strolls leisurely away, enwrapped in *Gemuethlichkeit* as in a garment, and is home by eleven at the very latest, having spent his evening rationally and cheaply. In the latter respect he has a great pull over the Londoner and Parisian. A stall at the Berlin Opera-house costs six shillings, save on those rare occasions when the engagement of a foreign "star" *als Gast* is held to justify the Royal administration in exacting "Hohe Preise," that is, fifty per cent. more than the normal charges. This only happens half-a-dozen times or so during the winter season. It is always announced in all the newspapers forty-eight hours before each performance at the augmented rates of admission takes place. "Hohe Preise" are sometimes demanded when a brand-new opera is being given, the setting, mounting and dressing of which have proved unusually expensive. Throughout my eight years' residence in Berlin only three cases in point occurred within my cognizance; two were Wagnerian productions, the *mise en scène* of which would not have dishonoured the Lyceum, and the third was an amazingly gorgeous ballet hight "Militaria," upon which Herr von Huelsen had lavished some sixty thousand marks. Prices run even lower at the Schauspielhaus, a subventioned theatre at which tragedy and comedy are admirably played by the best actors in Prussia. It may rank with and after the Théâtre Français in Paris; there is nothing at all comparable with it in London. At the Friedrich Wilhelm (operetta) and the Wallner (farcical comedy) the price of a stall is three shillings, less than half the sum charged for similar accommodation at the theatres of the Parisian Boulevards, and exactly three-tenths of that which the lessees of our minor theatres feel justified in demanding for performances of curiously unequal quality. The subscription-concerts at the Opera-house, on a par with those for which the Society of the Friends of Music in Vienna has acquired a world-wide reputation, can be enjoyed at the rate of four shillings apiece, and very few of the concerts given at the Academy of Singing cost their patrons more than a thaler for the best place in the room. Partly in consequence of the moderation displayed by theatrical managers and concert-givers in connection with their tariffs, and partly because the German propensity to temper labour with recreation is a peculiarly strong one, all classes of Berlin society attend dramatic and musical performances much more frequently than do the corresponding varieties of Londoners. Amusements of this description constitute an integral part of German life—not an "extra," as with us. The outlay they necessitate is methodically provided for—frequently by sacrifices in other directions—in the vast majority of German domestic budgets; and, as there is no sort of boredom to which the average German—particularly the Berliner—entertains so deeply-rooted an objection as to that inflicted upon him by a dull "evening at home," theatres and concert-rooms in the Fatherland, even when their attractions scarcely rise above a dead level of artistic mediocrity, fill nightly with intelligent and orderly audiences, well content to sit out three hours' fourth or fifth-rate performances in stifling heat and vitiated air, those being the periodical conditions in which they have always been accustomed to take their periodical doses of post-prandial diversion.

The Berlin musical audience, as those who have attentively perused the foregoing paragraph will readily understand, entertains—in common with that of Vienna—a strong aversion to performances that encroach upon its supper-hour. Its members are not compelled, like the more tractable Kaiserstaedter, to pay a fine for entering their own dwellings after eleven p.m. But they resemble the hero of Sam Weller's inimitable crumpet story in the respect that their "habits is reg'lar, and they don't intend to be put out of their way by nobody." Shortly after half-past nine has struck they develop symptoms of restlessness, which soon pass through the preliminary stage and assume a confirmed and alarming character. Up to that time their behaviour as a rule is irreproachable, from a German point of view; but I have ventured in days long past to take exception to two of their practices which—in Munich and Dresden, as well as in Berlin—always struck me as highly objectionable. In the first place, whether opera, symphony, stringed quartet, or any other variety of concerted music be announced in the bill, all the German youths and maidens present who have a mind to prove by demonstration that they know all about it, and no mistake, bring full scores, oblong in form, with them, and turn over the leaves during the performance in a flappy way that is peculiarly irritating to the auditor who happens to be listening for his pleasure, and not to show other people how intensely, absorbingly, far-more-than-professionally musical he is. I used to find a gloomy consolation for the annoyance inflicted upon me by these disturbers of my peace in observing how hard Nature had been upon them in connection with their personal appearance. No pretty girl or tolerably good-looking younker ever turned over the leaves of a score in any Berlin theatre or concert-room when I was present. Only guys did so; and I may remark that the German variety of guy, male or female, is a peculiarly formidable one, including as it does— amongst other special Teutonic terrors—goggles and long hair, apparently combed with a knife and fork. The other practice to which I demurred was that in which these out-and-out musicians were wont to indulge when anybody a thought less offensive than themselves in aspect and bearing ventured to whisper a comment on the performance, whilst it was going on, to his or her neighbour. The merest ghost of a remark would cause these unsavoury fanatics to turn sharp round upon its utterer, glare at him with blood-chilling ferocity, and give vent to an angry hiss, resembling the hostile warning which a cantankerous old gander addresses to a dog seeking whom it may devour on a village green. This proceeding is not wholly forlorn of a comic element, and it rather entertained me the first time one of the Berlin prize musical scarecrows made me acquainted with it. But I found it pall upon me after a while; and eventually it bored me so intensely that I left off attending concerts, all except Joachim's, at which I used to sit and watch dear old Moltke positively wallowing in silence, his favourite luxury.

There is another peculiarity of Berlin musical audiences which no lover of the divine art who has spent a winter in the German capital can have failed to notice. Perhaps it is the outcome of intrinsic amiability. I think this unlikely. Perhaps, on the other hand, it is the corollary of that lack of ear which, side by side with musical culture and erudition of an extremely advanced character, characterises the average German *habitué* of opera-houses and concert-rooms. The peculiarity I refer to is an amazing tolerance of false intonation. Men may sing sharp, and men may sing flat; but the Berliner endures them for ever—that is, to borrow a term from Bret Harte, if he "likes their style." To be persistently, remorselessly, homicidally out of tune is no offence in a popular vocalist, male or female, belonging to the Royal Opera Company, or to any of the leading operetta casts in Berlin. All the public favourites *di primo cartello* whom I heard in the house on the Opernplatz between the years 1867 and 1878, with those distinguished exceptions—Pauline von Rhaden, better known by her spinster name of Lucca, Amalie von Voggenhuber, otherwise Frau Krolop, and Ernst, the lyric tenor—sang more or less out of tune. Mathilde Mallinger, good musician and superb actress as she was, has often curdled my blood by singing a whole *scena* an eighth of a tone below the orchestral pitch; so has Albert Niemann, far and away the finest heroic tenor singer and actor in Europe, but incapable, for many years past, of keeping unswervingly in the middle of the note. Dr. Betz, the great baritone of the Hofoper, is a musician of musicians, a dramatic artist of the first water, an ornament to the lyric stage; but he sings out of tune. Fricke, the *basso profondissimo*, is a phœnix of talent, sublime in tragic, inimitable in comic rôles; the best Marcel and the best Falstaff I have ever seen in my life; but he sings out of tune. So does Frau Sachse-Hofmeister; so do Fraeulein Lehmann, Grossi and Lammert, all well-trained vocalists and efficient actresses. So does Schmitz, the second tenor who is always cast for Oberon, in the bewildering opera of that name, and sings his music in a manner that no love-lorn tom-cat need envy. So does the little podgy gentleman, who warbles fioriture with more effort than accuracy, and to whom, therefore, the florid parts of Don Ottavio and Count Almaviva are invariably entrusted—I forget his name, and this particular lapse of memory does not convulse me with a single remorseful pang. So did

Diener, whose C sharp in "Suivez-moi" still makes me shudder whenever I think of it, although more than a decade has passed away since I last heard him do his worst in the *ut de poitrine* line of business. So does Mierzwinski; with this difference, that, while all the previously-named artists merely sing out of tune, Mierzwinski bellows out of tune. I have named the leading favourites of the Berlin opera-going public. None of them can sing in tune straight through a part; or if they can, they don't. And yet I have never heard them called over the coals, or even gently rebuked, by a Hofoper audience for committing the atrocity which the Germans describe as "detonation." On the contrary, I have over and over again heard them, one and all, vehemently applauded and enthusiastically called before the curtain for singing in a manner that set my teeth on edge, and caused cold shivers to flutter down either side of my spine. I used to ask my Berlin friends —some of them were veritable mines of musical learning —why these dreadful sins were condoned. Once, when Fricke had been called out after some achievements in the way of false intonation for which nothing short of his instant execution could have fitly atoned, I said to poor Eckert, who was sitting next to me in the stalls (Radecke was conducting that evening), "Why is this man summoned to receive blessings instead of curses; or rather, why is he not led away to prompt but painless death? He has sung every note of his part a quarter-tone flat; is that what your public likes? Muss man denn detoniren, um die musikalischen Berliner zu befriedigen?" "You mean the good Fricke, my dear?"

replied my gifted friend the Royal Kapellmeister; "true is it, he sings out of tune a little now and then (er detonirt ein klein Bischen ab und zu); but what a fine artist he is—what an accomplished actor—what an excellent man, staunch friend, loyal subject! Do you know, my worthy one, that he paints quite delightfully in water-colours, and plays upon half-a-dozen instruments? Ein gar zu ausgezeichneter Mann, mein Bester; daher wird er auch gerufen; mann soll's ihm nicht verdenken!" (A really admirable fellow; that is why he is called out; we must not grudge him the compliment.) I did not believe, as I told the Kapellmeister, that the opera-house audience summoned Fricke before the curtain because he executed water-colour sketches which they had never seen, or was a true liege-man to the Hohenzollern, which they could not know for certain. It seemed to me far more likely that they thus distinguished him because they admired his acting, which was truly excellent; and, above all, because they were insensible to his "detonation."

Eckert was seriously annoyed with me when I expressed this opinion to him. During my residence in Berlin I found, indeed, that musical Germans almost invariably resented my doubts of their susceptibility to the *peine forte et dure* of false intonation; and it struck me that their displeasure was all the keener because those doubts happened, in my case, to be expressed by an Englishman. A very few years ago the conviction was still strong and general throughout Northern Germany that no native of these brumous isles could possibly be a musician, or form any opinion worth listening to in connection with matters musical. I had not lived long in Prussia before I found this to be a dogma—the dogmatic vein runs large in the Borussian character—and ceased to struggle against it. At first I had taken great pains to persuade my German acquaintances that, in denying to us, as a nation, the possession of musical taste and culture, they were in error; I even went so far as to point out to them that England could boast of a fine, vigorous school of creative and executant musicians at a time when the Germans, musically considered, were in a condition of barbarism, the sumptuary equivalent of which might be appraised at the bear and wolf-skin class of garment, worn loosely over an epidermis gaily decorated with rudimentary devices in woad and ochre. They did not seem, oddly enough, to relish this statement; nor, I am bound to say, to believe it, although it was supported by the evidence of history. But I never happened to know a German who was not a *doctrinaire*, or who was capable of being convinced by the most luminous arguments that his own view of any conceivable subject was not the only right one. So, as I said before, I soon gave up my endeavour to demonstrate the inborn musicality of Englishmen as a hopeless emprise, and submitted with decent cheerfulness to the inclusion of my own humble person in the sweeping sentence of musical incapacity pronounced upon my fellow-countrymen in general by Teutonic prejudice. I could not, of course, fail to perceive that Berlin society regarded any expression of opinion on my part, having relation to music or musicians, as an impertinence, and estimated the utterance (of which I was never chary in musical circles) of my conviction that the German ear, with respect to shades of intonation, was even less discriminating than the English, as a more than Bulgarian outrage. But all this left me calm; for, like one of the late Mr. Anthony Trollope's novelistic heroes, I knew I was right. And I defy any person, himself gifted with a correct musical ear, who has assiduously observed the attitude of a Berlin musical audience towards a false note sung by a favourite vocalist, to contradict me.

The Berlin Opera-house is a marvel of discomfort. Not the slightest provision is made by its directors for the comfort of the public, which is expected to contribute its money gratefully for inferior performances and wretched accommodation. There is no *foyer*, no *tabagie*, no ventilation. For the privilege of being slowly boiled and listening to third-rate singing you have to pay from six to nine shillings, if you select the stalls—into which officers are forbidden to enter—as your abiding-place for the evening, and the prices of seats in the other parts of the house vary between one and five marks. The temperature, about ninety degrees Fahrenheit when the overture begins, rises to one hundred and ten degrees or so by the time the performance is ended. The only concession made to public convenience by the directors of this torture-chamber is a regulation by which the evening's entertainment is punctually brought to a close at half-past nine, ten o'clock being the supper time of the eminently respectable class that delights to mortify its flesh at the Opera-house. For its *own* convenience, furthermore, the management has decreed that the *entr'actes* shall last a quarter of an hour each; so that, what with the earliness of the closing hour, and the length of the intervals between the acts, there is nothing for it but to mutilate the great works produced upon the stage. Some years ago I underwent the sorrow of hearing the noblest opera of modern times, Gounod's "Faust," so carved, clipped, and mangled as to be almost unrecognisable. It was, in fact, a mere abridgment of the original work—not only were whole scenes left out, and others amalgamated or fused down into one another, to the utter destruction of the unities, but Niemann (Faust) cut out the second part of "Salve dimora," and Mdlle. Baumgarten (Marguerite) omitted more than half of the jewel song, and a whole verse of the "Rè di Thule." For such wholesale and unscrupulous barbarism I was altogether unprepared in Berlin, which is ever being vaunted by its inhabitants as "die Hauptstadt der Intelligenz."

Amongst the musical audiences of Berlin is one which I believe to be, of its kind, unique in Europe, probably in the world. It is exclusively composed of Prussian officers, and frequents the concerts given during the winter season by a full orchestra of guardsmen, every member of which bears his Prussian Majesty's commission. Shortly after the conclusion of the Franco-German war I attended one of these entertainments at the Guard Artillery Barracks, which are situated in a melancholy district, unpenetrated by any of the frequented thoroughfares that are household words to an *habitué* of the Northern Kaiserstadt—a sort of debateable land, called "Am Kupfergraben," or "By the Copper Ditch," close to the Linden, to the Museum, the Academies, the University, and the Royal Palaces, and yet which a foreigner might never happen to traverse during a life-long residence in Berlin, unless he were invited to mess with the gallant gunners, or to be their guest upon such an occasion as that which on the night I refer to drew a brilliant company to the grim old *caserne*, built in the reign of Frederick the Great. In the mess-room of this enormous building—some notion of its size may be derived from the fact that it accommodates a whole brigade of artillery, officers, men, and horses—have for thirty-four years past been held the weekly meetings and practices of the "Officers' Orchestral Union." This society numbers over sixty members, fifty of whom are executants, and forms a complete orchestra capable of performing the most elaborate concerted works of the great masters. Colonel von Treske, who has been associated with the "Union" since its origin, was in 1874 its President and leader of the orchestra; Colonel von Ribbentrop, of the General Staff, one of the most distinguished scientific officers in the Prussian army, was its treasurer; and the members are officers of all ranks, from lieutenant-general down to second lieutenant, each of whom has qualified himself for admission to the "Union" by a certain degree of proficiency upon some musical instrument. There are more than a score of first and second violins—good store of serviceable, steady celli—a couple of vigorous "grunters," and the proper proportion of violas. Every instrument of wood or brass is duly "filled up;" and the drumsticks were for many years wielded by a soldier-prince, now a major-general and aide-de-camp to his Majesty, who resigned them some time ago to their present holder, and retired from the class of "executant members" into that of "listening members," in which he now holds exalted rank and honours.

With respect to these classes of membership into which the "Union" is divided, I must explain that, shortly after the constitution of the Society, the humorous idea of founding an Order occurred to its managing committee, which straightway drew up the statutes of "The August and Illustrious Order of the White Napkin," in five classes, to be conferred upon members distinguishing themselves respectively as executants, arrangers and composers. There were, however, then as now, "listening members" of the "Union," and presently it was suggested that they—inasmuch as they were expected to hear the performances given by the "executant members"—were at least as deserving of some honorific distinction for their services in this respect, as those members who enjoyed the advantage of improving their practical acquaintance with their respective instruments weekly, and whose meritorious endeavours to attain perfection might be held to be occasionally somewhat in the nature of an infliction upon the nerves of their audiences. So a second Order was founded, that of the "Golden Ear," to be bestowed on these listening associates; and I had the pleasure of witnessing the conferment of its highest class—carrying with it the strictly local title of "Excellency"—upon the amiable and accomplished Prince von Hohenlohe-Ingelfingen and one or two other "Zuhörenden Mitglieder" of assured merit and long standing. Every member of the

"Union" who has been decorated with one or both of these knightly Orders is under the obligation of wearing the insignia at the society's meetings; should he fail to do so, he is fined the sum of sixpence. A similar fine is imposed for late attendance or unnotified non-attendance. These fines are duly collected by the "Strafmeister," or Master of Punishments, of the "Union," and expended in a gigantic "Bowle"—a sort of cup, made of moselle, champagne, slices of pineapple and orange juice—which is solemnly imbibed at the last *réunion* of the annual season by members executant and listening.

The particular festivity to which I had the honour of being invited was held in celebration of the twenty-first anniversary of the society's birthday, and was characterised by the utmost jollity and good-fellowship. The first part of the entertainment was altogether musical, and consisted of orchestral and solo performances by members of the Union. The programme opened with an "occasional" overture by Kalliwoda, correctly and spiritedly rendered; another of the "numbers" was Mendelssohn's Grand Concerto (pianoforte and orchestra) in G minor; and a third was the slow movement of a quaint old concerto by Haydn, redolent of pulvilio, and suggesting, at every bar, bag-wigs, clouded canes, knee-breeches and silk stockings. A Saxon artillerist sang the great tenor song out of *Freischütz*, and a Blue hussar—who figured very creditably in the orchestra amongst the first violins—warbled a sentimental ditty, with *cello obbligato* by the regimental doctor, to everybody's unbounded gratification. At the conclusion of the programme the tables were rapidly laid, and we all sat down, over a hundred strong, to an excellent supper, the chief event of the occasion. As Colonel von Treske took his seat in the presidential chair, a transparency was hoisted up behind his throne, being an allegorical and emblematic presentment of the society's origin, career and prospects, depicted by an executant member, Knight Grand Cross of the White Napkin. This transparency was divided into eight compartments, to each of which a stanza of the medley *d'occasion*—subsequently performed by the whole body of members and guests with immense vigour and relish—was devoted. As soon as the first course had been removed, the President read the annual report, the Statutes of the Orders, and the congratulatory telegrams from kindred "Unions" in Breslau, Mayence, &c., which had reached him in the course of the anniversary; winding up with an eminently humorous speech, the culminating point of which was, of course, the toast of the evening. Then followed the Treasurer, Colonel von Ribbentrop, who proved a balance in the society's favour of forty-one shillings—showing a condition, it appeared, of unprecedented financial prosperity —and laid before the members a plan for investing their floating capital in a State Lottery share, as well as a project for the laying out of the £22,500 which that share could not fail to produce ! A flourish of horns, in the "*Katzenmusik*" manner, then introduced the interpreter of the transparency, who, armed with a wand, proceeded to expound the application of that graphic chronicle of the society's annals. Each explanatory strophe was furnished with a supplement in the shape of a commentatory stanza set to a popular tune, and these were intoned with an harmonious vehemence that threatened more than once to raise the roof of the building. The next great and impressive ceremony was the conferment of various classes of the Orders by the Grand Master in full chapter—each recipient of a cross, star, or collar paying up his capitular fees like a man before his insignia were handed to him.

How jolly it all was, and how harmless! What perfect *camaraderie* between old and young, noble and simple, general and subaltern, all wearing the "Kaiserkleid," and indulging in these innocent "high-jinks" with the fervour and joyousness of clever schoolboys! Truly it was one of the pleasantest sights I ever saw in a cheerless city, where every man seems to be eternally on his guard against his neighbour. I must, however, except army men from this rule, otherwise all but absolute. The feeling and bearing of officers towards one another and their foreign comrades are in every respect admirable. The exceptional privileges they enjoy, and the restraints imposed upon them in virtue of the uniform, cause them to be stiff in manner towards civilians in general; but a brother soldier, of whatsoever nationality or rank, is sure of a hearty welcome from them one and all. And not only do these gallant gentlemen work harder at their profession than does any other specialist that I know of labour at his *métier*, but for the most part they spend their leisure hours in rational amusements or profitable study. One of the "listening" generals took me aside between the parts of the concert, and described to me the various uses to which the old-fashioned, low-ceilinged mess-room in which we were standing was put by the "Offizierskorps." "It is really a club to these fine fellows," said his Excellency, "and even more than a club. There is not an evening in the week upon which our officers, young and old, do not gather together here for some social or instructive purpose. One night there is a practice, another night a lecture upon some matter of scientific or topical interest, another night a discussion on professional subjects; and they like the old walls and the old faces they see within them so sincerely that it is the deuce and all to get them away! Here are thirty and more young fellows—leaving out the oldsters and fogies like myself—who turn to and rasp or blow away for dear life week after week with the greatest possible enjoyment. They are able to play any concerted music you can put before them. Do you think that does not do them good? And when they leave us, as they must in time, through promotion or transfer to other garrisons, is it not a preservative against many temptations and follies that they carry with them the cultivated taste for art—the exercised faculty of passing their time agreeably and innocently? Not only are these boys kept out of mischief by their fiddling and tootling, but they keep their comrades out of mischief as well." And the general was right. As for the illustrious Orders of the "White Napkin" and the "Golden Ear," they are institutions for which I entertain a lively respect; for they confer, to my mind, a deal more appreciable distinction on those who have the honour to wear them, than a good many of the complimentary decorations that adorn the breasts of persons who have so frequently done nothing to deserve them.

Yet another Berlin musical audience, and I will pass to "fresh woods and pastures new." During the winter of the year 1872 I had the pleasure of attending a meeting of the Orchestral Knitting-and-Roast-Veal Association, held at No. 48, Leipzigers Strasse, in Athens on the Spree. The institution in question was founded upon that thorough comprehension of the "fitness of things" characterising North Germans in general and Berlinese in particular. It offered to its members a happy combination of concerted music, seasonable industry and solid nourishment, thus gratifying at once their intellectual, moral and physical cravings. Admission to participation in the enjoyment of the attractions it proffered to those who like their harmony served up hot with gravy, and garnished with coloured wool, was not trammelled by the protective process of ballot. To become a member of the Orchestral Knitting-and-Roast-Veal Association it was not necessary that you should be proposed, seconded and subjected to the ordeal of the black ball. When you presented yourself at the portals of its meeting room, you were not required to produce your baptismal certificate, vaccination papers, and other documents of legitimation; all that was expected was that you should pay your entrance fee, which varied in amount between the sums of sixpence and eighteenpence. Having discharged this obligation, you received a voucher, which passed you into a noble hall, brilliantly illuminated, and fitted with spacious boxes furnished like *salons*, wherein the servants of the association provided you with " every luxury of the season," at so many thalers a head. If knitting were your " strong suit," you had to enter the body of the hall, secure a table, order your roast veal, and produce the implements of your craft. You found yourself surrounded by its votaries. Knitting to right of you, knitting to left of you, knitting in front of you, knitting in rear of you, clicking and rustling, would, if you were susceptible of emulation, stimulate you to extraordinary efforts in that line. Should you not be sufficiently versed in the mysteries of "drop three, pick up one," &c., to take rank in the army of knitters, it were better that you mounted a staircase, and took a seat in a box, limiting the exercise of your rights as a member to the consumption of an "orchestralisches Kalbsfleisch." Knitting was optional, not compulsory; and you might smoke all over the establishment. The Perpetual Grand was a gentleman adorned with several glittering decorations, of home and foreign manufacture. His name was Bilse, and he was a leader of men. He ruled them with an ebony silver-tipped wand of office; his sway was just, absolute and undivided. That he knitted, and eat roast veal, in his character as chief official of the Association, I have no reason to doubt; but I did not see him perform those functions. During my three hours and a half membership I was witness to his admirable fulfilment of other duties attached to his responsible position. P. G. Bilse was an excellent conductor, and a man of refined musical taste, judiciously conservative in his fidelity to the classics, and yet tolerant of innovation where innovation is justified through intrinsic merit. Composers of the day had nothing to complain of at his hands; and he appeased the manes of the great dead by frequent and reverent worship. It was something gained to the cause of art that large audiences, chiefly recruited from the sixpenny class of society, should night after night be enabled to enjoy the glorious works of such masters as Beethoven, Haydn and Schubert, even with an accompaniment *pizzicato* of knitting needles, or knives and forks *obbligati*; and thoroughly well performed, too, by an orchestra of about forty artists, including a few remarkably good soloists. Nor could even a St. James's Hall purist take exception to the admission of such delightful latter-day melodists as Strauss, Offenbach, and Suppé, into the august company of the aforesaid giants upon such neutral ground as the platform of the O. K. and R. V. Association. Herr Bilse's programmes were models of the sort of entertainment that should be offered by the directors of popular concerts to a thrifty but appreciative public; and few conscientious people who have sat out an oratorio or a matinée of classical chamber music will deny that they have longed for something to do, and above all for something to eat and drink, during the dismal intervals usually devoted to changing legs, hopelessly striving to get something new out of the printed "Synthetic Analysis" or Book of Words, and whispering commonplaces to your neighbour, that elapse between the performances of the several "numbers" set down for execution. The joys of knitting and roast veal (not to mention tobacco), taken in connection with orchestral music of a high class, may be unorthodox, utilitarian, and grossly materialistic; but there is a good deal to be said on the other side. Perhaps it is better to knit stockings or comforters—a mechanical employment that in no way interferes with the intellectual faculty of enjoyment—than to sit with your hands before you doing nothing. A good supper conduces to the establishment of a happy frame of mind; when a man is hungry—and the German appetite asserts itself every three hours with such vigour that the arrangements of business life and of all public amusements have long since been made utterly subservient to its demands—he listens with comparative indifference to the sweetest strains, and is apt secretly to wish that their duration, instead of being "long drawn out," should be abridged or curtailed. Again, in this our Victorian age it may confidently be asserted that ten men of every twelve are smokers in a greater or less degree; smoking is become a part of our lives, and a good cigar enhances every pleasure that must be partaken of in comparative idleness.

However, even admitting the validity of these arguments in favour of the German *praxis,* as carried out by the above-mentioned association, I must say that the *coup d'œil* presented by the interior of the "Concert Haus" on an O. K. and R. V. night—the institution still exists, though not under Herr Bilse's direction—is calculated to strike an Englishman as affording one of the queerest spectacles that he ever set eyes on. Were it not for the orchestra, the festive garnishment of the wooden supper-tables, and the wreaths of tobacco smoke floating upwards toward the roof—where they stop, no means of exit being provided for them—he might fancy that he had strayed into the bosom of a Dorcas Society. Family groups, consisting of mamma, aunt Minna, and four or five strapping Fräuleins, are gathered round huge workbaskets, as busy as bees in the honey-making season. Click, click, go the needles—chatter, chatter, the tongues—clink and clatter the plates, knives and forks, with a surprising din that is only partially abated now and anon, when the Kapellmeister raps his desk energetically with his bâton. Anything more strictly respectable than the *matériel* of which the assembly is composed cannot be imagined. Upstairs in the boxes, where seductive young plungers, belonging to the garrison of Berlin, do congregate, a few gaudy sylphs with top-heavy chignons and stilt-heeled boots may be seen fluttering about in search of prey; but the five-groschen part of the audience consists exclusively of decent tradespeople and *employés* with the female members of their families. Materfamilias brings her whole brood of daughters, leaving pater at home to mind the shop or read his paper in peace and quiet; the buxom young chickens range themselves decorously round the "good fat hen," and stick to their Berlin wool as if the one aim and object of their lives were to knit an indefinite number of comforters. Presently, however, comes a refreshment interlude: large mugs of beer and smoking piles of *Braten* are brought to the table, which is promptly cleared of wool-balls, scissors, and other industrial impedimenta, and the ladies fall to with appetites worthy of Uhlans. Meanwhile the orchestra is playing a rhapsody of Liszt, an overture of Weber, or a waltz of Gungl. The programme is alternately music and a bill of fare. Musical *motivi* are interpolated between the items of the *Speisekarte;* roast pig and plums become mixed up in your mind with a triumphal march or a doleful dirge, as the case may be. The entertainment runs something in this wise—a plate of red cabbage, an adagio of Beethoven, and the foot of a stocking. It is as confused as the incidents of a dream, but pleasant and highly diverting for all that.

An excellent Italian baritone, Aldighieri, who was one of my most intimate friends during my residence in his native land, once told me in the fulness of his heart —we were strolling through the quaint old gardens of Monza one lovely autumn afternoon—that the provincial audiences of Italy were the only ones in Europe of which he stood in fear. He was a man of large professional experience, an admirable vocalist and fine actor, and had won public favour in every European capital; but nervousness impaired his powers, so he assured me, whenever he found himself called upon to sing to his compatriots in the smaller theatres of the Peninsula. "All Italian audiences are terrible" (he observed) "to the executant artist whom Nature has afflicted with keen sensibilities, or has forgotten to arm with the panoply of ignorance and conceit that renders so many operatic vocalists invulnerable to the shafts of criticism. For my fellow-countrymen are intensely critical; not after the German manner, which subordinates the faults of detail in a performance to its general efficiency, but in their own, which regards each individual shortcoming as a heinous offence, and is comparatively indifferent to the merit of an operatic production, considered as an entirety. They are by no means particular about correctness of *mise-en-scène*, appropriateness of costumes and accessories to the period in which the action of the opera is assumed to take place, orchestral excellence or choral correctness; but they are fiercely intolerant of faulty style or inaccurate intonation in the principal vocalists, and—when these fail to satisfy them—are prone to express their dissatisfaction with an angry vehemence that is little less than appalling to singers whose nerves—like my own—are not fortified by the supreme tonic of inexpugnable self-satisfaction. It matters not to Italian opera-goers how high the professional standing of an artist may be, or how great his international renown; if he fail to fulfil their expectations they do not hesitate to hound him down as unmercifully as though he were an assassin or an incendiary, caught in the very act of delinquency. As excitable as they are exacting, they by no means restrict their demonstrations of displeasure to hisses, whistlings, yells, hootings and other more articulate vociferations couched in terms of astonishing vigour. I have seen many a wretched singer, panic-stricken and livid under his paint, pelted off the stage with damaged fruit and vegetable refuse, culled from the market-place during the entr'acte by the vengeful occupants of pit and gallery; and, in cases when the luckless offender has belonged to the softer sex, it is customary in most of our provincial theatres to call her before the curtain ten or a dozen times in succession in order to assail her, over and over again, with storms of hisses and abusive epithets. To nervousness or physical indisposition—in a word, to any of the accidents which cause the best of vocalists, at times, to sing slightly out of tune—our country-town audiences show no pity. The Italians are in the main a good-natured, easy-going, and even, I will venture to say, courteous folk; but they rarely display these characteristics in their attitude towards the exponents of dramatic and musical art. Disappointment, in connection with the quality of operatic performances more especially, seems to turn their abundant milk of human-kindness into gall. They are lambs in their homes, and leopards in their theatres. As a set-off to their ruthlessness when discontented, however, they demonstrate their approval with an exuberance of enthusiasm unknown in every other European country, except Spain. Please them, and their gratitude keeps no bounds, at least in its visible and audible expression. Annoy them, and they thirst for your blood."

My own experiences of Italian audiences, undergone in every province of the Regno Unito (with the two exceptions of Sicily and Sardinia), and at all seasons of the year, confirm those of Aldighieri, summarily set forth above, in every respect. Nearly twenty years ago, when I sojourned in the fairest of European lands, I was an inveterate theatre-goer; moreover, it was the fashion in Italian society at that time to spend some portion of every evening at the theatre—not necessarily to attend to the piece, but to exchange the news of the day, pay visits to one's friends in their boxes, and, above all, to talk scandal—and I did as everybody else did. Indeed, there was nothing else to do, for the clubs were deserted between the hours of nine and twelve P.M., and receptions at private houses rarely commenced until at least the second act of the opera *en vogue* had come to a conclusion. The only recreative, or even social, resource of the "intelligent foreigner" whose lines are cast for any length of time within the old-world precincts of a provincial Italian town—not excluding from this category large cities, the former capitals of kingdoms and duchies—is the theatre in which the lyric drama is performed; the minor houses being generally affected to the representation of farcical comedy in the local dialect of the district, utterly unintelligible to all save those to the manner born. Fantoccini are fascinating once in a way; and "talking-shadows," when stage-managed by a caustic wag—many such pick up a living in the popular entertainment line on Italian soil—are eloquent with excellent fooling, at which one may laugh one's self sore the first time one hears it; but as "a constancy," to borrow a term from Miss Nipper's vocabulary, these funniments are apt to pall upon anybody but an out-and-out Italian. After I had exhausted their joys I fell back upon the stock amusements of the natives—opera and ballet, repeated as a rule night after night throughout the *stagione*, save when a flaming announcement of "Gran Riposo," affixed to the entrances of the leading theatre, leads the public to infer that the *prima donna* has had a more than usually painful difference with the *impresario*, or that the robust tenor's digestive faculties have proved unequal to grapple with macaroni enough for seven, followed by double portions of *frittura mista*, *polpette*, *stuffato* and *bomba alla strega*. The Italian robust tenor, I should observe, is an all but unrivalled trencherman, though the *tenore lirico*, as far as appetite and stowage capacity are concerned, is not the variety of *edax rerum* that one could hope to nourish satisfactorily on a small income. "Gran Riposo" is a term susceptible of interpretation in many several ways. That it may mean either of the calamities above alluded to I have on more than one occasion been enabled to ascertain beyond the possibility of doubt.

Asking forgiveness for this digression, and harking back to my subject, I will endeavour to reproduce in black and white some of the impressions made upon me by Italian musical audiences. In the first place, when I was a novice in Ausonian "tricks and manners," I was surprised to observe that, except on so-called "gala" nights, next to nobody attended operatic performances in evening dress. The stalls were never occupied by ladies "of society," as they are in English theatres, and the men of "high life" and "sport" who sometimes sate in the three front rows generally wore black morning coats and coloured trousers. The "dress circle" institution had not, at that time, been introduced into any Italian opera-house, but the prevalent distribution of accommodation was as follows: stalls, pit, standing room in a seat-less parterre, four or five tiers of private boxes, and a spacious gallery, affording a (literally) bird's-eye view of the stage. Even in the boxes, ladies and gentlemen seldom appeared *en grande toilette*, unless they happened to be going to a ball or reception after the theatre. Hence the general aspect of the audience was seedy rather than festive. In the pit and gallery—which, with the stalls, constituted the emotional element of the house on ordinary nights—no objection appeared to be entertained to those unconventional patrons of the lyric drama who kept their hats on their heads throughout the performance. I observed that applause, as well as its converse, was almost invariably led and insisted upon by *dilettanti* of this class; while society in the boxes, as a rule, only gave expression to its approval in *sotto voce* murmurs, and rarely vented its displeasure in sibilation or whistling. All the box-people seemed to know one another, and to pass their time in animated conversation, instead of listening to the opera. The pittites and gods, on the other hand, were eagerly attentive and audibly critical; no flaw in the accompaniments, no false note in the singing, no hitch in the stage business escaped their notice, or failed to elicit from them some appropriate utterance. Aldighieri was right; these were terrible audiences indeed, not only to the artists engaged to entertain them, but to the music-loving alien unaccustomed to their restless demonstrativeness, and suffering from the nervous irritability provoked by a succession of disturbing noises that only ceased when the opera itself came to an end. It never seemed to strike any native member of an Italian audience that he might possibly be marring his neighbour's enjoyment by ventilating his own feelings *vivâ voce*. I have frequently sate between able-bodied *fanatici* to whom every well or ill-sung phrase suggested a sonorous cry of "Bene!" or an ireful growl of "Male!" all through an opera; and have remembered how savagely I had been snubbed in Berlin, by fanatics of another variety, for daring to whisper a word or two in the ear of my companion for the time being, while some popular *cantatrice* was singing steadfastly out of tune.

This irrepressibility of utterance in Italian musical audiences, even when everything behind the footlights went smoothly and well, was my normal drawback at all the Peninsular opera-houses I ever attended. But it was nothing to the discomfiture that befel me upon one or two occasions, when really vicious performances raised the public temper to fever-heat, and speedily led up to scenes of disorder, sound, and fury such as I have never witnessed in any theatre north of the Alps. During the spring of 1868 I was engaged in the fulfilment of a special mission that took me into several nooks of Tuscany and the Papal States, comparatively unfrequented by foreigners, and on more than one occasion was compelled to stay for two or three days at a stretch in small out-of-the-way towns of fossilised aspect, in the *piazze* of which grass grew with significant luxuriance, traffic of every kind being conspicuous by its absence from the grey flagged thoroughfares, flanked on either side by huge houses of tawny and dusky stone, with massive closed doors and barred open windows. In old-world places of this kind, remote from the highways of progress, dull, poor, lethargic, and hopeless, I was more than once surprised to find large and handsome theatres, well-built and tastefully-decorated, spacious enough to contain thrice the visible population of the towns to which they belonged, and—as far as their acoustic properties are concerned—everything that could be desired. How it is with them now I know not, but at the time I refer to they were closed for eight months of the twelve in the year. Throughout the winter, backed up by some small state or municipal subvention, the local lessee contrived to keep them open four nights in the week, with the aid of touring companies and migratory stars; and—although their stock orchestras, costumes and accessories were as a rule very marvels of weakness, decay and archaism—I found them almost invariably well-attended, by audiences, moreover, of the exacting or "terrible" class to which Aldighieri's above-quoted observations referred. Not that they were rough upon the old-established shortcomings of the local executants, scenery and dresses, which they appeared to regard as inevitable evils, to be endured in silence and under gesticulatory protest of sardonic shrugs. They reserved their utmost severities for the vocal "strangers within their gates"—the "principals" in troupes engaged for half-a-dozen performances by an enterprising management, and "billed" all over the town as "the egregious tenor Malandrino," or "the inclyte first-lady Pettegola."

It was in one of these theatres, thronged for the nonce, that I happened to be seated, hopeful of whiling away a long idle evening by the aid of the *Trovatore*—announced for performance by a galaxy of stars that professed to have sparkled in Royal Opera-houses without number—when the ire of the audience, justly aroused by the *laches* of the robust tenor—let us continue to call him Signor Malandrino, in recognition of his vocal turpitude—broke all bounds, and gave rise to an episode of riot and clamour compared to which Irving's version of the Brocken orgies might rank as a mild and orderly Sunday-school entertainment of the bun and sky-blue order. Malandrino was a comely and stalwart artist; when he first "came on" his appearance so far prepossessed the public in his favour that he was received with a round of polite applause. But he had not terminated the introductory phrase of his opening recitative, when an apprehensive shudder ran through the house, and a few sonorous voices were heard exclaiming "Non stuonar!" (Don't sing out of tune!). As he proceeded, however, regardless of this timely prohibition, to sing flatter and flatter, the outcries grew louder, more general, and, I regret to say, more objurgatory in their character. Amongst the uncomplimentary epithets hurled at the wretched Malandrino were "Bestia!" "Asinaccio!" "Infame!" and others (the Italian popular vocabulary teems with such amenities) less fit for publication; one sustained high note of peculiar atrocity elicited a terrific yell of "Boja!" (executioner), a term of dire reproach throughout the Realm of the Boot. No sooner had the curtain dropped than the occupants of the pit and gallery vanished from the auditorium with extraordinary rapidity. I followed them at my leisure, fully expecting to find lobbies and entrance-hall crowded with infuriate citizens, in full cry over their wrongs, and stimulating their just wrath by a more than usually passionate consumption of the indescribably revolting cigars at five a penny with which Italians were wont to poison the atmosphere of their native land in the days when Unity was not—even in the matter of cheap and nasty tobacco—and the Peninsular taste was divided between "Cavours" of home production, "Veveys" imported from Switzerland, and "Virginias," hollow horrors pierced by a straw, which afforded rank internal evidence of having been invented and manufactured by the Foul Fiend himself. All the usual places of rendezvous during the "waits" were deserted. Amazement prompted me to ask the official who gave out the entr'acte checks what had become of the audience. With a sad smile he replied "Si sono recati al mercato!" (They are gone to the market-place!) The true significance of this mysterious statement was revealed to me half-an-hour later, when Manrico the untuneful, reappearing upon the stage, was assailed by a heavy and continuous shower of stale fruit, minor vegetables and other unconsidered trifles which speedily caused him to beat an ignominious retreat into the wing, vainly endeavouring to shield his head from the missiles aimed at him. This "demonstration of reproof," as a gentleman sitting by me happily described it, was accompanied by an altogether inconceivable and indescribable clamour, which lasted through the remainder of the performance—that is to say, whenever the miserable Malandrino was "on;" for the audience would not allow the *impresa* to carry out its desire to drop the curtain and return their money, but insisted upon hearing the opera out, threatening to wreck the theatre if the management attempted to baulk them. And so, at intervals, they howled at Manrico until nearly midnight, calling him forward again and again in order to overwhelm him each time with fresh floods of opprobrium. The poor fellow's agony of mortification and fear might have melted a heart of stone; "but," as my ingenious neighbour put it, "we other Italians are inflexible in our attitude towards impostors presumptuous, who dare to desecrate the temples of our national art." Next morning "Gran Riposo" was placarded on the walls of the "temple of art" above referred to. Malandrino had disappeared during the night, like a dream.

The average Italian theatrical orchestra would not be tolerated in any third-rate English theatre. That of the Florentine Politeama was peculiarly atrocious in the early days of Italian Unity. The Politeama is an enormous amphitheatre, open at the top like the Coliseum, but resembling in the arrangement of its galleries rather the huge ruin hard by Pompeii than the mightiest of all ancient places of amusement. The arena is filled with seats, pit, first and second stalls; there are about thirty private boxes on the ground tier, including one of modest dimensions, though draped in crimson velvet, for the King; and an enormous gallery, containing about 3,000 persons, stretches away above these to where the roof would be if roof there were any save the deep blue sky. The principal chandelier of this delightful theatre is the moon, of course, and brilliantly she does her work, considering how inexpensive is the abundant light she yields; but there are jets of gas galore besides, and the gentlemen in wideawakes, gathered together in the orchestra, are supplied with the regular green-shaded burners in plenty. I am sure I do not know to what purpose; they could not possibly play worse in the dark!
Par parenthèse, not the least startling anomaly in a country of contradictions, is the quality and execution

of the music provided for public entertainment. It is the fashion to admit, without troubling one's self about taking evidence on the subject, that Italy is the *pays musical par excellence*. If this postulate be founded on fact, why are the harmless but harmony-loving stranger's ears insulted in every Italian town by combinations of sound so vile that a German audience of street-sweepers would not tolerate them for a moment? In Naples, at the Villa Nazionale, where the cream of an accomplished aristocracy assembles nightly to eat ices and listen to sweet strains, the musical refection provided for their decidedly appreciative palates is a military band, so weak that, being quite close to it, I could only compare it to a donkey barrel-organ with a cold in its inside. In Rome—but no, I will not describe what I heard there in the way of concerted music, further than to say that the players of many trombones appeared to have got something firmly wedged into their dreadful instruments, and to be engaged in a tremendous but fruitless effort to blow it out with many a groan, gurgle, and eccentric interval. In Florence I have heard dragoons play at the Casino, *horresco referens!* and have moreover patiently suffered the braying interludes of the Politeama—interludes occurring four several times, by reason of the moral drama's historical number of acts. The brass band wont to "attend" weddings in London, if multiplied by ten, will give the exact musical result attained in the largest and best-attended theatre in the former capital of Italy. And yet you shall hear an ostler, or a chambermaid, a *facchino*, or a flower girl, unconscious of their gifts, trolling out *canzoni popolari*, or chanting *stornelli* in perfect tune, with admirable accent, and oh, such wonderful voices! How is it that such a people will listen patiently, even cheerfully, to trash so shameful as that trumpeted out every evening at the Politeama? I can ascribe their endurance to nothing but the profound *insouciance* of the national character.

To return to the theatre. It is a sublime institution in a southern climate—a place where for a franc you can sit in the open air, on a cool iron chair, see excellent acting, and smoke your cigar the while, filling up the entr'actes with natural lemonade, beer of Chiavenna (a sort of malt tea, very effervescent and altogether guiltless), or threepenny ices. Hundreds of pretty girls— the Florentine girls *are* pretty, deny it who can—do not lessen the charm of the scene, to which the open roof, shelving galleries, and moonshine impart an indefinable *cachet* of classicality. And when the performance is over, the walk homewards, Lung' Arno, along the glittering river studded by tiny boats, each bearing on its prow a coloured lantern—is it not almost too lovely to be real? At night Florence becomes a city of enchantment; it is wrapped in ghostly light and shadow—troops of phantoms, diaphanously clad, glide about the white quays, dive into dark, narrow alleys, or float across the bridges spanning the golden Arno; it takes but little elasticity of faith to believe that you are transported into a world of dreams, of which the City of Flowers is the *chef-lieu*. If your fancy wants confirmation, stray to the square, where the Duomo and Campanile stand side by side, objects of inexhaustible wonder and admiration; or linger under the shade of the Santa Croce, and mark how everything outside that shade's sharply defined limit glows in living light. Or still better, get away out of the town to the heights, a couple of miles distant, and look down upon Firenze la Bella, la Cara, bathed in a silver flood. Nobody will ever make me believe that Florence is merely an ordinary, prosperous, prosaic city *comme une autre*, any more than Venice Anadyomene. No, it is a spirit-abode; one in which to write poetry, to paint pictures, to think in melodies, to make love, to inhale the perfumes of flowers and fruit; but not to work in, to make money in, to have butchers' bills, protested acceptances, water-rate in.

An operatic company engaged at an Italian theatre seldom takes upon itself the rendering of more than one opera, to which the répertoire of three-fourths of its *personnel* is limited; and thus the musical public finds itself compelled throughout a half or quarter season to listen night after night to the same strains sung by the same people, the only occasional variation being the interpolation of a stray overture between the first or second act of the opera and the ballet. Thus, let us suppose you to have been staying at Venice during the month of January, and to have taken an *abonnement* at the Fenice; you would have heard *Dinorah* twenty-two times in four weeks. Spending your February in Florence, you would have had nearly as many opportunities of becoming familiar with *Martha* at the Pergola, and would have been so much refreshed by Flotow's delicious music that you would have been equal to a March full of *Dinorah* at Turin. Coming on in April to Genoa for a " sea-change," you would have found the *Ballo in Maschera* well settled down in the Carlo Felice, and would have probably, in the course of a month or so, made an exact and intimate acquaintance with that highly sensational work, as well as with a ballet called *Brahma*, in which the unities suggested by its title are admirably preserved—the scene being laid in China, and a large proportion of the costumes being strictly Polish. As, however, the *habitués* of Italian opera-houses take up their accustomed places nightly with the settled intention of doing anything rather than listening to the music or looking at the stage, the sameness of the programme, ineffably vexatious to the foreigner, does not so much matter to them. According to Puritanical views, theatres are wicked places—I should say nowhere more so than in Italy—but certainly not by reason of the musico-histrionic performances offered by the management for the public entertainment. It is not the poor players who provide the vice—the audience bring that with them, in all sorts of states of development, and devote themselves with remarkable energy and perseverance to perfecting it. Queer stories the boxes in these Italian theatres could tell—the ground tier of the Scala, for instance, every private box in which has attached to it, or rather divided from it by the corridor, a luxurious *cabinet particulier*, with table, sofa, gas, and all complete!

Spain and Roumania are by no means so productive of *fanatici per la musica* as Italy is, although both the kingdoms in question are mainly populated, like the Ausonian Peninsula, by the descendants of music-loving Latin races. Consequently, the Italian characteristics distinctly manifest in their musical audiences are not so strongly marked in attitude or so vehemently expressed in gesture and sound as they are in the cradle of the legions that of yore colonised Hispania and Dacia. The genuine passion and fierce enthusiasm that underlie the outward calm and dignity of Spanish demeanour seldom make themselves visible and audible, save under the stimulus of bull-fighting or political excitement; whilst the average Roumanian is restrained from extravagant demonstrations of delight or disapproval by a strange blending of Oriental phlegm and French *insouciance.*

The Spanish love of music—the strength and genuineness of which I am far from wishing to impugn—concentrates itself upon song-melodies and dance-tunes rather than upon operatic works; it is curiously insensible to the charms of symphonic compositions and of what is conventionally designated "chamber-music." Iberians revel in narrative ballads, sentimental lovesongs, and all the provincial varieties of their national dance-music. To *seguidillas,* in the just rendering of which singing and dancing are combined, they listen with unflagging attention and obvious pleasure, and never weary of the lively measures of the *bolero, fandango* and *cachucha,* or of the *jaleo's* and *rondeña's* plaintive strains. My own recollections of the *seguidilla* are exclusively Andalusian; but this quaint song-dance is indigenous to Don Quixote's province, and its orthodox variety still goes by the name of " Seguidilla Manchega," in distinction from the gipsy *seguidilla* (Seguidilla Gitana), performed in slow time and with little movement of the lower limbs compared to that of the torso and arms;

from the "Seguidilla Bolera," a majestic dance unaccompanied by song; and from the "Seguidilla Taleada," which affects the impulsiveness of the Bolero, and is altogether of a less droning melodic character than are the other varieties of *seguidilla*.

It was at Seville that I last saw and heard them all performed by a very skilful troupe of Spanish minstrels, consisting of five men (vocalists and guitar-players) and three extraordinarily handsome girls, who did all the dancing, but sang not at all, and played upon no instrument but the castanets. The performance took place in a long low garret of an old Sevillan palace—a sort of lumber-loft, about fifty feet in length and twenty in breadth—and was attended by the élite *pollos*—mashers they would be called in London—of the old Andalusian city, including the Capitan-General for the time being, whose guest I happened to be. No payment was demanded for admission; one of the *chitarreros* was told off to show the "patron cavaliers" to their seats and attend to them generally, while the other four, squatting cross-legged on the floor, formed a small hollow square in the central portion of the room, which was kept clear for the dancers. These latter—Anita, Dolores and Carmencita—were really charming creatures, very young (the eldest, Dolores, had just entered her nineteenth year), and tastefully dressed in the style rendered familiar to London audiences by frequent performances of Bizet's *chef-d'œuvre* at Covent Garden and Drury Lane. Two of them were very dark—I found out, upon inquiry, that they were natives of the Triana, a gipsy-breeding suburb of Seville—and the third was a dazzling Valencian blonde, with languishing violet-blue eyes and bright golden hair hanging in thick plaits nearly down to her knees. The entertainment furnished by the troupe to some fifty or sixty gentlemen, for the most members of the Circolo Sevillano, an aristocratic club to which very few of even the wealthiest local merchants and professional men were admitted as members, lasted from about nine in the evening to two of the next morning, by which time the guitar-playing vocalists were hoarse with chanting innumerable *seguidillas,* and the three pretty dancing-girls were fairly worn out with fatigue. Meanwhile they had taken (as I was afterwards assured by a knowing young aide-de-camp of my guide, philosopher and friend, the military governor of Seville) over sixty pounds in gold and silver, had been laden (the girls I mean) with bonbons, comfits and tiny bouquets, had been treated to a plain but substantial supper — no champagne, but a little ordinary Val de Peñas and plenty of natural lemonade, orangeade, and fruit syrups diluted with water—and had danced every sort of dance known in Spain, including triumphal *hotas* and *jaleos* executed towards the end of the festivity on the supper-table, amongst the plates and dishes, with a single breakage.

It is, however, rather of the audience than of the performance or performers that I desire to treat in this place. The dancing had scarcely commenced—true, it was super-excellent of its kind—when Spanish frigidity began to thaw, and Spanish thrift to display a conspicuous tendency to transform itself into lavish and even reckless generosity. Many of those present were grave and stately *caballeros*—some few, well advanced in years—but, as *bolero* followed *seguidilla,* and *fandango* succeeded *bolero,* they warmed to a heat of enthusiasm I have seldom seen the like of in any Southern country of Europe. When they were sufficiently excited to have become oblivious for the time being of the principles of frugality instilled into them in early childhood, and thereafter practised by them inflexibly with relation to all their ordinary habits and avocations, the dancing-girls began to subject them to an ingenious process of pecuniary depletion, hallowed by ancient custom in connection with terpsichorean performances for the contemplation of which no charge is made by their executants.

Here I may parenthetically remark that experience has taught me—and at no inconsiderable cost—that professedly gratuitous entertainments are invariably the most expensive recreations in which the pleasure-lover can indulge. It comes cheaper to attend a Maskelyne and Cooke *séance,* having duly paid for your stall, than to patronise an open-air magician in Egypt; to hire a ground-tier box at the Italian Opera on a Patti-night than to accept a Pasha's invitation to see a Cairote choregraphic celebrity go through the "Bee-Dance;" to purchase a front-row place on the shady side of a bull-ring when El Tato is announced to appear than to witness a dancing *divertissement* in an Andalusian cock-loft as the honoured guest of a club-committee, or even a Captain-General. I have partaken of all these "gratuitous" joys in my time, and of many others of a similar character, to the serious minishment of my monetary resources; and I earnestly exhort persons of moderate means who crave for professional amusement of any kind to find out beforehand exactly how much it costs, and to pay at the doors.

The method of collecting fees adopted by Spanish dancers of the "select and exclusive" class to which Señoritas Anita, Dolores and Carmencita belonged in the year of grace 1868 was the following. I should premise that the spectators were seated on chairs and backed-benches (like those set up for public accommodation in our London parks) arranged in the form of an oblong circle some thirty feet long and twelve feet broad. In the space thus surrounded the girls danced in succession—sometimes two at a time—to the accompaniment of the strumming and chanting quartet seated tailor-wise in the centre of the boarded floor. Shortly before the closing measures of any particular dance, the *bailarina*—as though moved by a sudden and irresistible impulse—plucked her pocket-handkerchief from her girdle, and whilst gyrating and tripping past the front rank of the excited *pollos*, tossed it saucily into one of their faces. Etiquette required that the gentleman thus distinguished by her special attention should knot up a coin in one corner of the handkerchief, and restore the latter to its pretty owner during the next interval between the dances. This obligation having been punctually discharged, it was not considered the correct thing for that particular *bailarina* to "compliment" the contributor in question again in the course of her performance; unless, indeed, his own uncontrollable enthusiasm should prompt him while she is dancing later on to exclaim, "Quiero el pañuelo!" (I solicit the kerchief), when she might once more throw it at him without committing any breach of professional decorum. But each dancing-girl had the right to " lanzar el pañuelo" once in the course of the evening at whomsoever it might please her to favour with that delicate attention; and base, sordid, despicable would have been considered the insensible wight who should have restored the kerchief to her unweighted by Spanish currency. The least valuable coin he could offer, with any respect for himself, his family and his ancestral tree, was a *peso fuerte*, or Spanish dollar, a clumsy coin about the size and weight of a five-franc piece. But silver was looked down upon by a *bailarina* of any standing, who expected at least a half-isabellino in acknowledgment of her *complimiento;* I have seen such an one burst into tears of rage and mortification upon finding a *peseta* in the corner of her kerchief when she untied the knot; and I regret to say that that inadequate tribute emanated from a middle-aged English clergyman, unversed in the "customs of the country," and who—as he naïvely confessed to me—had made offering of the sum he would have thought it his duty to "put into the plate at afternoon collection." The intensity of the girl's humiliation at receiving tenpence when—the contributor being a *caballero estranjero*—she expected at least ten shillings, was chiefly attributable to the accident that her rivals were eagerly looking on with envious curiosity whilst she undid the handkerchief, and broke out into a tempest of scornful laughter and cackling chaff as soon as they caught sight of the humble *peseta* usurping the place of the expected *isabellino*. The latter coin was the proper one to have given to a dancer of established provincial renown, although its moiety—a fat, comfortable-looking little gold piece, bearing the effigy of the Reyna muy Española—was, as I observed, invariably acknowledged by a bright smile or (when contributed by an exceptionally good-looking youth) a blown kiss. The Capitan-General, as beseemed his Excellency's exalted station and large emoluments, gave a golden *onza* in the prescribed manner to each of the *bailarinas* in succession, the recipients duly stepping up to him, curtseying and presenting first one cheek and then the other to be kissed by their generous patron. His evening's amusement cost him nearly twelve pounds; but, as he told me afterwards, he considered it well worth the money. He also explained to me that, had the form of Government then obtaining in Spain not been Republican, he could not, in his official position, have attended the performance; that even under the existing *régime* certain prescriptions of etiquette precluded him from engaging a troupe of dancing-girls to entertain him in the Palacio; and that *las bailarinas renombradas* of the class to which the Señoritas Anita, Dolores and Carmencita belonged hardly ever appeared on the theatrical stage; so that, as he drily put it, but for the "enterprise" of his friends, Serrano, Prim and Topete, he might have been doomed until his retirement from public life to drag on a gloomy existence, never brightened by the sparkling feats of the *lindas muchachas* which had enraptured us both that evening! Worthy simple-hearted Capitan-General; that he, the supreme representative of authority in Seville, arrayed in the splendid uniform of his rank and attended by two gorgeous aides-de-camp, should be seen by illustrious natives and " distinguished foreigners" sitting all night long in a cockloft, gloating over the singularly suggestive dancing of three girls "of the people," and giving free vent to his enthusiastic admiration of their significant contortions and provocative gestures, did not for a moment strike him as an anomaly. *Cosas de España!*

I learnt from him that the "gifts" bestowed upon the *bailarinas* in the course of their performances were always put into the common purse of the troupe, and divided amongst the executants in shares, the proportions of which one to another had been settled by verbal agreement at the commencement of the tour. Any attempt on the part of the dancer to secrete a *réal* of the money personally given to her—and frequently one girl would happen to take eight or ten pounds more of a night than either of her companions—was, as he assured me, unheard of. "They are keen about their money, as you may perhaps have noticed," he added, "but quite honest to one another; *niñas muy caballerescas* I assure you, who never throw their handkerchiefs at any men for whom they really care, it being quite against their principles to put a *cortejo favorecido* to any unnecessary expense." "And what becomes of these pretty girls, Excellency?" I ventured to ask. "Temptation dogs their dainty heels by day and night—their vanity, fed as it is by passionate Spanish admiration, must be something tremendous; do they finish their career in the hospital or the poorhouse, after the manner of so many French and Italian *figurantes?*" "*Nada, nada* (not at all)," he replied. "They are thrifty, they drink nothing; they take care of their money and save it up for their dowries; generally, when they have been dancing for five or six years, they marry *empleados* (Government clerks) who cannot make two ends meet on their own salaries, and are glad to find pretty wives with a few thousand reals in their aprons, and to ask no embarrassing questions. Those girls whom we have admired to-night, and after whom all the *pollos* of Andalusia are running just now, will take husbands some day, and be very fond of and true to them, too. But they must have their *dote*, in order to settle respectably in life, and they know it; so meanwhile they work hard and spend next to nothing, except what their families—and sometimes their lovers—contrive to squeeze out of them. I know of two or three ex-*bailarinas* here in Seville, and of one in Cadiz, where I was formerly in command, who are married to good plodding fellows in the Customs and Excise; mothers of families, too, and pinks of propriety. But they soon lose their bright looks and lithesome gait when they take to respectability!"

On the whole, after living nearly a year in Spain, I came to the conclusion that Spanish musical audiences were amongst the most enthusiastic I had ever encountered; but, as a rule, only when the music of their predilection—every phrase of which lends itself to the practice of the sister-art, dancing—constitutes the entertainment provided for them. I have seen them sit, frigid and silent, through excellent operatic performances; and for classical compositions they have neither inclination nor patience. In the national *zarzuela*—a sort of *vaudeville*, interlarded with saltatory episodes— they take the liveliest delight; and no wonder, for more amusing and better played pieces I have never seen, even in Paris. But, when all is said and done, what goes straight to their hearts is the *seguidilla*, in which the strains they love and the steps they admire are triumphantly combined.

Before concluding this chapter, I will venture to say a very few words about that variety of English musical audiences which is more particularly to be observed within the walls of the London opera-houses. Nothing is more eminently calculated to strike an observant Englishman habitually resident abroad and visiting his native country but rarely, than the growth of tolerance in general London society with respect to advanced or eccentric opinions. Pharisaism is still deeply rooted in British soil, but its superficial growths, formerly so obtrusively luxuriant, have been so mown and clipped by the shears of science within the last twenty years, and so unmercifully dealt with by the pruning-knives of free-thinking *littérateurs* that they can only be seen here and there cropping up in sparse tufts—feeble caricatures of their pristine vigour. Who, for instance, would have deemed it possible a couple of decades ago that the lessee of Her Majesty's Theatre would have obtained the Lord High Chamberlain's permission to bring out an opera the first scene of which is laid in the heaven of Christianity—not of Buddhism or Brahminism—the entire action and interest of that scene being centred in a wager between the Deity and the Prince of Darkness respecting the ultimate destination of a doubtful human soul? Yet such was the entertainment presented by Colonel Mapleson during the 1880 season to the wealthy and aristocratic frequenters of his opera-house, and by them greeted with an enthusiastic welcome, expressed in tempests of applause such as I never before listened to within the walls of an English theatre. Towards the end of June, 1879, when, seated by Adelina Patti in her ground-tier box at Covent Garden, I witnessed the production of Massenef's *Roi de Lahore*, I could not help thinking that we English were getting on apace in the way of emancipation from old-fashioned prejudices and hallowed traditions; for the third act of that extremely remarkable work is also transacted in the celestial regions, its "leading business" being appropriately confided to the First Person of the Trinity, who promotes human souls to eternal bliss or condemns them to its converse in solemn strains (to the accompaniment obbligato of four trombones), seated on his throne and surrounded by his angels—cherubim and seraphim—who dance "ballets of rejoicing" whenever a virtuous spirit obtains advancement or a sinner's ghost is bundled off to the infernal regions. True, the Deity thus presented on the boards is a member of the Brahminical, not of the Christian Trinity; but, considering that Brahma, Vishnu, and Shiva are devoutly worshipped by many millions of British subjects, who hold them to be the only true gods, it struck me that the lyric stage of our Empire's capital was perhaps hardly the most fitting place whereupon to exhibit even the Indian Creator as a dramatic personage "with a song." The rôle of the Omnipotent was rendered in an admirably dignified manner by worthy old Capponi, a veteran "heavy father" with a potent bass voice, excellently suited to the majestic exponence of a mimic divinity's decrees; and the surpassing humour of the whole episode consisted in the circumstance that the crowded audience (including several members of the Royal Family) was obviously unconscious that anything unusual—far less irreverent or blasphemous—was going on, and absolutely insisted upon a repetition of one of the angels' ballets, interrupting a divine recitative for that purpose. If any one present happened to reflect that, after all, there was something a trifle queer in representing heaven other than the Olympian realm freely dealt with in several modern operettas upon the boards of Covent Garden, he or she probably jumped to the conclusion that "an Indian god did not so much matter, especially when set to such pretty music." To me the bass Deity and his capering seraphs seemed to point unmistakably to the fact that English convictions are far less stubborn than they were in my youth, and that tolerance of trifling with sacred personages and subjects, whether it be real or affected, is become a fashionable institution in the upper classes, at least, of British society.

The impression then conveyed to me was materially strengthened by my experience of the reception accorded by *élite* London audiences to Signor Boito's *Mefistofele*. Not only was the above-alluded-to bet between God and the Devil, with all its accessorial *intermezzi* of archangelic fugal choruses and cherubic comments, in monotone, upon the terms of the wager, rapturously applauded and even redemanded, but Faust's singularly immoral adventures in Greece, to which the fourth act of the opera is devoted, elicited a deafening clamour of approval from the spectators, as did that singularly dishonourable person's final breach of faith with his infernal "guide, philosopher and friend," which exhibits Faust himself as a psychical swindler, and his august backer as by no means an uncompromising advocate of fair play. No more startling, and at the same time ludicrous, examples of stage "business" had hitherto met my gaze than when I saw Faust, upon Mephistopheles claiming the fulfilment of his bond, snatch up a promiscuous Bible (for the presence of which upon his library table there is certainly no warrant in Goethe's tragedy) and hold it up menacingly before the very nose of the terror-stricken fiend, who cowers, shrinks, and shivers, subjugated by its uncalled-for interference, and ultimately vanishes through a practicable panel of the laboratory " set," driven from his legitimate prey by a shower of rose-leaves, rained upon the expiring voluptuary by seraph hands in the flies. This amazing anti-climax, however, was not greeted by the audience with shouts of derisive laughter, according to its intrinsic merit, but with vociferous plaudits, reiterated recalls of the leading actors, and a thundering summons to the composer, who came on between the Devil and Faust whilst the celestial petals were still falling! It should be remembered that this performance took place in one of our two great operahouses, the lessees of which have been steadfastly prohibited for years past—and still are so—by the Royal censors from bringing out Rossini's *Mosé in Egitto*, and Rubinstein's *Maccabäer*, on the ground that the subjects of those glorious operas are borrowed from Scripture—a circumstance constituting an insurmountable disability as far as their production on the British stage is concerned. Permission, however, having been granted to the enterprising Mapleson to represent heaven and hell upon the boards of Her Majesty's, surely the day is not far distant when we shall be allowed to contemplate Moses in the full exercise of moral suasion upon Pharaoh by means of ingenious mechanical miracles, got up "regardless of expense;" or to gloat over the incremation of the three younger Maccabees, chanting loud hosannahs on their way to the oven; and the homicidal triumph of Judah over Israel's unprincipled oppressors. Within a few years doubtless the Passion plays at present drawing crowded houses in the Ober Ammergau will be given at Drury-lane, where they will be brilliantly stage-managed by gallant Augustus Harris; and "Revelations," deftly travestied into a Christmas pantomime, will furnish delectation to thousands of juveniles at the Alhambra with its "entirely novel effects, gorgeous costumes, and scenery of unprecedented splendour."

END OF VOL. I.

www.ingramcontent.com/pod-product-compliance
Lightning Source LLC
Chambersburg PA
CBHW032010220426
43664CB00006B/198